HOSTILE CLIMATE

report on anti-gay activity
1999 edition

PEOPLE
FOR THE
AMERICAN
WAY
FOUNDATION

CONTENTS

For many in the gay civil rights community, the singular event of 1998 occurred off a lonely road in Wyoming, where a young man paid the ultimate price just for being who he was. The horrific murder of Matthew Shepard cast a long shadow over our nation and has prompted national soul-searching about hatred and its consequences.

This volume, our sixth report on discrimination against gay men and lesbians, is not an examination of hate crimes like the one perpetrated against Matthew Shepard — these horrible injustices are well-documented elsewhere. Instead, we examine the context in which such crimes occur. We ask, as a nation: How have we arrived at such a place, where someone could commit such a heinous, heartless crime? The answer, as this book reveals, is that we start down this path whenever we deny people their basic human rights and dignity. The hostile climate that gay men and lesbians face — with its powerful undertow of partisan rhetoric, public and corporate policy — fosters hate by validating and perpetuating discrimination.

The events that followed Shepard's assault show the depth and pervasiveness of this hostile climate. While Shepard lay dying in a hospital just a few miles away, a college fraternity's parade float rolled down the street in Fort Collins, Colorado, featuring a scarecrow lashed to a fence, painted with the words "I'm gay." In New York City, 70 people were jailed when they attended a vigil for Shepard. In Duluth, Minnesota, the mayor refused to sign a certificate of appreciation adopted by the city's Human Rights Commission to honor students who had organized another Shepard vigil.

In the years that we have been reporting on anti-gay discrimination, the number of reported incidents has grown exponentially. This 1999 edition of *Hostile Climate* includes 292 incidents — more than ever before and twice as many as last year's report. While we can't say conclusively what caused the jump in incidents, it seems clear to me that as more and more gay men and lesbians assert their fundamental human rights, they encounter a commensurate amount of resistance in their own lives and in the broader political sphere. The same holds for the growing ranks of companies, colleges and city governments that move to end anti-gay discrimination: they push, and the opposition pushes back. Quite often, the opposition wins.

In all, I'm struck by the number of family-related issues among these pages: marriage, foster parenting, adoption, child custody. As I write this, I celebrate the birth of a new grandchild, and the intense bond between child and family is very much in my mind. But how many gay men and lesbians must endure separation from their children, or never know parenthood at all, because they remain invisible and powerless in the eyes of the law?

Those feelings of powerlessness resonate sharply in this edition of *Hostile Climate* through 14 personal reflections by advocates, lawmakers, authors, artists and ordinary people who have suffered the kind of discrimination outlined in the rest of the report. Beyond the venomous rhetoric spewed out by the far right, beneath the debates over public policy, these essays speak truly of the real harm that prejudice inflicts upon people trying to lead normal lives. Their voices appeal powerfully to the common bonds of family and community that connect us all. It's humbling to realize that for every personal story told in these essays, there are thousands more to be told.

Still, the essays reflect not just despair and frustration, but also a uniquely human welling of hope. David Mixner says, "we no longer surrender our dreams to those who seek to divide the American people." Chris Camp says, "I have rediscovered my faith — deeper and more intense than before." Utah teacher Wendy Weaver writes that her ordeal gave her "a freedom that most gay people have never had in their lifetimes." And Alicia Pedreira, who was fired from her job in Louisville, Kentucky, converted her painful experience into action to help pass a Fairness Ordinance in her city.

Some of the incident reports show encouraging signs as well. At Goucher College in Baltimore, for example, a wave of anti-gay vandalism brought students together in an unprecedented display of support for the gay community there. And in Lafayette, Indiana, after several teachers received anonymous mail and phone calls threatening to expose them as gay, parents, citizens and officials united to condemn the campaign. A city council member said the hate mail "galvanized the community in support of diversity. It's just been wonderful to see."

I'm heartened by those stories. I'm inspired by the people whose will and spirit remain strong despite personal wounds and constant setbacks, who turn their pain into hard work. Many of us in America have been moved to activism that way, pushing for change in our states, towns, schools and employers. For all those battles, it's essential that we understand the battlefield — and this book offers an important lesson in that geography.

Carole Shields
President, People For the American Way Foundation
October 1999

INTRODUCTION

In Kentucky, a woman returns from vacation to find she has lost her job after a photo of her with her female partner was shown at a state fair. In Alabama, a woman loses custody of her child to an abusive father, solely because she is a lesbian. In Oklahoma, the state legislature takes up a bill barring gay men and lesbians from working in public schools. In Arkansas, the state prohibits gays from becoming foster parents.

These are a few of the hundreds of incidents of discrimination and intolerance chronicled in the 1999 edition of *Hostile Climate.* * They are evidence that in spite of the heightened visibility of the gay community in popular culture, and in spite of the Religious Right's claims that gays have political power, there is still a tremendous amount of institutional prejudice against gay men and lesbians in this country. Whether this current of intolerance emerges as legislation, or in the workplace, or in family issues, or in court rulings, it harms all of us — and it runs against all the beliefs that make up the American Way.

This year's edition of *Hostile Climate* includes more than twice as many incidents as the 1998 edition. As in previous years, our focus is not on the hate crimes and physical attacks that are documented exhaustively by other organizations. Thus, you will not find an account here of the vicious torture and murder of Matthew Shepard. What you will find is a chronicle, incident by incident, of the individuals, government bodies and institutions that shape public policy and public opinion — the decisions that create a hostile climate in which discrimination, hatred and even violence become permissible.

This year's report also has a new feature: personal essays by 14 people who have first-hand experience with anti-gay discrimination and the struggle to end it. The voices of these writers — artists, activists, clergy, students, lawmakers, working citizens — show us the very real fear and suffering that bigotry wreaks upon human lives, in a way that *Hostile Climate's* incident reports alone cannot.

A Look at Trends

The 292 incidents described in this book represent marked increases from last year's edition, in all categories of discrimination. The upswing may reflect better reporting by media outlets or a broad increase in anti-gay activity, though it is likely caused by a combination of the two. Incidents related to **marriage and family** issues — such as same-sex marriage, adoption, child custody and foster parenting — doubled from 20 in 1997 to 40 last year, which may be attributable to greater assertiveness on the part of gay men and lesbians seeking the same legal rights that all families enjoy. In the area of **education,** which includes all incidents that occurred within an academic setting (either secondary

*The incidents in this book occurred in 1998, though their status was updated throughout much of 1999. New incidents from 1999 will appear in next year's edition.

schools or colleges), the number again doubled — from 34 in 1997 to 76 in 1998. *Hostile Climate's* reporting has always included high proportions of incidents in schools, partly because the public school environment remains a singular target of right-wing groups. Another distinct increase took place among incidents related to **religion.** The report lists 32 such accounts, compared with only nine in 1997. These incidents often relate to same-sex marriage or commitment ceremonies and the consequences they bring for ministers who perform them.

In the area of **employment,** the number of incidents increased from 27 in 1997 to 36 in 1998. Our report has usually described an abundance of firings and other disputes between employers and gay workers; this year's edition also lists many incidents linked to the issue of whether an employer would offer benefits to its employees' domestic part-ners. Another striking trend in the report is the 32 **anti-discrimination ordinances** it men-tions (regardless of passage or defeat), proposed at the federal, state and local govern-ment levels. This category had no parallel in the classification system used for 1997; that report also did not have a separate category for **censorship** incidents, which number 20 in this edition. **"Culture war"** incidents — related to events such as protests, gay pride parades, speeches and vandalism — increased from 25 in 1997 to 36 in 1998. Under anoth-er new category in this edition, **politics and government,** the book lists 44 incidents. These include anti-gay political rhetoric by public officials or candidates, and legislative or executive decisions that could not be classified elsewhere.

An appendix that describes these categories and indexes all the incidents according to their category appears on p. 240. Some incidents were grouped under more than one heading — for example, a school censorship incident could be classified both as censor-ship or education. For that reason, the totals above add up to more than 292.

As we note every year, *Hostile Climate* represents only a "snapshot" of anti-gay activity around the United States, not a comprehensive accounting of all discrimination across the country. While our researchers conduct several personal interviews, the incidents are largely compiled through secondary material, such as newspaper stories, Internet reports and direct mail from anti-gay organizations.

The Role of the Religious Right

In 1998, the Religious Right fought harder than ever to marginalize gay men and lesbians, pouring thousands of dollars into an advertising campaign to convince Americans that being gay is a choice that can be reversed. Millions more flowed into political campaigns to deprive gay men and lesbians of their civil rights, to tear apart their families and codify discriminatory practices. With the "Truth in Love" ad campaign, Religious Right groups are pushing a scientifically discredited treatment into the mainstream media. They perpetuate false stereotypes of gays as child molesters in their direct mailings. Right-wing radio hosts such as Laura Schlessinger and others dwell obsessively on homosexuality — spreading distorted "news," quack science and vicious rhetoric intended to demonize gays.

By calling efforts to protect students from harassment "indoctrination," by labeling laws against hate crimes "thought policing," and by telling their constituency that anti-discrimination measures will force their churches to rewrite the Gospel, the Right has forged a solid base of frightened voters:

▌ In **Maine,** after the legislature had passed a law prohibiting discrimination on the basis of sexual orientation, the Christian Coalition led a successful referendum drive to repeal it. The Maine Christian Civic League, which also backed the referendum, said: "We believe that … if a Maine businessman or landlord wants to discriminate against a person because of their sexual orientation, they should be able to do so."

▌ In **Florida,** the Christian Coalition — trying to repeal a non-discrimination law — distributed a fraudulent document purporting to be a "Gay Manifesto." It warned: "Homosexuality must be spoken in your churches and synagogues… [Homosexuals] will in all likelihood expunge a number of passages from your Scripture and rewrite others, eliminating preferential treatment of heterosexual marriages…If all of these things do not come to pass quickly, [homosexuals] will subject Orthodox Jews and Christians to the most sustained hatred and vilification in recent memory."

▌ The **Hawaii** Christian Coalition posted the following on its website: "[S]ome, but not all, homosexuals are pedophiles, preying on children and wanting the age of consent laws for sex removed all over the world. Just as they call gay marriages a 'civil right,' some — again, not all — say children are being deprived of their 'civil right' to have sex."

Bigotry in the Workplace

Gay men and lesbians face blatant job discrimination from employers, and from lawmakers bent on denying them the same protections that all workers enjoy. In all but 11 states, the District of Columbia and certain cities in other states, it is still legal to fire or refuse to hire someone because he or she is gay.

▌ In **Oklahoma,** the legislature debated a bill that would have prohibited gay men and lesbians from working in the public schools in any capacity. The lawmaker who sponsored the proposal said his goal was to "drive [gays] back in the closet like the way they were."

▌ In **New York,** a software company employee said he was fired because he was gay, even though his company has a policy protecting gay men and lesbians from discrimination. In court, the company maintained that because there was no local anti-discrimination law, it was not required to follow its own rules.

▌ In **New York City,** a 13-year veteran police officer who is gay alleged that his fellow officers hung him from a coatrack with handcuffs, locked him inside lockers, forced him to simulate a sex act with another officer, and subjected him to relentless verbal harassment. The officer ultimately had a nervous breakdown. And in **Oregon,** a decorated 21-year veteran police officer accused his force of demoting him because he is gay, jeopardizing his safety by assigning him a squad car without a police radio or siren, and launching an investigation in which he was interrogated about his "sexual positions" and the names of his partners.

▌In **Kentucky,** a child therapist returned from vacation to find she had been fired because of her sexual orientation. Alicia Pedreira's personal account of her experience appears on p. 29.

Marriage and Family Issues

One of the Religious Right's biggest myths is that "family values" are the sole province of heterosexual, two-parent, middle-class families, and that any other family structure is not only detrimental to the people in the family, but also to the institution of marriage. This lie is the foundation of their arguments against same-sex marriage and any other codified recognition of same-sex relationships and families, such as adoption, foster parenting and domestic partner benefits. The Right uses this rhetoric to justify taking children away from their parents and denying health benefits, hospital visits and other legal rights to the partners of gay men and women.

In 1998, 17 anti-same-sex marriage bills were introduced in 14 state legislatures. Voters in Alaska and Hawaii adopted ballot initiatives to amend their state constitutions with language forbidding recognition of same-sex marriages (in Hawaii, the initiative allowed the legislature to do so). Thirty states have laws banning recognition of such unions. All these laws have been passed within the past five years with the exception of Louisiana's law, which was passed in 1803. This year, attacks on gay and lesbian families included bills to prohibit gay men and lesbians from serving as foster parents and from adopting children.

▌**Arkansas** became the second state in the nation to prohibit gay men and lesbians from serving as foster parents. The state's Child Welfare Agency Review Board passed the ban despite the warnings of an assistant state attorney general, who said, "[Y]ou can regulate what someone does, but not who someone is."

▌In **Alabama,** the state Supreme Court refused to grant custody of two children to their mother because she is gay and lives with a partner, with whom she "openly displays affection." Instead, the court sent the children to live with their father, who a dissenting justice described as a violent, abusive drunk driver. (The father had been cited for driving under the influence with the children in his car.) The mother is now allowed to visit her children only in the presence of her parents.

▌In **Florida,** laws prohibiting recognition of same-sex marriages and adoptions by gay men and lesbians cost a woman custody of her daughter and even the right to visit her, because she and her partner — who is the child's birth mother — ended their relationship.

Prejudice and Censorship in the Schools

The Religious Right's continuing battle to have its own political and social views taught in American public schools dovetails with its desire to squelch any rational discussion of homosexuality in the public sphere. Organizations like the Family Research Council and the Christian Coalition have waged a campaign of fear, telling their members that the "homosexual agenda" is taking hold of the schools and that their children are being taught how to have homosexual sex. Through censorship of books, plays, and entire curriculums they have succeeded in keeping gay issues out of many classrooms.

▌In **California,** a school allowed the parents of 15 students to transfer their children out of a teacher's classroom, because news stories had quoted him objecting to the anti-gay remarks of a local official. The local school board dismissed the teacher's complaint, and he ultimately decided to retire.

▌A week after Matthew Shepard's murder, a middle school in **Provo, Utah,** had a "wish ceremony" in which students divided into groups of 20 and read out the wish they have all agreed on. One student stood up and said his group wished that "gay men be crucified on Main Street and lesbians be burned at the stake."

▌In **South Dakota,** administrators objected to a high school play's allegorical theme of tolerance for gays. When the students tried to win approval by removing parts they thought might offend the administration, the publisher forbade them from performing the play.

▌A transgendered teenager at a private school in **Georgia,** whose handbook says it prizes "diversity in opinion, culture, ideas, behavioral characteristics, attributes or challenges," was kicked out because he dressed as a girl. "Alex wasn't causing any problems," said a fellow student. "She wasn't trying to change anybody to be like her or anything."

In the wake of school shootings over the past two years, students' safety has received new attention. Recognizing the impact that anti-gay harassment has on students, many schools have adopted policies prohibiting it. Through open discussion and the formation of gay/lesbian clubs, some students are finally receiving the support they deserve from school staff and peers. But instead of welcoming this trend as a step that will foster the acceptance and safety of all students, groups like Focus on the Family have called the harassment policies "indoctrination."

▌In **Florida,** the Florida Family Association deluged Pinellas County School Board members' home mailboxes with hundreds of postcards and letters to protest the county's first high school Gay and Straight Alliance (GASA). David Caton, the president of FFA, said the mail campaign's goal was not only to shut down Largo High School's GASA, but also to deter other area schools from attempting to start new clubs.

▌In **California,** Alana Flores, the lead plaintiff and the first female student in an anti-gay peer harassment case, alleges she found violent pornographic photos and death threats in her locker and that although she reported the incidents to administrators, it took weeks to have epithets scratched into her locker removed, and she was not permitted to change lockers. In addition, when she reported the incidents to an administrator, she asserts the response she received was, "Well, *are* you gay?" Flores wrote an account of the harassment for this book that appears on p. 23.

Harassment, censorship and discrimination against gay staff members, students and organizations take place at the collegiate level, too. Gay and lesbian groups' funding, advertising, and even guest speakers were censored or challenged in 1998.

▌ In **Montana,** a state senator threatened to cut state aid for higher education if a literature course focusing on literature by, for and about gay men and lesbians was not dropped. And gay/lesbian student groups were either stripped of funding, disciplined or threatened at Florida State University, Western Kentucky University, Nebraska Wesleyan University and Catholic University in Washington, D.C.

Religion: The Power of the Pulpit

For some time, the religious community has been embroiled in a debate over the acceptance of gay men and lesbians. While many congregations and ministers have informally embraced the gay community, this often clashes with official doctrine. The Religious Right views all of these gay-affirming incidents with horror. When men and women of faith are seen as embracing gay men and lesbians for who they are, recognizing their relationships and affirming their role in society and religion, it undermines the Right's claim to speak for the religious community — and its assertion that gays threaten that community. While each faith and each congregation must reach its own conclusion as to how these issues will be resolved with its own theology, we include these incidents to give the complete picture of the "climate" in which gay men and lesbians live.

▌ In **Iowa,** at a dinner sponsored by conservative activist Edward Atsinger III, local pastors were asked to speak out against homosexuality from the pulpits. And as part of the anti-same-sex marriage ballot initiative campaign in **Hawaii,** the Christian Coalition asked clergy members to "stand up in their pulpits and denounce the evils of homosexuality."

▌ Holding signs that said "Unrepentant sodomites risk hell" and "Sodomy is not a family value," 30 protesters caused Josie Martin and Carol Parker to cancel a "friendship blessing" ceremony in May at St. Elizabeth Seton Catholic Church in Pleasanton, **California.**

Oklahoma minister Leslie Penrose has written an essay for this report about how she withdrew from the United Methodist Church after performing commitment ceremonies for same-sex couples. It appears on p. 35.

The National Scene

In 1998, Tammy Baldwin, who is openly gay, won election to Congress. In June 1999, James Hormel, who is also openly gay, was named U.S. ambassador to Luxembourg with a recess appointment, despite an intense campaign against him. These high-profile advances help shift the way gay men and lesbians are seen in American culture, and they represent the mainstream acceptance of homosexuality that Religious Right groups fear so much. This is why they have tried to censor positive portrayals of gays, and why they have fought so hard to portray themselves as the victim of the gay rights movement. One way to combat the general acceptance of gay men and lesbians is to promote homophobic stereotypes: When respected figures say that homosexuality is comparable to kleptomania, the disparagement resonates with some members of the public. The rhetoric may be somewhat gentler than that of Rev. Fred Phelps, who preaches that "God hates fags," but the same point is made: homosexuality is a disease. If you're sick, you should get treated — if you don't, then whatever happens to you is your fault.

▌ In June, U.S. Rep. Joel Hefley (R-CO) sponsored a bill in the House that would have prohibited any funds from being used "to implement, administer or enforce" President Clinton's executive order prohibiting discrimination against federal employees on the basis of sexual orientation.

▌ Senate Majority Leader Trent Lott taped an interview on "The Armstrong Williams Show" in which he stated his belief that homosexuality was a sin. He continued, saying he believed homosexuality was a problem, "just like alcohol...or sex addiction...or kleptomaniacs." This interview was recorded just a month after Lott and other high-ranking Republicans met with disgruntled representatives of the political far right, some of whom were threatening to bolt from the Republican Party.

▌ Football star Reggie White was honored by the Family Research Council and became a national spokesman for the "ex-gay" advertising campaign after he stated, "Homosexuality is a decision, it's not a race. People from all ethnic backgrounds live in this lifestyle. But people from all ethnic backgrounds are also liars and cheaters and malicious and back-stabbing."

A Look Ahead

While *Hostile Climate* documents the injustices faced daily by gay men and lesbians, it also shows the progress being made in the fight for equal rights for all Americans. But those who oppose this move forward aren't giving up — on the contrary, they have become more intense in their efforts to reinforce the hostile climate that exists. Fairness and justice will advance as our institutions — businesses, government, schools and communities — recognize gay men and lesbians as human beings, and afford them the equal treatment and dignity that is the birthright of all Americans.

Fourteen voices from
across the country reflect
on discrimination and
its consequences

ESSAYS

DAVID MIXNER

As a gay man in his fifties reflecting back on my journey, I have mixed feelings of pride, sorrow and pain. I am proud that I was able to survive the oppression and hate that dominated my childhood. I am in sorrow because over 280 friends have died of AIDS. I remember the pain that came from the discrimination and hate directed toward me simply because I am a gay American.

Growing up in rural America in the late 1940s and '50s as a gay child was an ordeal. There were no movies of the week, Time magazine covers, community centers, role models or in-depth coverage of being gay or lesbian. We were hidden and expected to live in shame and disgrace. Many young gay people took their own lives, or surrendered their dreams at an early age. I remember when a young neighbor boy committed suicide at age 16 because he was gay, and my father declaring that the young man's family was better off being rid of such a burden. Every institution in our life — our families, religious communities, schools, community organizations, media, the medical community — reminded us on a constant basis that we were abnormal and had no role to play in American society. The fear and pain were a constant companion in my early years.

High school and college were an especially a difficult time for me. I was blackmailed, contemplated suicide, made up identities in order to avoid being discovered. I was not allowed to mourn the death of my college lover. In those college years, I didn't build my plans for the future around my dreams — I based them on what I thought I would be allowed to do as a gay man. All of my energy went into hiding the truth from my family and friends. There wasn't a day or a week that went by when that struggle was not foremost in my mind.

As I began to work with the civil rights and anti-war movements of the '60s, I understood that if I was known to be gay, I would no longer be able to contribute my gifts to those causes. Alcohol and drug use too often became a companion, so that I could numb the fear or find the courage to have a personal life. I had to navigate an unbelievable maze of lies, entanglements and logistics simply to love, calculating every move to prevent any exposure that might identify me as gay. I listened to "faggot" jokes from friends, and the

David Mixner is a consultant and civil rights activist in Los Angeles.

ridicule they heaped on people they knew to be gay or lesbian. There was no doubt in my mind that I would receive the same if they knew who I really was.

Finally, facing Anita Bryant's 1977 campaign to deny us the basic rights of other American citizens, I came out of the closet. It was an extraordinarily painful process that caused several years of turmoil in my family; during that time, I had a nervous breakdown and was certain that my professional career was over. But I knew, like so many others, that I had to fight back for my basic freedoms — and most of all, for my dignity. In many ways, publicly acknowledging my sexuality was like being reborn. For the first time, my life was honest and I no longer had to hide.

Coming out has not ended the bigotry. My partner and I had a consulting firm. In the early 1980s, as we bid on contracts, our competitors would send a plain envelope to corporations, with news clips describing our work to promote gay civil rights. One Fortune 500 company was a particularly painful experience. They needed our unique services, but no one in the company wanted to be the one who hired an openly gay person. Apparently they thought it would hurt their careers, or feared that

> The hotel manager took some pleasure in pointing out that he had a legal right to discriminate against us.

someone might assume they were gay. My partner and I were made to sit in a meeting of the company's Board of Directors while they discussed whether they could hire an openly gay person to allow us to save them money. It was one of the more humiliating experiences of my life.

On another occasion, my partner and I were traveling and had booked a reservation together in a well-known hotel chain. As we checked in, the clerk refused to rent us a room because we answered "yes" when asked if we were gay. I remember staying at the reservation counter for hours, refusing to move. The hotel manager took some pleasure in pointing out to us that no laws protected us, and that he had a legal right to discriminate against us. Ultimately their shifts ended, a young woman whose brother was gay took over the front desk, and we got our room.

Circumstances are much better today, but we still have so far to go. There are still apartheid-type laws against gay men and lesbians serving in the military, marrying and adopting. On the other hand, there's no doubt in my mind that the world is a better place for us. I can go on a college campus and see gay youth groups and dances. I look with pride at our community centers. I see the progress we have made in many states and cities toward gaining protection against discrimination. Young gays and lesbians are being elected to office. We no longer surrender our dreams to those who seek to divide the American people. With amazement, I watch many straight people stand by our side in the battle for justice and freedom. The struggle is far from over, but millions of people confront less fear and hatred, and their lives are filled with promise. ■

THE HON. TAMMY BALDWIN

I'll never forget the phone call I got back in January 1993. It was the day of my swearing-in as a member of the Wisconsin Assembly. A newspaper article had run statewide about the fact that I would be the first openly gay or lesbian person to serve as a member of the Wisconsin Legislature. The voice on the other end of the phone sounded young and frightened. He identified himself as being from northern Wisconsin, then he said, "I just read about you. I had never heard about you before. I just want you to know that I feel differently about *myself* today."

I never learned anything more about that young man. But I can't help thinking that reading something positive and exciting about a gay or lesbian person stood in stark contrast to other messages he had heard. It gave him hope.

A decade before I got the phone call, I was engaged in a search of my own. A search for information to challenge the screaming silence about gay, lesbian, bisexual, and transgender issues that emanated from all the educational institutions that I'd been affiliated with. My public schools and my liberal arts college were viewed as outstanding institutions. But my passage through each left me with no information about the young woman I had become. So I set out to fill the void — to give some social and historical context to my own coming out as a lesbian. And what I found made me so proud and so angry.

I was proud because so many gay, lesbian, bisexual and transgendered people had taken the time to document the stories of the gay civil rights movement, to tell the stories of our courageous leaders, to make our world's history whole and truthful by including our part in shaping it. These people had taken the time to write books, research historical documents, produce documentaries, and record oral histories.

Tammy Baldwin was elected to the U.S. Congress in November 1998 after serving three terms in the Wisconsin Assembly. She is the first woman elected to Congress from Wisconsin, and the first open lesbian to serve in Congress.

My anger came because no one in my educational background had ever uttered the words "gay" or "lesbian." I had never been taught about Stonewall or about any of the leaders of the gay and lesbian civil rights movement. Nor had a teacher ever taken the time to share that an author, an artist, or a scientist whose work we were studying happened to be gay. It was only then that I realized how damaging silence can be.

Silence compounds the isolation, the sense of shame, the lack of self-esteem experienced by children. Young people with gay siblings, parents, or other relatives experience many of the same fears as do those who are themselves gay. But arguably, the silence is equally harmful to those children who believe they have never met anyone who is gay. Because no respected adult has suggested otherwise, those youngsters have no information at all with which to challenge the negative myths and stereotypes that persist about gay people.

> Silence compounds the isolation, the sense of shame, the lack of self-esteem experienced by children.

Of course we know that we live in a world where we have more than silence to contend with. We have those who openly espouse their hate toward gay, lesbian, bisexual and transgendered people. Some artfully "disguise" their hate rhetoric under the rubric of "special rights" or "condemning the lifestyle, not the person." But the impact of such rhetoric can be equally as harmful as the unveiled hatred that we hear so much about.

I remember all too well fending off anti-gay legislation in the Wisconsin Legislature. The authors of such proposals would invariably deny that they held any anti-gay animus. Yet they could not understand that when a public figure stands up in an effort to codify discrimination against gays and lesbians, she or he is sending an explicit message that it is OK for others to do the same. Such anti-gay legislation has the impact of threatening the safety of gays and lesbians in our communities.

We need and must support a public policy response to anti-gay hate at the local, state and national levels. And we must work toward a day when there are no further accounts to fill the pages of a book such as this one. ∎

An account of Rep. Baldwin's House race appears on p. 230.

ARTHUR DONG

PHOTO: TOM LeGOFF

I was asked by a student at a recent presentation of my films: "What keeps you going after all these years?" My answer: "Anger. Anger that the world is an unfair place. Anger that after over 25 years I still need to make films that attack social injustices. And most of all, anger that any sexuality other than heterosexuality is condemned equally by all sectors of our society, regardless of race, religion, nationality, class or gender. My films are my weapon, it's what I know best."

"Coming Out Under Fire" was my first major film to probe the hypocrisy of our heterosexual-oriented society. Based on the book by Allan Bérubé, it documented the World War II origins of the military's anti-gay "don't ask, don't tell" policy. Working on the film, I learned how a branch of government, without consent from the governed, officially sanctioned the discrimination of an entire class of citizens by creating a policy that branded homosexuals as mentally ill and unfit to serve. I learned that subjective personal views were sufficient grounds to relegate an entire community into second-class citizenship, as the military did when gay soldiers were stripped of all rights, discharged, and shipped back to their hometowns — stigmatized forever as sexual perverts. Above all, I realized the power held by public servants and how their prejudices could lead to devastating consequences for the individual lives they were charged to protect.

Coincidentally, as we began production on our film in January 1993, President Clinton proclaimed that he would lift the ban on gays in the military. The ensuing public debate brought the issue of homosexuality openly into the halls of Congress, and created unprecedented media headlines. Untruths spewed from politicians, ordinary citizens, and religious and community leaders alike. Suddenly it seemed as though everyone who disapproved of homosexuality felt free to unburden himself; it was open season.

Arthur Dong is a Peabody Award-winning independent filmmaker. His work includes "Licensed To Kill," nominated for an Emmy this year; "Coming Out Under Fire"; "Forbidden City, U.S.A." and the Oscar-nominated "Sewing Woman." For more information, visit his website at www.deepfocusproductions.com.

This was the first time I truly understood that achieving equal footing with heterosexuals would be an uphill battle — not only in the military, but in all the institutions that govern our daily lives. This realization was reaffirmed by the evidence that our government did not learn from the history of World War II and was blatantly perpetuating the military's distorted views a hundredfold. More detrimental than before, these ideas were being transmitted without limits to the mass public as certified fact, via modern media technology.

It was no surprise, then, that incidents of anti-gay violence saw a dramatic increase across the nation immediately after the military controversy, and continue to escalate as I write this essay.

As for myself, my first of two gay-bashing experiences occurred in 1977. My initial thought was, "Why me?" This quickly grew into the larger question: "Why does this happen at all?"

It took me 20 years to find a way to explore this inquiry: I would go to prisons and visit killers who have been convicted of murdering gay men. I would ask them directly: "Why did you do it?" This formed the basis for my film "Licensed to Kill."

> If anger is what pushes me forward, I hope that compassion is what comes forth.

As I set out to meet these prisoners, to discover what these men were made of, I did not find misfits, outcasts, fanatics or lunatics. Instead, I found a deeply disturbing reflection of American society. I saw that while individuals are responsible for their actions, individual minds can also be nurtured and molded by social conditioning.

One killer told me he was taught by his junior high school librarian that homosexuality was wrong. Another inmate recalled how he was told that gay men were weak, and that "you could take theirs and they wouldn't put up a fight." A third murderer claimed that the Bible preaches that homosexuality was a sin worthy of death, and if that's what the Bible says, it must be true. He remembers: "They were trying to sink into our heads then when we were kids that what's written in the Bible is right."

What they represented was not the freedom and liberty that America so proudly parades. On the contrary, they illustrated the deterioration of human values to a point where respect was no longer a virtue, where moral standards were set by charismatic, powerful leaders determined to impose their deep-seated, intolerant dogma on all Americans. For these leaders — be they national figures or small-town teachers and those in-between — there is no compromise on moral authority.

If I could go back to the day when that student asked me to discuss the motivation for my films, I would add: "As I work on each of my projects, I find that there is much still to be done to create a world in which I can be a proud citizen. And if anger is what pushes me forward, I hope that compassion is what comes forth." ∎

An account of the campaign against the PBS broadcast of "Licensed to Kill" in South Carolina appears on p. 199.

THE HON. SHEILA JAMES KUEHL

Three times, during each of my terms as a California State Assembly member, I have tried to gain sufficient votes to pass a simple piece of legislation that would add sexual orientation to the list of protected categories in the anti-discrimination sections of the California Education Code. In the course of writing, promoting and fighting for this legislation, I have heard testimony from a number of young people, some of them still in the public school system, who have been the targets of harassment and violence because of their perceived sexual orientation.

I talked with a young man whose head was plunged into toilet water by his fellow students; a young woman who was roughed up, followed home and threatened with rape; a young man who was pushed down a flight of stairs, and these stories are not all that unusual. Many young people have faced endless rounds of harassment. Some of the individual incidents they experienced are not as extreme as those I've described here and might seem small by themselves, but, as an almost-daily occurrence, the threats, slurs and pointed ostracism turned their school days into an endlessly excruciating ordeal.

Some of the young people I spoke with were able to tough it out and graduate from high school. Some have gone on to college, where they have resolved to turn the pain of their experience into positive lessons about the value of pluralism, diversity and simple civility in society. Others felt that they had no choice but to drop out of school. Some were able to complete their high school equivalencies and get on with their lives. Others are still trying to repair the damage.

Most of the people who have come forward to testify about their experiences really are lesbian or gay. But a substantial number are not. They are heterosexual young people whose appearance or behavior does not conform to someone's idea of what proper heterosexuality looks like. These students don't even have a community of support to come out in.

There are, of course, a number of young people I will never have a chance to meet, because they didn't make it. They are among the shockingly high number of lesbian and

Sheila Kuehl is a member of the California State Assembly, where she chairs the Judiciary Committee. She served as Speaker pro Tempore in 1997-98, becoming the first woman in state history to be named to that position.

gay youth that commit suicide, broken by the omnipresence of hate. Others have fallen into depression, substance abuse or the absolute depths of the closet, locked into fear and convinced that only invisibility can guarantee survival.

It is especially disheartening to realize the extent to which some school authorities ignore the problem or, in some cases, make a public show of endorsing the prejudice that gives rise to so much pain. While some school districts — notably those of San Francisco, Los Angeles and Santa Monica (a city I represent) — take positive action against bigotry in all its forms, others are passive to the point of complicity in the face of anti-gay violence.

I wish I could end this story on a happy note by telling you that the California legislature passed legislation that would give school districts a mandate to act when harassment or violence because of perceived sexual orientation rear their heads. However, this summer this legislation was, once more, narrowly defeated, losing by only one vote. The radical right wing in California spent more than $300,000 misrepresenting my bill in the targeted Assembly districts of legislators whom they believed they could scare.

> I have learned that any move toward a just society will be fought at every step along the way.

Among the Big Lies repeated over and over — on call-in radio, in letter writing and phone campaigns to undecided legislators, in full-page print ads — was the assertion that my bill would mandate teaching the "gay lifestyle." Spanish-language fliers with those same twisted, hateful messages were sent to families with Spanish surnames. Groups around the state, my staff and fair-minded legislators did everything they could to counter those messages. However, at the time of the vote, a number of legislators continued to say they were "uncertain" about the bill's meaning, although the language was plain. Others were more honest and said that voting for the bill would just be too politically expensive.

The bill was defeated. Out of 80 Assembly members, no Republicans voted for the bill, and eight Democrats voted no. Thirty-nine Democrats and the one Green Party member voted aye. We only needed one more vote.

I have learned at least two things from my experiences in trying to pass anti-discrimination law dealing with sexual orientation. I have learned that the opposition is unprincipled and determined, and that any move toward a just society will by fought at every step along the way. But I have also learned that there is a deep yearning within our society's fair-minded people for justice. Every term, when we re-introduce this legislation, we pick up a few more votes. For the sake of all those young people, straight or gay, who are counting on us to make their schools safer and more civil, we can't afford to quit.

EPILOGUE: I decided to allow this essay to be printed just as it was written earlier, in order to demonstrate the level of discouragement and sorrow one can reach in the course of work-

ing to change the world. However, I'm very happy to report on how that sorrow gave way to a happy ending.

On October 2, 1999, Gov. Gray Davis signed AB 537, the reborn "Dignity For All Students Act," which prohibits discrimination in all of California's public schools on the basis of actual or perceived sexual orientation or gender identity (as they are defined in California's existing statute on hate crimes). By linking the new bill to our state's anti-hate crime law — which also, in its language on gender, protects transgendered persons — we actually strengthened the bill in several important ways.

So, we went from dejection to triumph in one short legislative session. There are two lessons here. The first is that the best antidote to despair is renewed action fueled by the conviction that justice really will have its day. The second is that people will, eventually, live up to their best selves, given half a chance. When I look at the enormous amount of positive change I have seen in my lifetime, I am in awe, and I feel so proud of us. AB 537 passed with the help of dogged community activists and lobbyists, our indefatigable allies in the legislature who spoke up in support and took the flak, and the courageous youth whose testimony about the outrages they suffered moved a majority of lawmakers to do the right thing. When we stand together, there is no limit to what we can accomplish. ■

ALANA FLORES

There is no way to describe the despair I felt for 10 years of my life prior to coming out of the closet in terms of my sexuality. I can say, however, that when I did finally come out to my family, to my peers and most of all to myself, I felt a great deal of angst lift from my soul.

It was a long and winding road to self-acceptance. I'm still making my way along its path daily, but two simple words said aloud took me miles closer to a comfort within. There are a million different things that make me who I am today. But it is my sexual orientation that society chooses to look at, judge me by, and finally label me under. I will be labeled for life as an "out-of the closet bisexual," and it will be my sexual orientation that defines me, not the millions of other things that also make me who I am today.

My family moved to Morgan Hill, Calif., when I was a freshman, the summer after I met my first girlfriend. I was the new kid in a new town and everyone was curious. Going to Live Oak High School my sophomore year would be the beginning to a twist of fate that will affect my life forever. I was fairly popular at Live Oak; my oldest sister was a senior and I got to hang out with all of the coolest seniors because of her. I was also on the dance team and in the school plays. People liked me, but no one knew that I was bisexual. One day I found a note in my locker that read "Dyke Bitch Fuck Off!!!" I was terrified at the thought of someone knowing my darkest secret — who could this possibly be from, how could they know?

Before anyone could see the note, I destroyed it, trying to ignore the fact that it ever happened. But the notes became more and more frequent and it was becoming too hard to ignore the fact that I was being stalked by someone who wanted to hurt me. I was

Alana Flores, 20, is the lead plaintiff in the lawsuit *Flores vs. Morgan Hill Unified School District*, which is scheduled to go to trial in California in fall 1999. She plans to attend the California Institute for the Arts next year.

afraid to tell anyone because the last thing I wanted was attention. I still wasn't ready to accept myself.

One day, toward the end of my hellish sophomore year, my friend Brennah came running into one of my classes and was very upset. She shared my locker with me once in a while, and when she'd gone to get one of her books, she found a particularly disturbing note that said "Die you fucking dyke bitch, leave our school or we'll kill you!!!" There was also pornography attached of a woman who was bound and gagged with her throat slit wide open. Seeing Brennah so upset made me start sobbing, too. She persuaded me to report it to the school administration. We went crying up to the administration office and tried to get the vice principal to do something about this, and at least change my locker. Instead of helping us, the vice principal asked, "What is this trash?" I told her that I had been getting those sorts of photos in my locker for months. Then she asked, "Well, *are* you a lesbian?" That question scared me more than any of the letters I got — no one had ever asked me that before. "No," I replied, "I'm not!"

> "Why are you crying, why do you care?" she said. "If you're not a lesbian, then why are you getting these notes?"

I lied because I was scared and scared of her and what she would have done if I had said yes. "Why are you crying, why do you care? If you're not a lesbian then why are you getting these notes?" I didn't know what to say. I stared at her blankly with tears running down my cheeks. I can still hear her words: "Go back to class, stop complaining, and stop bringing me this trash!" She crumpled the letter and threw it away. What could I say, what could I do, where was I going to go for help?

The threatening notes and pictures were persisting and got more graphic each time I got one throughout my junior year. By then I didn't even bother to look at them; I would crumple them up and throw them away — that's what the administration did when I talked to them about it, so I thought I might as well do it myself.

In my senior year, things took a turn for the worse. I was constantly depressed, I was contemplating either dropping out of school or ending my life completely. I feel that suicide is a very selfish way of escape, but I was in an unhealthy state; I didn't want to go through this hurt any longer. I was locked away in a personal hell, and it seemed like there was no other way to escape.

So one night in October, I intentionally took an overdose of drugs I'd taken from a friend. I went home, saw my mom and knew I wanted to tell her and my whole family that

I was gay before I died. Fortunately I failed in my suicide attempt. My friends and family amazed me. They were supportive and understood all the pain I was going through. They didn't care about my sexual orientation because they loved me for who I was, not what I was. My classmates, on the other hand, were anything but understanding. My coming out of the closet didn't just give my harassers a better reason to hate me; it also gave people who didn't know me a reason not to like me. Food was thrown at me on a daily basis, and one student actually handed me pornography, telling me and a friend that heterosexual sex was what we should be doing. Except he didn't use that phrase.

After I graduated, I was no longer afraid: I was angry! I realized I was treated so unjustly that I had to do something about the corruption at Live Oak. I couldn't let this happen to anyone else. I wanted to get involved in making policy changes to help queer youth at Live Oak. I wanted to make sure that other gay students at that school had equal rights in terms of sexual harassment. But everywhere I turned, I got the same response: "sue." I could work the rest of my life on councils, but nothing seemed like it was going to change the policies that applied to people like me — nothing but a major lawsuit, that is.

I was shocked by the number of people who wanted to help me, when at one time I had no one who was willing to support me. Today I have five attorneys, two from the National Center for Lesbian Rights, two from the American Civil Liberties Union, and two private attorneys who wanted to be a part of the lawsuit because they believe in the cause. There are five other plaintiffs in the lawsuit besides me, including some from nearby Murphy Middle School. They heard about what I was doing, had reached the end of their rope and wanted to tell their stories too.

I could give you a fistful of statistics on the suicide and high school dropout rate among queer youth, but I don't think I need to do that. Just look around: a face in a crowd of hundreds is already pleading for your help. Action must be taken in order to make change for the faceless, voiceless teenagers who are powerless in a corrupt school system. It might be someone you know and love who is going through such horrifying isolation, it could be your son or daughter someday, it could be you right now! I can't take back the years that I suffered, but I can give some justice to a person who might never know who I am. I can make change for someone like me, and I know I will. ∎

An account of Alana Flores' lawsuit appears on p. 83.

DEBRA CHASNOFF

PHOTO: KATHLEEN MICHAUD

Once word got out that our film, "It's Elementary: Talking About Gay Issues in School" was going to be broadcast on public television stations this past summer, the phone calls, letters, and e-mails started pouring in. For the first three years that our small nonprofit company had been distributing the film, the correspondence had been overwhelmingly positive. Hundreds of teachers and parents had contacted us, brimming with emotion, full of thanks for creating a resource they could use to get people to talk about how to prevent anti-gay discrimination and to make sure schools were safe for all children.

But now groups like the American Family Association, Concerned Women for America, the Family Research Council, Coral Ridge Ministries, radio talk show host Laura Schlessinger — even Oliver North — had decided "It's Elementary" was evil incarnate. Distorting one boy's comments in the film to make it look like we were trying to get children to hate Christians, they fanned the flames for a massive campaign to stop the broadcasts, the likes of which PBS affiliates across the country had never seen.

The e-mail chime on my computer goes off:

Your film is child abuse. Your group is nothing more than nicely dressed thugs. The makers of this film are more dangerous to our children than the tobacco and alcohol industries combined!

I wonder what they would think if they came into our office. Saw the four of us opening our Tupperware containers to eat leftover casseroles for lunch. Saw the row of pictures of her daughter that Helen, my co-producer, keeps over desk, or the one I look at all day of my two sons dressed in their Superman costumes.

Christy, our office manager, opens the mail.

This video is slick propaganda to convert children to homosexuality. Once a lezzy homo was trying to get close to my daughter. It's disgusting and makes me sick. May all homos burn in hell!

Christy gets ready to leave for her regular Thursday night commitment, reading books out loud to an elderly blind woman.

Line three on the phone lights up:

Debra Chasnoff is an Academy Award-winning documentary filmmaker whose work includes "It's Elementary," broadcast on PBS this summer; "Deadly Deception" and "Choosing Children." For more information on her films, see the Women's Educational Media website at www.womedia.org.

Instead of promoting this crap you should spend your time searching for a cure! Keep your immoral behavior in the closet or under the rug where it deserves to be.

My girlfriend calls to rearrange our plans for the weekend. Can we work in the garden on Sunday afternoon instead of earlier? She wants to go to church in the morning.

Eat shit you bunch of faggots. You are permitting the disintegration of the family and therefore the country!

I leave and go food shopping. I try to guess whether the kids will go for spaghetti or chicken tonight.

Leave our kids alone. "It's Elementary" is a stealth campaign to cultivate a new generation of sex partners.

I pick up my youngest son from preschool. He is beaming with pride over the picture he drew of his brother and his two moms. I get to my oldest son's soccer practice and pile him and three other mud-covered 10-year-olds into the van.

> I glance at myself in the mirror, surprised that my face is the one they think poses such a threat to so many children.

The child [in the film] who has two lesbian mothers shouldn't have two lesbian mothers in the first place. I was completely disgusted to watch children of elementary school-age discussing how it is okay for gay or lesbian couples to have a family with children.

I help my son finish his homework. Then, since I'm the room parent for the fifth-graders this year, I make phone calls to find other parents who can go on next week's field trip.

Stay out of our schools you damn dykes. It's bullshit that you are teaching our kids that lesbians and gays are all right.

Everybody's tucked in to bed. I cuddle with my youngest son. "Mommy I love you," he whispers in my ear before he hunkers down with Tuffy, his favorite Beanie Baby.

Little girls can't hold hands any longer because women like you are snickering in the shadows. The world wishes you had better parents.

After the kids are asleep, the phone rings. I have an interview scheduled on a national talk radio show — one of hundreds I've been asked to do since the broadcasts started. I put on my Radio Shack wireless headset, pull out the laundry basket, and start folding little pairs of socks as the show's host takes callers.

Stop preying on our children. We don't approve of this film. We are a family of good values.

"And what are we?" I wonder to myself, grateful that the boys can't hear this. I glance at myself in the mirror, surprised, once again, that my face is the one they think poses such a threat to so many children.

"Mom? can I have a drink of water?" I push the mute button and scramble to fill the glass and bring it into the kids' room before the next caller comes on.

If PBS continues to show "It" then let us hope they air it in the middle of the night when the queers are more than welcome to watch it while me and my NORMAL family are sleeping.

This goes on for weeks as "It's Elementary" gathers steam and picks up air dates in North Dakota, Hawaii, Nevada and Louisiana. In Idaho, the Christian Coalition puts up billboards across the state screaming: "Do you want public television promoting homosexuality to your child? Stop the broadcast of 'It's Elementary.' "

Die! I will kill you!

I try to remember why we made the film in the first place. I think of another mom, Judy Shepard, getting the phone call informing her that her son was murdered by two young men who thought torturing a gay guy would be a fun way to spend a Saturday night.

I go on CNN live for an hour and I am reassured by all the children in the studio audience who are not swayed by the other guest, a representative of one of the conservative groups that has opposed the broadcasts. Every student who gets a turn at the mike says something to the effect of: "That lady [me] is right. You should hear what goes on at our school. Everyone is really horrible to the kids who are gay and everyone says 'faggot' all the time. It would help a lot if our teachers talked to us about this in school."

I don't hate homosexuals. I love them. I love everyone. But it is a sin and school is not the place to teach children about sin.

I remember Katherine, a third-grader in the film who explains what happens on the playground: "It's amazing how teachers don't notice all the stuff that's going on. Kids say 'oh, what are you? gay or something?' It makes you feel weird in your stomach."

What is the real sin?

I just have to trust that giving millions of people a chance to see the young children in "It's Elementary" air their concerns about anti-gay name-calling, to see talented teachers find age-appropriate ways to end the invisibility of gay people in school curricula, and to see schools warmly embrace all kinds of families is worth the abuse. That there really is no excuse for another generation growing up believing that gay people are some lower subcategory of the human race.

We'll stop at nothing to keep this show off the air. Parents everywhere should be on alert! We'll fight to the end.

Fortunately, in more than 100 cities and in almost all of the top media markets, they lost the fight. Hundreds of parents, teachers, and religious leaders refused to let these voices speak for ALL parents, teachers, and religious leaders. Gay and lesbian adults recalled their own painful experiences in school and demanded that the children in "It's Elementary" be heard. Other viewers, sickened by the rise of anti-gay hate crimes, asked for the opportunity to see how some adults are trying to prevent hatred before it starts. And scores of programmers at public television stations stood their ground amidst a deluge of opposition and threats to their financial support.

I think America inched forward a little bit this summer. No one used to talk about gay issues in schools at all. Now, at least, the dialogue has begun.

But hey — I gotta go; there's a PTA meeting tonight. ∎

ALICIA PEDREIRA

In August 1998, I was working as a therapist and residential counselor for Kentucky Baptist Homes for Children (KBHC) in Louisville. I could never have foreseen that by the end of the month I would be riding an emotional roller-coaster that would end with my being fired on Oct. 23.

I had been recruited five months earlier to work for a special unit for behavior-disordered adolescent boys. During the interview process I told the clinical director, my future supervisor, that I was a lesbian. The director told his supervisor and he was told the special unit was his creation and responsibility, and that he should hire the best person for the job. He hired me, and said there was no official policy against hiring gay people, but that I should be discreet. Being discreet goes with being a therapist, so I didn't think this was unreasonable. He also warned that should people higher up than his supervisor find out, there could be problems.

Although my partner, Nance Goodman, and I had reservations about my working for a Baptist organization, I decided I wanted to for several reasons. First, my boss was a well-known clinician and I wanted to be under his tutelage. The Spring Meadows campus, at that time, was one of the few long-term residential homes left untouched by the state's drive to cut costs through managed care. Also, I wanted to work with the adolescent population, and KBHC paid its clinicians well.

On Aug. 22, 1998, Nance and I returned home from vacation. It was the opening weekend of the Kentucky State Fair. To our surprise, an 11-by-14-inch photograph of the two of us that had been taken a year earlier was being displayed in the amateur photo contest. When I returned to work on Monday, co-workers began telling me about the picture. One of my co-workers, who knew I was gay, told me that I was standing in front of Nance and

Alicia Pedreira, a clinical therapist by training, is currently a loan officer at a Louisville bank. Together with Kentucky's Fairness Campaign, she has worked to pass laws that prohibit discrimination based on sexual orientation. The photograph on this page is the one mentioned in her essay.

wearing a tank top with a map of the Aegean Sea that read "Isle of Lesbos," which is a real island off the cost of Turkey. In that moment I knew I had lost my job.

I immediately called Nance and she sent a friend to investigate. The next day, Nance went down to the fairgrounds and had the photo taken down. The people in charge of the photo contest didn't seem to understand that we did not find the photo lewd or vulgar in any way, but that merely showing it could cause me to lose my job. After some difficulty they took down the photo, but by then thousands of people had seen it.

> They said there was a photo of me wearing a shirt that said "Isle of Lesbos." In that moment I knew I had lost my job.

It was a week before I heard the first rumblings. One of the eight counselors I supervised complained to the manager of the unit. A week after that, I was asked to resign by KBHC's cabinet, which consisted of the president and five vice presidents. My supervisor was stunned. He honestly did not believe I would be fired. The cabinet told him to ask for my resignation. Through his tears, he did. I refused to resign because I felt I had done nothing wrong. I had been honest from the beginning and I had been discreet, as I had been asked.

Some people have said I was not discreet because I wore a "queer" shirt in public. My response is that I will not live my life worrying about infinite negative possibilities. That photo was taken at the local 1997 AIDS Walk, a year before I came to work for KBHC.

So, that Friday, I refused to resign and fully expected to be asked to pack up my office and leave on the next working day. This was not the case; there was a great deal of ambiguity for another week. Every day I went to work and there would be no word. After a week of tense anticipation, I decided to ask my supervisor what was happening. He said that Human Resources wanted me to pick a date that was to be my last day. I refused to do that because that would appear as if I were resigning. At that point my supervisor, under protest, chose the date of Oct. 2 as my last day. I spent those three weeks trying to find another job while working full time, asking the president of KBHC for an official letter of termination, and telling the eight teen-age boys in my care what was happening.

Up to this point, they hadn't known anything was going on. In those three weeks I had to tell them I was gay, something I would never have done otherwise. I had to tell them I was being fired and help them deal with their anger and emotions as well prepare them for goodbyes.

During those three weeks, the boys were angry and very supportive of me. Fellow clinicians and social workers were outraged and stood by me. To my knowledge, seven people have resigned from Kentucky Baptist Homes in protest. Most of the other workers at Spring Meadows did not know what was happening until a few days before my last day.

When they were told, the majority of them were angry. Several people made a point of coming to me and telling me they were sorry about what had happened, and that they didn't agree with the decision.

The counselors in my unit knew what was going on almost from the beginning. Therefore, I endured passive-aggressive behavior, ignorant comments, avoidance, etc. One of the counselors told the boys that my "sin" was as bad as being a murderer. Another told a boy he would be "bad" if he chose to follow through on his bisexual feelings. At the end of the three weeks, I had been refused an official letter of termination from President Dr. Bill Smithwick twice. I was eager to leave. It had been very stressful.

On Oct. 3, after my goodbye session with the boys, I went to sign my papers of termination. I was surprised when the vice president of Human Relations and another executive did not want me to sign the papers. They asked if I had found another job. I had not. They wanted to know why this day was picked to be my last. They said that they would find another job for me to do until I found another job. They offered a job placement agency. I was stunned, but I didn't want to give them one more iota of my time and energy. All I wanted was to leave, so that I could look for another job and put this behind me.

To describe what happened in the next three weeks would be too tedious, so I will summarize. Kentucky Baptist Homes wanted to transfer me to a clinical job in the central office. The transfer would have been against their own policy and procedures because transfers were not allowed until a person had worked with the agency for nine months, and I had only been there for six. If I had taken that transfer, I would have been working at same office with the people who voted to fire me. The pay would have remained the same, but the job was a demotion. I used every rule and procedure I could find to decline the position without being insubordinate. I did not want to give KBHC a reason to fire me.

In the end, they must have tired of my volleying. On Oct. 23, I was called in to the central office, where I was suspiciously ushered into the president's office. He then told me that the whole situation had caused uproar in the agency and that he wanted me to know that it was not personal. I wanted to scream, but I just signed my papers and left. I was relieved to leave, even though I was unemployed and unsure of my future. My employer instituted an official policy against hiring gay people on the very day I signed those papers.

The good news is that the publicity surrounding my departure helped: the city of Louisville passed a part of the "Fairness Ordinance" three months later. This part of the ordinance forbids city employers to discriminate on the basis of sexual orientation. Ironically, it would not have covered my case — because KBHC is in the county, not the city, and it is a considered a religious organization even though it gets 80 to 90 percent of its money from state and federal grants. The Fairness Campaign and I will continue our struggle to have discrimination in public housing and public accommodations prohibited also. ■

An account of the controversy surrounding Alicia Pedreira's firing also appears on p. 143.

RANDY BLOCK

This is the story of my partner and dearest friend, Gerry Crane.

Gerry was hired by the Byron Center (Michigan) Public Schools in the summer of 1993 to teach high school vocal and instrumental music. He previously had been employed by another public school system, where he had attained tenure status, as well as by the Christian school system in Grand Rapids.

The Byron Center school system knew that Gerry had impeccable teaching credentials. They did not know that he was also gay. Gerry and I had been in an exclusive relationship for over

Randy Block, left, and Gerry Crane.

two years, and we made a conscious effort to hide his homosexuality from the schools. Whenever I would attend one of his concerts, marching performances, or presentations, I would take a friend with me (usually female) or attend with a group of friends.

During the summer of 1995, while attending the commitment ceremony of two of our closest friends in Massachusetts, Gerry and I decided to have our own commitment ceremony. We chose Oct. 21, our fourth anniversary of living together, for the ceremony, and we went about making plans that summer-arranged for the pastor of our church to officiate, met with caterers, informed our friends and families, hired a string quartet, ordered flowers, designed invitations — all the things that heterosexual couples do to prepare for their marriage ceremonies.

Gerry's first day of school that year was Aug. 30. At the end of that day, he was asked to report to the Administration Office. When he reported to the assistant superintendent at the appointed time, he was first told, "This is an informational meeting per the master contract with the teachers' union." The high school principal and assistant superintendent then proceeded to inform him, "We know that you are a homosexual and that you are planning to marry another man sometime within the next two months." They did not even ask him if this

Randy Block is a manager at a home improvement retailer in Grand Rapids, Michigan, and serves on the board of a gay Christian organization there. Gerry Crane's story was featured on the ABC-TV news magazine "20/20" in 1998.

was accurate. Gerry was shocked, to say the least. He asked what the school intended to do. They responded that at this time they were contractually obliged to inform him that they held this information, but that they weren't prepared to discuss any future plans.

Gerry and I had already scheduled our first premarital pastoral counseling session for that very afternoon, and we arranged to meet at the church immediately after school. When he arrived, he was noticeably upset and told me and our pastor about the meeting. We discussed postponing or canceling our plans but decided to carry on, but with some minor changes. We changed the venue of the ceremony from our church to a botanical garden. We took additional steps to ensure privacy, even adding the phrase "confidentiality is appreciated" at the bottom of our invitations to try to keep students and their parents from learning about the event.

Our commitment ceremony took place as planned on Oct. 21, with 90 of our closest friends attending. The next day, Gerry received a phone call at home from one of his students, who informed him, "One of the other students is distributing a copy of your marriage ceremony program to people all over town." We were stunned, confused, and frightened. Who could have obtained this evidence and passed it on to someone in the community?

Gerry had taken a personal day for the Monday following the ceremony. When he returned to school Tuesday, he quickly found out that many of the students were talking about him. During one of his classes that day, a student asked, "What did you do over the weekend, Mr. Crane?" He avoided a direct answer, and then the student asked, "Is that a new ring on your hand? Did you get married?" Gerry replied that he would not discuss his personal life with them.

Later that day, he was again called into the Administration Office for a meeting. There, he was informed that the school board would be discussing any actions to be taken against him at their next meeting. Gerry and I contacted several lawyers and the teachers union to determine what the school board could legally do. We were told that despite his excellent teaching record, tenure status, and the absence of any inappropriate interactions with students, the Board could legally terminate him after following procedures in the teachers' contract. Gerry was directed not to discuss the situation with any students, which he never did in the following weeks and months.

The school board met in November to discuss the matter. Many students, supporters, opponents, teachers, parents, and the local media attended the meeting. The Board decided only to continue investigating its options. The following weeks brought many more meetings between Gerry and the administration. It also brought much tension. Many parents withdrew their children from Gerry's classes during this time. Local churches put pressure on the community to discharge him. During morning services one Sunday, letters were placed on windshields of cars calling for the "dismissal of the sodomite music teacher" and urging local pastors to "preach against this sin." Discussion and public debate continued for the next month, and almost daily Gerry had meetings with lawyers, union representatives and school officials.

Finally, on Dec. 18, 1995, the School Board made a decision. In a five-paragraph statement, the board said it would not terminate Mr. Crane at this time. It would "continue to monitor the situation and take appropriate, lawful action when justified." As one district parent observed, "It means he'll be coming back to school and looking over his shoulder."

When school resumed after the holiday break in January 1996, students continued to withdraw from Gerry's classes. In February, a mailing was received in the home of each of his students. The mailing contained the video, "Setting the Record Straight: Inside the Homosexual Agenda," and a 98-page booklet that condemned homosexuality. Two teachers at the school, it was later learned, had provided a group with class lists and student addresses for this mailing. Those two teachers were later reprimanded for "not cooperating with school officials" during the investigation of their actions. Meanwhile, Gerry was constantly reprimanded for a sundry list of items: disciplining a student for calling another student "faggot," questioning one student about why he was dropping out of class, and for including the song "Colors of the Wind" (from the movie "Pocahontas") in one of his concerts. It seemed to Gerry that everything he did was suspect.

> "One of the other students is distributing a copy of your marriage ceremony program to people all over town."

In June 1996, two new members were elected to the school board. They had both campaigned on a platform of anger that the previous board had failed to dismiss Gerry Crane.

Finally, that July, tired of the struggle and the constant chaos in his personal life, Gerry decided to seek a negotiated resignation from his position and move on. He made an agreement with the school whereby they would pay him one year's salary plus benefits in exchange for his resignation, payable over a one-year period. To Gerry, this represented a defeat for the school and the Byron Center community. In September, he returned to college to begin work on a degree in social work.

On Dec. 27, 1996, Gerry suffered a heart attack and lapsed into a coma at the age of 32. One week later, he died. When the autopsy was performed, the medical examiner determined that Gerry had died of a congenital heart valve defect of the type that was not usually fatal. In the examiner's opinion, the stress of the previous 16 months had contributed to Gerry's death. As the minister at Gerry's funeral said, "Gerry died of a broken heart."

The day Gerry died, Jan. 3, 1997, I was informed through school sources that they would no longer be making any additional payments on the severance agreement. In January 1999, I filed a lawsuit against the school district on behalf of Gerry's estate to obtain the balance of the unpaid settlement agreement. The Senior District Court judge filed a summary judgment against the school district, ordering them to pay the balance due with interest and legal fees. The school filed for an appeal in April 1999. The fight continues.... ∎

REV. LESLIE PENROSE

"We are lifelong Methodists," the card said, "but today we withdrew our membership from the United Methodist Church. We have a gay son, and when he read your story in the newspaper, he said he could never go back. If he can't, then we won't."

"Three more losses," I thought to myself as I placed the card in the growing stack of cards and letters I had received that week. The cards and letters were mostly expressions of support for "what I had done," but each one also bore witness to the underlying grief of the person who sent it. "I thought their welcome was real this time," one young man wrote, "shame on me for being fooled twice." "They have sacrificed my dignity for the illusion of unity," another said. And on the back of a Sunday bulletin handed to me as a tearful young woman left worship, was the single sentence: "I'm so angry I can't feel my heart breaking — yet." So many losses... and for what gain?

I was appointed by the Oklahoma Bishop of the United Methodist Church in 1993 to begin a "base community" ministry in Tulsa — a ministry that would embrace and empower those persons who had "fallen through the cracks"; those who were economically, socially, and religiously marginalized. From the beginning, those who became the congregation of the United Methodist Community of Hope committed to try "to act as the Body of Christ." We committed to invest half of our time, energy, and money working for justice and reconciliation both in and beyond our congregation and our local community. Each Sunday we gathered, gay and straight together, in one borrowed or rented space after another. And each Sunday, we lit our rainbow-colored Christ Candle, and proclaimed: *"We light this candle as our witness that in all things we choose to hope rather than curse the darkness!"*

In March 1994, the Community of Hope, a growing, diverse congregation of about 50 participants, voted to become the first Reconciling Congregation in Oklahoma, and in July

Originally a Methodist elder, Leslie Penrose is now a minister in the United Church of Christ and still serves as pastor of Community of Hope Church in Tulsa, Okla.

of that year, we held our first holy union for two gay men, both of whom were living with AIDS. It was a grand celebration, with seven United Methodist ministers and one Unitarian minister in attendance.

Although the resistance to our ministry was strong, both in the local community and in the United Methodist Church, support for it was also strong and consistent. Members of Parents, Families and Friends of Lesbians and Gays (PFLAG), United Methodist Women chapters, church youth groups from several denominations, and clergy and laity across the state supported our ministry physically and financially. As the Community of Hope's ministry to and with gay and lesbian persons grew, so did the hopes of many in Oklahoma that a new spirit of hospitality and compassion might be dawning in the church — that, at last, there might be a place in the church, other than corners and closets, for men and women who were both Christian and gay.

> How do you even begin to imagine the costs to people you cherish, if you apologize for affirming who they are?

That hope was severely challenged in 1996 when the United Methodist Church added a statement to its Book of Discipline declaring that "Ceremonies that celebrate homosexual unions shall not be conducted by our ministers and shall not be conducted in our churches."

We asked ourselves: Does it make sense — or make hope or wholeness or justice — to say we affirm homosexual persons, but condemn homosexual relationships? Can we "act as the Body of Christ" by prioritizing *who* one loves over *how* one loves? And I asked myself, "Can I, with integrity, pastor half of my congregation differently than the other half, based simply on their sexual orientation?" The only possible response to all three questions was "no!"

Therefore, choosing to ground our discernment in an ethic of 'right-relationship,' the community continued to evaluate all relationships based on their "fruits" (Gal. 5:22-23) rather than their gender makeup. I continued to bless the unions of *all* those "whom God had joined together" (Mark 10-9) — homosexual or heterosexual — and we entrusted the consequences to God.

In the next three years we blessed over 20 life-partnerships, gay and straight, and hope made a comeback. Then, early in 1999, my participation in the holy union of two women drew two complaints. Further charges were threatened. There were three options: 1. stop and apologize; 2. withdraw; or 3. go to trial.

"Count the cost before you do this," a mentoring pastor once urged me about going into the ministry, "the Gospel always has one!" My personal costs were fairly clear — lose your integrity, lose your denomination, or lose your ministry. But how do you count the costs to others?

How do you even begin to imagine the costs to people you cherish, if you apologize for affirming who they are? Or to persons you don't even know — to men and women still trapped in closets of silence and fear; to the children growing up in our churches who will someday have to wrestle with the awareness that they are in love with someone of their same sex; to the teens who think they'd rather die than tell someone they are gay? How do you count the cost to gay men and lesbians who have started to trust God again, or to their parents who have finally learned to reconcile their faith in God with their love for their gay child, if you stop to save your job? If you choose this door, everyone loses — you, those you pastor, the church.

Or, if you withdraw, abandon the struggle, how do you count the cost to the clergy and laity who have invested their energy, their reputations, their hope in the possibility your ministry represents? Or to all the United Methodists — gay and straight — who yearn for a more open and inclusive denomination? Or to those to whom you have said, "change only happens from the inside"? If you choose this door, everyone loses — you, those you pastor, the church.

And how could you possibly anticipate the terrible costs to members of a community — especially its already wounded and weary members, or fearful, still-secreted members — if you drag them through the national attention of a public trial? Or to your ministry, if all your time and energy are being spent creating a defense? If you choose this door, everyone loses — you, those you pastor, the church.

There were no good options; no "right" choices. And even though there are some who may have convinced themselves that if I lost, they would win, the truth is that whenever God's people choose to deny God's bounteous blessing and grace to anyone, no one wins — there is only more alienation, more division, and we are all losers.

"You have no right," my Bishop had preached at my ordination, "to tell a brother or sister 'God loves you,' unless you are willing to stay with them until they experience it." I painfully and prayerfully chose Door No. 2 and all the losses it would bring. On March 4, 1999, I withdrew from the United Methodist Church in order to transfer my orders to the United Church of Christ. The Community of Hope is still painfully and prayerfully discerning its future. ■

CHRISTOPHER C. CAMP

I was raised in a loving, conservative family in Southern California. I was close to my father and mother. But as far back as I can remember, I always felt "different" from the rest of my family. When I was in kindergarten, I had a crush on David, the boy in first grade who lived across the street from me.

In the third grade, I stumbled across the word "homosexual" in the dictionary and knew immediately that it applied to me. I also knew that I would have to do every-thing that I could to conceal that fact from my family and friends, that I would never be accepted if they knew who I really was. Seeking to immerse myself in "masculine" activities to avoid detection, I was active in football, soccer, track and the swim team. I always had a steady girlfriend.

In junior high school, I felt increasingly different from my peers. I felt that if I only had enough sexual experiences with enough girls, I would not be a homosexual anymore — but nothing changed. I didn't dare confide in anyone, lest they humiliate me by revealing my dark secret to the world. I felt hopeless, and soon became suicidal. It was at that point that I became involved with a Campus Life group sponsored by Youth for Christ, and at the age of 16, I entered my new life as a "born-again Christian." I hoped that also meant I could become "normal" like everyone else.

I quickly rose through the ranks and became a student leader in our high school Christian Student Union. I went through leadership training with Campus Crusade for Christ. I began spending time with my local pastor, who taught me how to pray, share my faith and study the Bible.

In my freshman year of college, when everything seemed to be turning out well for me, something happened that shook me to the core. I fell in love with my best friend, and

Chris Camp has been an AIDS activist since 1982 and frequently speaks on his experience in the "ex-gay" movement. He is a training specialist with the AIDS Administration in the Maryland Department of Health and Mental Hygiene.

ended up making love with him. Feeling unclean, I felt that my world had fallen apart. I felt I had let God, my family and my friends down. Desperately seeking help, I turned to my college pastor for guidance. After going through many, many hours of intensive counseling, prayer and study with my pastor and therapist, they referred me to a support group for "ex-gays" that met at our church. The group leaders had been trained by a group called Exodus International.

All of us in the group would meet together for Bible study, prayer and fellowship. If any of us felt "tempted," we were to call on someone else in the group for strength and support. Soon it became apparent to me that most of the men in the group still seemed to be homosexuals. While overt homosexual behavior was condemned, the hint of homosexuality was still present — in the clasp of a handshake, the closeness of an embrace, or a lingering gaze.

The group's definition of a homosexual as "someone who practices homosexual behavior" was too shallow for me. If it was true, as I understood it from my study of the Bible, that *"out of the abundance of the heart the mouth speaks,"* then even though I was not having homosexual sex, I was still a homosexual. My thoughts and feelings had not substantially changed, though I did try to deny them. I knew that the only way I could change was to immerse myself in memorizing the Bible. I felt that if I was devout enough, somehow I could be changed from the inside out.

Throughout my college years, I was active as a student leader in the Baptist Student Union and numerous other organizations: I was trained by the Navigators and helped to start the local chapter of Inter-Varsity Christian Fellowship. I led Bible study groups for fellow students twice a week. I conducted college workshops for L'Abri Christian Fellowship. My college co-pastor and I assisted in the research for the Family Discipleship series in Focus on the Family, led by Dr. James Dobson. I also assisted my pastor and co-pastor in the development of programs for the Institute of Basic Youth Conflicts — a course developed by Bill Gothard. I followed a rigorous daily Bible memorization, study and meditation regimen. In 1979, I entered Dallas Theological Seminary, as a World Missions major.

I was twice elected class representative to the Student Missions Fellowship, and organized groups of "prayer cells" for former seminarians then on the mission field. I had a steady girlfriend, and we were discussing the possibility of marriage.

It was while I served on a new church extension team overseas that I had a profound realization: through seven years of countless hours of Bible study, intense counseling sessions, prayer vigils, agonizing and soul-searching, I was still a homosexual. My thoughts, my desires and drives had not changed. More than that, I also realized that as far back as I could remember, I had always felt the way I did. At no time did I ever *choose* to be a homosexual — no more than someone chooses to be heterosexual. I just was. My experiences were in direct contrast to what I was taught in church and seminary.

I came to view my homosexuality as something I was born with — a moral neutral, like my hair or eye color, or my ethnicity. It was what I did with my life that made it good or bad, not who I was.

> Through countless hours of Bible study, counseling sessions, prayer vigils and soul-searching, I was still a homosexual.

Where are my friends and companions from Exodus International and other "ex-gay" groups now?

▌ Many were so unhappy about not being able to change their orientation that they committed suicide.

▌ Others live double lives — one publicly as heterosexuals, with wives and children, active in church work, seminary or bible college teaching and other ministries, while having to maintain another one, a secret life as a closeted homosexual.

Where am I now? I am happier with my life now more than ever, knowing that I don't have to hide anymore. I have rediscovered my faith — deeper and more intense than before. And, knowing that I am called into the ministry, I intend to complete my seminary training in the near future.

What do I hope and pray for? I pray for the day when gay, lesbian and bisexual teens will no longer feel estranged and isolated for being different. That they will not feel compelled to engage in self-destructive behavior, including drug abuse, unsafe sex and suicide. And I pray that they gain strong self-confidence and self-esteem — so that they can grow up to become happy, healthy, well-adjusted, responsible people. ■

JEFFREY MONTGOMERY

The Triangle Foundation has been one of the leading anti-violence projects in the country for gay, lesbian, bisexual and transgendered people since it began such work in 1991. As is the case in many fields where people deal with gruesome circumstances, we like to think we become inured to it. Unfortunately, that's not possible.

During the early hours of a Thanksgiving weekend Saturday in 1994, two killers beat a gay man to death in his suburban Detroit home. A second man, the deceased's friend, was brutally beaten in the same attack. The four had met earlier in the evening at an area gay bar.

The victims were closeted gay men.

The man who died, Gary, a 41-year-old Ford Motor Co. engineer, was deep in the closet. He was known to be gay by a small circle of friends, his pals at the bar; the bar where he would meet his executioners. That bar, those friends, formed the boundaries of his gay world. His family and co-workers had no idea.

He was outed in death. His brutal strangulation was the device that brought Gary out to his family, his co-workers and neighbors.

From their first response to the scene, the police recognized this as an anti-gay bias crime. Without hesitation, they accepted Triangle's assistance and relied on gay community involvement in conducting the investigation.

The news media also accurately portrayed the story as an anti-gay hate crime. They broadcast the sketches of the suspects; they did a good job, without sensationalizing it, without making a tabloid item of it.

Those efforts paid off when police had both suspects in custody within five days of the killing. All parties agreed that the quick result was due to authorities' willingness to treat

Jeff Montgomery is executive director of Detroit's Triangle Foundation, which has a web site at www.tri.org.

the crime as what it was: the murder and assault of two men purely because they were gay. Police credited Triangle as essential in apprehending the assailants.

We were actually feeling pretty good. There had been great cooperative police work, serious attention and help from the media... and then we were hit.

Gary's family, which hadn't had an inkling about his sexuality, was outraged. His co-workers, who also had been in the dark, were incensed. How dare we — the police, the media, the Triangle Foundation, Jeffrey Montgomery — how dare we claim that Gary was gay!

They said Gary was in the bar by accident. He did not intend to be there. They said he was definitely not gay. His father knew he wasn't. His co-workers knew he wasn't. In fact, they could produce women who knew better. They had joked with him about gay-bashing and he had never said anything. They had worked with him for a long time. They *knew* he wasn't gay. They reviled us. They would seek legal action if this slander was not corrected!

> Gary was living the double life forced on anyone who has to remain so deeply inside the closet.

It was jarring. We knew that Gary had been going to the bar, was a regular there, for at least ten years. We knew people who had been involved with Gary. We knew he had never been able to tell his family. We then became aware of some people at his company, people who knew he was gay, people like Gary, who also could never share that fact with people at work. We knew Gary had lived a double life.

Not a double life like in a spy novel, nothing nefarious. Gary was living the double life that is forced on anyone who has to remain so deeply inside the closet. The two worlds are defined in crystal. Crystal clear, night-and-day definitions. Fragile.

We found ourselves dealing with an angry, grief-stricken father who had just learned — at the same time — that his son was viciously murdered, and that he was gay. In all the experience that I have had dealing with dctails of death and mayhem, this was one of the worst moments I can recall.

There is no more stark an example of the tyranny of the closet.

Gary's family and friends found a literal corpse inside that closet. Often another kind of corpse occupies the closet-tomb's interior. It is a living, zombie-like, damaged corpse.

During the last five years, I have not stopped thinking of just how tragic Gary's murder was. Tragic beyond the murder, brutality and loss.

His family was not able to grieve as most would. They must have coped with the guilt and shame of not really having known their son. Gary's colleagues must be embarrassed, perhaps recalling when, or trying to remember if, they engaged in conversations that were inappropriate or hurtful. None of them will ever be able to tell Gary that it's fine he's gay, that it's OK, that they still love him anyway.

So they were angry. At Gary, the police, the media, at Triangle, at me — at themselves. They joined the actual survivor, the one who lived through the attack, as additional victims in Gary's murder case.

When the suspects were captured, Gary's family issued public statements forgiving their son's killers, in the spirit of their Christian faith, they said. They also used that opportunity to blast Triangle for identifying him as gay. They forgave the killers, but not their son.

Whether closets are blown open or opened slowly to allow a peek inside, skeletons are found inside. Gary's case still haunts us, but it will not deter us from our mission and work to honestly and diligently work on behalf of GLBT victims.

"You can't out a dead person," we often say. But for those who remain, it is a grave responsibility to act on behalf of the one who has passed on.

Epilogue: Gary's killers were found guilty of first-degree murder. During testimony they admitted to having hunted gay victims in the past. They said they knew gays never report being victims. The survivor of the attack that killed Gary admitted that had both he and Gary survived, they would not have reported the attack. The killers are serving life sentences without possibility of parole. ■

WENDY C. WEAVER

I struggle to know how to define my journey — because for so much of it, I believe, I was in a relatively unconscious state. I grew up in the small farming community of Buhl, Idaho, the youngest of 10 children. I worked on the farm and spent a lot of time on my own, creating my own fun and adventures. My memories don't include a lot of people.

I feel as if I spent most of my school years quietly and without a lot of deep attachments. I left high school a year early and attended Utah's Brigham Young University, where I majored in physical education and minored in psychology. I became involved in competitive sports and made many lasting and wonderful friends. Over the last few years, I have learned that many of them have traveled a similar path

Wendy Weaver, right, and Rachael Smith.

as I. We didn't speak much about our personal lives in those days. The environment at BYU didn't give us many options to share our lives with each other.

I started my teaching and coaching career almost 20 years ago. I came to the local high school in Spanish Fork, Utah, when I was just 21. I started coaching right away — basketball, track & field and volleyball. I wasn't a very good coach in those days, I had a lot to learn. Eventually I focused exclusively on coaching volleyball. Even though it was the sport I knew least about in college, I determined to learn all I could about volleyball. All the team camps, coaching clinics, training videos and publications eventually paid off for me. My coaching and my teams got better and better. Meanwhile, I was a well-liked and proficient teacher. I enjoyed talking to the kids and getting to know them.

I was active in the Mormon Church. Through my career and my religion, I met Gary, who was Spanish Fork High's school psychologist. I had been taught since I was a child that my destiny was to marry in the Mormon temple and to have an eternal family, so I

Wendy Weaver is a psychology teacher and coach at Spanish Fork High School near Provo, Utah. Her volleyball teams won four Utah state championships in the 1980s and '90s.

determined that marrying Gary was what I was supposed to do. I was 24. From the beginning, Gary and I took foster, youth-in-custody boys into our home. We were immersed in the care of these kids and in our respective careers.

Gary and I had some similar interests, but we didn't spend a whole lot of time together in those formative years of our marriage. I told Gary early in our marriage that I struggled with same-sex attraction, and I was encouraged to be faithful and to live close to my religion and to my husband and all would be well. I spent much of my married life in a subconscious state, emotionally close to death. At times I would meet someone who would allow me to feel alive and to talk about my feelings, but my religion and my marriage held me back from completely realizing myself.

Meanwhile, my career as a teacher and coach was going well. I had always been one of those teachers who did my job and did it well, getting excellent reviews with no complaints from administrators, parents or students. Our volleyball team was the pride of the school, we had wonderful support from parents and students.

In my personal life it was becoming more and more difficult to remain unconscious about my attraction to women. In 1995, I signed up for a cross-country bike tour. I felt like I needed to determine the direction my life would go. It was a wonderful experience, with nothing to think about each day but getting up, riding, eating, and getting ready to ride again. After seven weeks and 3,400 miles, I was more at peace and a stronger person than I had been in a long time. I determined that I needed to leave my marriage and be true to myself. I gave myself a two-year timetable.

> School officials took away my coaching job and forbade me to speak with students about my sexual orientation.

In April 1997, I left my marriage and started a new life. I bought a new home and moved in with my partner, Rachael Smith, and our kids. I was still teaching and had just come back to coaching after a two-year sabbatical to work on my master's degree. In June, I began to call my players, and in the process one of them asked me if I was gay. I answered honestly; she probably already knew the answer.

My honesty seems to have gotten me in a lot of trouble. I would not change that answer today — but it launched me and my family into a public arena of lawsuits, newspaper articles and evening news clips. Among other things, school officials took away my coaching job and imposed a gag order on me, forbidding me from speaking with students about my sexual orientation.

But the turmoil has also brought an honesty about myself and my relationships that has been more positive than negative. It has required me to be open to my family, friends, community and most of all mine and Rachael's children. Without this ordeal, I think, we wouldn't have reached the level of communication we now have in our lives. Rachael and I have had many talks with our children, our neighbors and community because of my dispute with the school system. It hasn't been easy, but it has been well worth it. We have a freedom that most gay people have never had in their lifetimes. We're seldom concerned with "being found out" or being anything that we are not — because, in reality, everyone knows who we are.

The ruling in our federal lawsuit could not have been more favorable. The judge even wrote law concerning sections of the civil rights laws that we hadn't sued for or addressed in our lawsuit. The civil lawsuit brought against us by a parents' group calling themselves "Nebo Citizens for Moral and Legal Values" has essentially lost its bite. Its ruling is not nearly as clear-cut, but the lawyer for that lawsuit, despite saying he would appeal to a higher court, has done nothing further on his case at this point.

I have called myself an accidental activist many times, and actually that title could not be more apt. In my insulated life, I was unaware of the pain and hurt that most of my gay brothers and sisters face. I have been vastly educated to the struggles that still go on everyday in our world. I look around me now and see kids in my high school, especially young gay men, who struggle with their identities and "fitting in" every day of their lives. If I have made life a little easier for gay educators, then I'm glad, and I hope it makes a difference. I would like to do more. Now that I have a background of discrimination and judgment, I see how impossibly unfair life can be for us. I hope for a better future for us all. ■

An account of Wendy Weaver's dispute with her school appears on p. 218.

MANDY CARTER

I guess all advocates have stories to share about how we came to activism. In my case, the story is how I became concerned with the work of the Religious Right.

I had always known about people like Jerry Falwell and Pat Robertson, and had been aware of their anti-gay and anti-choice positions. And as a black lesbian, I had known where they stood on issues of concern to people of color — such as welfare reform, prison reform, affirmative action, immigration and "English-only" laws, to name a few.

But my eyes were opened even wider in 1993, when I saw the Religious Right trying to bring their anti-gay message into the black community in Cincinnati, Ohio, which was then in the throes of debate over Issue 3, an anti-gay citywide ordinance. Issue 3 sought to repeal all laws banning discrimination against gays, lesbians and bisexuals, and to rewrite Cincinnati's city charter to prevent lawmakers from ever passing such legislative protections in the future.

The Religious Right employed a number of tactics. They used a conservative black minister as the "face and voice" of their anti-gay initiative, but in reality the all-white American Family Association (AFA) was calling the shots. The group Colorado for Family Values, which had successfully spearheaded a similar anti-gay ballot initiative in that state called Amendment 2, pumped $500,000 into the Cincinnati campaign.

The Colorado money was spent extensively on local broadcast, newspaper and billboard advertising in Cincinnati — and it bought a *lot* of them. You couldn't pick up a newspaper, turn on a radio or TV, or drive around Cincinnati without seeing ads decrying "special rights" for homosexuals.

The AFA was distributing a video made by Rev. Lou Sheldon of the Traditional Values Coalition called "Gay Rights, Special Rights," which had as its theme "the hijacking of the

Mandy Carter is a consultant to the National Black Lesbian and Gay Leadership Forum. She lives in Durham, N.C.

civil rights movement." So we now have our own video, an award-winning film called "All God's Children" that addresses, in a positive way, black gays and lesbians in the black church. It was produced by Woman Vision video.

(Sheldon later popped up again during the first-ever U.S. Senate hearing on the introduction of the Employment Non-Discrimination Act. He and local black ministers appeared with day-glo stickers that read "No Comparison"— i.e., you can't compare skin color with sexual orientation.)

We stopped Cincinnati from enforcing the law, and we thought we'd won the battle. But in 1998 the Supreme Court inexplicably allowed Issue 3 to stand — even though the Court had already struck down Colorado's Amendment 2.

> We need black members out and up front, as proof that "white, privileged gay people" aren't trying to "hijack" the civil rights movement.

Despite the Court's eventual ruling, I learned a few lessons from my Cincinnati experience. First: All of us working for gay rights need black members out and up front, so that others in the black civil rights community can't say that "white, privileged gay people" are trying to "hijack" the movement.

Second, gays and lesbians must have an ongoing relationship with the black community, working on common agendas — and not just go to the black community when anti-gay issues come up. This is especially true because the right has targeted the black community with their anti-gay message. Finally, there needs to be a relationship, even if it's adversarial, between the black church and local black gays, lesbians, bisexuals and transgenders.

As we head into the new century, the radical right will still be with us, but I'm very skeptical about whether they'll win over communities of color to their anti-gay effort. There are just too many other issues that matter to us in which the right is on the wrong side.

Nonetheless, lesbian, gay, bisexual and transgendered people of color must work in our respective communities. And not just on gay issues, but issues that include the full spectrum of economic, social, and racial justice. There's a lot of power among us waiting to be tapped, and when it all comes together, it's an incredible thing to watch. ■

An account of the Supreme Court's ruling on Cincinnati's Issue 3 appears on p. 60.

STUART HOWELL MILLER

In 1992, I made a decision that would forever change my life. I told my parents and family I was gay. There was just one catch — my parents are fundamentalist Christians.

It seemed simple enough. I would fly back to my hometown in Tennessee from my new life in West Hollywood, California and just *do* it. After all, surely they already knew. I had been working in the AIDS prevention field for three years — not exactly a career heterosexual men were flocking to at the time.

Plus, my family loved me. I was the golden boy: president of my college fraternity, successful in my career, the life of the party at family gatherings. They'd understand and forgive this just as they had understood and forgiven all the other "crazy" things their bleeding-heart liberal son had done.

Thinking back, I don't know who was more in denial — them or me. While I expected my strict, college-professor father to have the most difficulty with the news, I thought that even he would eventually come around. Nothing could have prepared me for the price I would pay for sharing my secret with those I loved most. Within 48 hours of coming out, I was embroiled in the biggest battle of my life. At the age of 26, I became not only an orphan but an enemy as well.

The first strike in this holy war was an eight-page, single-spaced letter from my father. In it, he laid out the battle plan for winning me back to the fold. "If you have never seen spiritual battle before, you are in for some of the roughest times of your life — as are we," he said. "This will not be stealthy jungle warfare but battle out in the open, exposing the forces of evil for who and what they are. Our battle plan will be public information, and you will be fully aware of every move. If God is for us, who can stand against us? One way or another you will be released, and God will be glorified."

Stuart Miller is the author of "Prayer Warriors: The True Story of a Gay Son, His Fundamentalist Christian Family, and Their Battle for His Soul," published this year by Alyson Publications. For more information, visit www.stuartmiller.com.

After a lengthy diatribe on what the Bible says about homosexuality — complete with a flow chart outlining my choices for salvation or physical death — my father informed me he had enlisted 27 "prayer warriors" to "join the brigade to petition the Father to rescue me from the enemy camp." He explained these prayer warriors would be praying for my salvation, and would also be asking God to maintain "unbearable pressure on me" until I sought "Him" once again or, if I sinned until death, until *He* took me.

Since that time, I have received hundreds of letters, phone calls, and e-mails from this merry band of God's warriors. Some have been funny, others infuriating, and many heartbreaking — like the one from my 12-year-old sister, who wrote "God can change you or kill you." Through it all, one message has been loud and clear: The radical right truly believes that homosexuals are worthy of death. So much for hate the sin, love the sinner.

> My father said he had enlisted 27 "prayer warriors" to "join the brigade to rescue me from the enemy camp."

Many of my friends have watched in abject horror during this seven-year war. They can't believe this kind of overt hate and homophobia still exists. But I know only too well that this form of religious persecution not only exists but flourishes in both urban and rural areas throughout our country. And it's not too much of a leap to go from preaching God's ultimate wrath (death for homosexuals) in the pulpit to actually "pulling the trigger." Just think about Matthew Shepard and Billy Gaither.

As for me, I am no longer in denial about the war being waged by fundamentalist Christians against us. No matter how it is cloaked, it is a war, and one that we cannot afford to be passive in. History shows us that religion has often been at the forefront of violence. My daily prayer is that we don't allow history to repeat itself. ■

INCIDENTS

AFA boycotts

The American Family Association (AFA) called on its members to boycott Mobil and Amoco Oil companies and AT&T because the three companies offer same-sex domestic partner benefits to their employees. AFA told their members that "The U.S. Centers for Disease Control statistics show that almost half of all new AIDS cases are still contracted by two men engaging in sex even though taxpayers have paid out millions of dollars for government 'safe sex' campaigns." The organization's public relations director, Allen Wildmon, also stated that "AT&T sees nothing wrong with their policy as long as a dollar can be made. There is nothing gay about the human suffering caused by AIDS and the tremendous cost to the taxpayers." AFA urged its members to call the companies to voice their complaints and to boycott the companies because "the best way to vote your convictions is often through your pocketbooks." Burke Stinson, spokesman for AT&T, supported his company's policies by stating "Gay rights is the issue of the '90s, just as civil rights was the '60s and women's rights was in the '70s."

Conan O'Brien show

When author and National Public Radio commentator David Sedaris was preparing to appear as a guest on NBC's "Late Night with Conan O'Brien," representatives of the program told him he could not discuss the fact that he is gay. Sedaris responded to this in UNo MAS magazine: "It's not like I have to talk about that every time I open my mouth, but you hate for somebody to say you can't talk about it." Sedaris said that he was given a list of things he would be talking about ten minutes before the show started, and it was made very clear that he could not talk about anything else, especially his homosexuality.

Restaurant chain rejects non-discrimination proposal

On Nov. 24, stockholders of the Cracker Barrel restaurant chain rejected a proposal made by the New York City Employees' Retirement System to implement an employment policy to hire workers "without regard to race, color, creed, gender, age, or sexual orientation." Cracker Barrel claims that it already complies with local, state, and federal employment laws and follows the equal opportunity practice of hiring employees without regard to race, creed, color, age, or gender and "does not believe that a specific non-discrimination policy relating to sexual orientation is appropriate or necessary." The shareholders' proposal was intended to counter the company's 1991 policy stating that it would no longer employ people "whose sexual preferences fail to demonstrate normal heterosexual values" because such employees do not conform to the company's "family image." The statement was followed by a number of employee firings for which there has never been any apology or compensation.

Out of a possible 51 million votes, 31 million were cast. Of those cast, 84 percent were against the proposal and 16 percent were for it. Elizabeth McGeveran, spokesperson for the Social Investment Forum, a national non-profit organization that promotes socially responsible investment, said a 16 percent favorable vote is above what most shareholder proposals get. "Very infrequently do resolutions like this one pass. Therefore, a 5 or 10 percent vote can be considered a huge victory. Those kinds of percentages are often a wake-up call to management. You don't have to get a majority vote to get the company to sit down and talk."

Hate Crimes Prevention Act

The Hate Crimes Prevention Act (HCPA), introduced by Sen. Edward M. Kennedy (D-MA), was designed to expand the existing federal hate crimes statute in two ways: by eliminating the requirement that the crimes be committed while the victim was participating in a federally protected activity and by including people attacked on the basis of sexual orientation, gender or disability. However, these crimes would have to occur in connection with interstate or foreign commerce. The bill, which had been introduced in November 1997, was the subject of hearings in July 1998, after the brutal murder of James Byrd Jr. in Texas. Byrd, an African American, had been targeted for murder because of his race and was dragged to death behind a pickup truck. Byrd's eldest daughter testified in support of the bill before the House Judiciary Committee. Rep. Bob Barr (R-GA), an opponent of the legislation, said he thought the protected categories were too broad, and that drug addicts could be covered, since some see addiction as a disability. The Religious Right was also quick to denounce the bill. The Traditional Values Coalition released a statement calling the HCPA "nothing less than a premeditated assault on Americans who oppose homosexuality." After this hearing, however, possible impeachment proceedings put the HCPA on hold for months.

Then, in October, the bill was once again thrust into the limelight, this time by the murder of University of Wyoming student Matthew Shepard. Shepard, who was gay, was taken out to a field by people who then pistol-whipped him, tied him to a fence and left him to die. On Oct. 14, an event that was part vigil, part rally was held on the steps of the Capitol building. After memorializing Shepard, some speakers, including Sen. Kennedy, pushed for passage of the Hate Crimes Prevention Act. Donald Wildmon, the president of the conservative Christian organization American Family Association, criticized the bill's supporters: "Gay activists have no shame, exploiting the death of a young man to ratchet up the rhetoric for one of their pet political projects." He also claimed the bill would "add criminal penalties to any crime that is committed with even a hint of anti-gay motivation." HCPA was not revived before the end of the 105th Congress, but on Oct. 15, Rep. Barbara Cubin (R-WY), whose sons knew Shepard, introduced a congressional resolution condemning the murder and calling for tolerance. The resolution passed by a voice vote.

Hefley Amendment

In June, Rep. Joel Hefley (R-CO) introduced legislation that would prohibit any funds from being used "to implement, administer or enforce" President Clinton's May 28 executive order protecting federal employees from discrimination on the basis of sexual orientation. Hefley said, "Bill Clinton has added a new category to the nation's civil rights laws. With this action, the President has effectively established institutionalized quotas for gays and lesbians." Conservative Christian organizations, including the Family Research Council (FRC) and Concerned Women for America (CWA), also attacked the executive order. Gary Bauer, then-president of the FRC, said that the order "[D]iscriminates against people with traditional views of sexual morality and lends the prestige of the U.S. government to promotion of homosexuality." FRC's Robert Knight said, "This is more than politics. It's a clash between a revolutionary group that is trying to impose moral anarchy on a society built on a Judeo-Christian worldview." Carmen Pate, president of CWA, claimed that the order "grants special privileges to gays. It is an attempt to force acceptance of homosexuality on those who view such behavior as immoral."

> "Being likened to an alcoholic, kleptomaniac is insulting, degrading. We're the most popular people to hate."
>
> — A protester outside Senate Majority Leader Trent Lott's Mississippi office, after Lott compared homosexuality to kleptomania in a TV interview.

House Majority Whip Tom DeLay (R-TX), a supporter of Hefley's legislation, lobbied other Republicans to support the effort to block enforcement of Clinton's order. Hefley's proposal was paired with another proposal to defund an executive order expanding federal jurisdiction in an effort to focus debate of the bill on presidential powers as opposed to discrimination. President Clinton, however, rescinded the second order, forcing Hefley and the other Republicans to address the issue of discrimination. Republican Party leadership foresaw what they called a "public relations nightmare," however, when it turned out that the bill to which they had planned to attach the Hefley amendment was sponsored by the only openly gay House Republican, Rep. Jim Kolbe (R-AZ). This delayed but did not deter Hefley, who decided to attach his provision to another spending bill, the Commerce, Justice and State Appropriations bill. His move increased the potential impact of the amendment, because while Kolbe's bill only applied to the executive branch of government, this bill applied to all areas of government. On Aug. 5, the House voted against the Hefley amendment, 252-176.

Hormel nomination

In 1997, President Clinton nominated James C. Hormel, an openly gay lawyer, businessman and former Assistant Dean of the University of Chicago Law School, to be U.S. Ambassador to Luxembourg. Although Hormel's nomination was quickly approved by the Senate

Foreign Relations Committee, and although Hormel had been approved by the Senate two years before for a UN post, a hold was placed on the nomination by Sens. Jim Inhofe (R-OK) and Tim Hutchinson (R-AR) and later by Sen. Bob Smith (R-NH). These holds prevented a Senate confirmation vote on Hormel unless Senate Majority Leader Trent Lott (R-MS) interceded. The objections to Hormel's nomination purportedly centered on his activism in and financial contributions to the gay rights movement, including a production gift toward the documentary "It's Elementary," co-founding the Human Rights Campaign and an endowment gift for the James C. Hormel Gay and Lesbian Center, a research facility at San Francisco's main public library. However, it was widely suspected that the real objection was that Hormel himself is gay.

Religious Right organizations including the Family Research Council (FRC) and the Traditional Values Coalition (TVC), were quick to attack the nomination as inappropriate and anti-religious. The two groups distributed information to senators in an effort to derail the nomination, including excerpts from publications at the Hormel Center that allegedly promoted "bizarre, immoral and illegal acts." The director of the Hormel Center has said that Hormel has no input into the selection of materials for the facility, and Hormel himself has said he finds parts of the collection offensive. TVC sent each senator a copy of a coloring book depicting female genitalia. Missing from the book was the forward by the author explaining that the book was intended for use by sex education groups as a means for helping women become more comfortable with their bodies-not for children. Enclosed with the coloring book were crayons and a note from Andrea Sheldon, Executive Director of the TVC, which read, in part, "I ... hope that [the coloring book] angers and shocks you enough to block any consideration of Mr. Hormel's nomination." The groups also accused Hormel of being anti-Catholic for officiating at a parade in which the Sisters of Perpetual Indulgence, a philanthropic group of gay men who dress in drag and wear habits, marched. A video of the parade was provided as alleged proof of Hormel's complicity in the Sisters' shenanigans. In October, Hormel's nomination was officially pronounced dead when the legislative session ended.

In January 1999, Clinton once again nominated Hormel for the Luxembourg post. Once again, the nomination languished. Finally, in June, President Clinton appointed Hormel during a congressional recess, bypassing the Senate. Sen. James Inhofe (R-OK) responded by threatening to block every single civilian nomination that came before the Senate. Inhofe eventually relented. Hormel was sworn in June 29 by Secretary of State Madeleine Albright.

'Nothing Sacred'

ABC's "Nothing Sacred," a critically acclaimed drama about a young priest, Father Ray, who explores his own faith and the meaning of spirituality, yanked one of its own episodes after an attack by Religious Right organizations. Before the series even aired, it had been denounced as "anti-Catholic." The series aired despite the controversy, but what was to be the second episode did not. The episode pulled was entitled "HIV Priest: Film at 11." In the episode, a fellow priest, Father Jesse, reveals to Father Ray that he has AIDS. Jesse is humiliated and wants to leave the priesthood. Ray has known that Jesse is gay, and although he is distraught by the implications of the breach of the vow of celibacy, he refuses to condemn him, telling Jesse that there is forgiveness and a chance to start over. He counsels Jesse and in the final scene, Jesse confesses his breach of celibacy and HIV status to a group of priests over a game of cards. Although all are shocked at first, they each slowly admit their own failings and urge Jesse not to leave the priesthood.

The Catholic League for Religious and Civil Rights (CLRCR), a conservative organization with a stated membership of 360,000, sent out newsletters and petitions urging people to pressure ABC to ensure that this episode did not air. The CLRCR had already been boycotting Disney (which owns ABC) as well as corporate sponsors of "Nothing Sacred" to protest the series. CLRCR was joined by Focus on the Family, another Religious Right organization, whose president, James Dobson, said the show "breaks new ground for its irreverence.... [a]nother insulting attack on Christianity." Dobson added, "if people care enough to use their voice, they can make a difference in the culture." Under the pressure of boycotts from both the CLRCR and Focus on the Family, as well as low ratings in its time slot, the show was canceled.

Riggs amendment on San Francisco

The House of Representatives passed a bill in July to deny federal housing monies to San Francisco. U.S. Rep. Frank Riggs (R CA) claimed he offered the legislation on behalf of companies and religious groups that opposed the city's equal benefits ordinance, which requires businesses that contract with the city to offer the same benefits to employees' domestic partners as to employees' spouses. The bill covered any city with such an ordinance; however, so far only San Francisco has one. The legislation was put in the form of an amendment to a Housing and Urban Development and Veterans Affairs spending bill and threatened a cut of about $260 million in federal funding to the city. San Francisco Mayor Willie Brown reacted angrily to news of the proposal, "We're outraged at this type of activity. Local autonomy is of the utmost importance, and Congressman Riggs has in the past been a supporter of that concept." Riggs, in a debate on the amendment, claimed that San Francisco was "trying to force a particular political belief, a doctrine..." on others and that "[w]e should not force or coerce [private business] to adopt policies they find morally objectionable." The amendment was narrowly passed, 214-212. Daniel McGlinchey of the National Stonewall Democrats reacted to the vote, saying, "One of the basic Republican tenets is smaller federal government and increased local control. Republicans immediately forget those principles as soon as a state or local government does something that they don't like." The Senate version of the appropriations bill had no similar amendment, however, and the eventual conference committee compromise bill, which the House passed 409-14, did not contain the amendment.

PAX Network ad

PAX Network, a television station whose stated mission is to screen non-offensive television programming, ran an ad that offended many people who considered it to be homophobic. The ad offered PAX as an alternative to networks where "so-called creative people seem to be using what was once the family viewing hour to peddle every kind of alternative language and lifestyle to our kids." The ad also stated that "anyone who doesn't share their sometimes bizarre and depressing views of family values gets vilified for being intolerant."

The reference to an "alternative lifestyle" was seen by many as a reference to gay men and lesbians. When confronted with complaints, PAX President Bill Paxson and marketing chief Steve Sohmer both apologized for the ad, saying that they had not meant it to be offensive. Sohmer said, "I didn't know that these [alternative lifestyle] were buzzwords" and claimed that he was referring to promiscuity. Despite his remorse, Paxson still said he would not allow shows that glamorize gay or lesbian characters to be shown on his network. He gave "Ellen" as an example, adding, "I think we have a right not to have that kind of alternative lifestyle promoted on television, especially the television that we control."

Sen. Lott's statement on homosexuality

On June 15, Senate Majority Leader Trent Lott taped an interview on "The Armstrong Williams Show," during which he stated his belief that homosexuality is a sin. He continued, saying that he believed homosexuality is a problem "just like alcohol...or sex addiction...or kleptomaniacs." The show aired on the conservative cable network America's Voice, which was started by Paul Weyrich — founder of the Heritage Foundation, president of the Free Congress Foundation and a key figure in the birth of Jerry Falwell's Moral Majority.

This interview was recorded just a month after Lott and other high-ranking Republicans met with disgruntled representatives of the political far right, some of whom were threatening to bolt the Republican Party. Conservative activists, including Gary Bauer of the Family Research Council and James Dobson of Focus on the Family, were becoming increasingly dissatisfied with the speed at which the GOP was moving Congress to the right. "We're not looking for scraps from the table," said Dobson during an interview with Larry King. Lott's remarks represented a positive step toward mending the relationship between the Republican leadership and its right-wing base. Soon after Lott's statement, House Majority Leader Dick Armey joined in, asserting that homosexuality is indeed a sin and citing biblical passages as evidence.

After Lott's comments aired, outraged citizens protested outside his home office in Mississippi. One attendee said, "Being likened to an alcoholic, kleptomaniac is insulting, degrading. We're the most popular people to hate." White House Press Secretary Mike McCurry said of Lott's statement, "I think there is extreme pressure on the Republican leadership in Congress to hew to a certain line. And it's being forced on them by Mr. Bauer, Mr. Dobson, and others. In fact, they're very proud of the fact that they are moving the Republican Party in that direction." Letters, phone calls, e-mails and petitions condemning the remarks flooded the Senate Majority Leader's office.

At the same time, a greatly encouraged right wing flew to his defense. Bauer issued a release saying, "I commend Senator Lott's courage in speaking the truth about homosexuality. Homosexuality is considered unacceptable behavior by every major religion in the world and by most Americans." Dobson issued a statement on the Republicans' comments saying, "Leaders willing to be set apart and stand solidly in the truth are rare in today's permissive culture. It is far easier to go with the tide than willingly subject oneself to the fury of homosexual activists, the media and the political elite. We applaud their boldness in the face of great personal risk." Christian Coalition Chairman Pat Robertson said on his "700 Club," "Mr. Lott is following the biblical mandate, as are a number of us. And this is neither extremism nor is it prejudice. And I congratulate a man who is in high political office of saying the truth according to the Bible."

Groups on the right capitalized on Lott's remarks, referring to him in a series of full-page ads run in the New York Times and the Washington Post as part of the "Truth in Love" campaign. Janet Folger of the Religious Right Coral Ridge Ministries, who masterminded the ad campaign, said Lott was part of the inspiration for the series. The ads urged gay men and lesbians to seek help to become heterosexual through ex-gay ministries. It was sponsored by myriad groups on the far right. One ad read, in part, "Recently, several prominent people like Trent Lott, Reggie White, and Angie and Debbie Winans have spoken out on homosexuality...calling it a sin. When I was living as a lesbian I didn't like hearing words like that...until I realized that God's love was truly meant for me." Other ads thanked Lott for his words and one ad defended him against "a tidal wave of harsh language from homosexual activists."

Supreme Court: AIDS as a disability

In 1994, Sidney Abbott went to Dr. Randon Bragdon, a dentist in Bangor, Maine, to have a cavity filled. When completing the forms about her medical history, she disclosed that she was HIV-positive. Bragdon refused to treat her in his office because of her HIV status, but said he would treat her in a hospital as long as she paid the additional cost. Bragdon's waiting room contained fliers asking readers to consider the "irresponsibility that causes AIDS" and he supported a 1992 Maine Dental Association proposal to build regional clinics for patients who are HIV-positive or have AIDS. A previous lawsuit had been filed against Bragdon by an HIV-positive man who alleged that upon calling Bragdon's office to schedule an appointment to have a root canal, he was told that the dentist's policy was not to treat anyone who was HIV-positive in the office. In that case, the plaintiff, identified as John Doe, passed away while the case was still pending.

Abbott, who at the time showed no outward symptoms of the virus, filed a lawsuit seeking an order requiring Bragdon to treat her. According to Gay and Lesbian Advocates and Defenders, who brought the case on behalf of Abbott, there has never been a documented case of AIDS being transferred from a patient to a health care worker. In 1995 U.S. District Judge Morton Brody ruled in Abbott's favor, applying the disability statute to Abbott because she was "substantially limited" in a "major life activity," namely, reproduction. The Americans with Disabilities Act prohibits discrimination based on disability in public accommodations. The First Circuit Court of Appeals upheld his opinion. Both the American Medical Association and the Centers for Disease Control have stated that people with HIV can be treated safely in a private dental office, and the American Dental Association also said it disagreed with Bragdon's refusal to treat Abbott, although it filed a brief on his behalf arguing that reproduction is not a major life activity. Bragdon appealed to the Supreme Court, and on June 25, the Court, in a 5-4 decision, affirmed that HIV-positive people are protected under the ADA, even if they do not suffer from any of the symptoms of AIDS.

Supreme Court: Cincinnati's Issue 3

The U.S. Supreme Court declined to hear a challenge to an anti-gay initiative in Cincinnati, allowing an appeals court ruling on the matter to stand. The appeals court upheld the constitutionality of a 1993 city charter amendment barring the city from adopting laws prohibiting discrimination against gay men and lesbians. The language of the amendment was similar to Colorado's infamous "Amendment 2," which was struck down in 1996 by the Supreme Court in *Romer v. Evans.* After the Supreme Court issued the *Romer* decision, the Court sent Issue 3 back to the 6th Circuit. In 1997, that court upheld its earlier ruling that Issue 3 was constitutional, and the case was again appealed to the Supreme Court. In an opinion issued with the decision not to hear the case, three of the high court justices wrote that while the state-level Amendment 2 in Colorado would have allowed the state to impose its policies on the local governments, Issue 3 did not interfere with the decision-making authority of other communities. The appeals court ruling is binding in Ohio, Kentucky, Tennessee and Michigan.

The American Family Association of Kentucky promised to push a similar anti-gay measure in Louisville "to make sure no one has special rights." National Religious Right groups including the Family Research Council, Focus on the Family and Concerned Women for America spread the word that Issue 3 would stand and called for further action to codify discrimination against gays. Then-FRC President Gary Bauer called the decision a step in the right direction in his radio commentary. "Overturning *Romer* would be a good next step. State and local governments must remain free to uphold traditional moral principles." Stonewall Cincinnati, a local gay-rights group, promised to collect signatures for a ballot initiative repealing Issue 3. The lawyer who challenged the amendment said, "Cincinnati now stands as an island of intolerance with discrimination built into the city charter, and we're challenged now to solve this problem politically."

'The Sissy Duckling' on HBO

"The Sissy Duckling," a children's television show written by gay writer/actor Harvey Fierstein that is described as a "gay version of the ugly ducking story," met with attacks from several Religious Right organizations. The show is supposed to appear as part of HBO's "Happily Ever After: Fairy Tales for Every Child" series. Voices include those of Sharon Stone, Ellen DeGeneres, Anne Heche, Melissa Etheridge, "Frasier's" Dan Butler, and Andy Dick, with Fierstein as the title character.

The show has been derided as part of the "homosexual agenda." Don Wildmon of the American Family Association (AFA) stated on a Focus on the Family radio program, "[T]hey know that if they can indoctrinate the children with the thought that homosexuality is the same as heterosexuality, that two homosexuals marrying is the same as two heterosexuals marrying, then they've got the minds of kids." Wildmon's guest on the program, psychologist Tim Stanford, claimed that the show creates gender confusion in the minds of kids who then think, "I can get as crazy as having sex with animals because anything is possible and I don't know if I'm a guy or a girl." In a newsletter aimed at its members, the Georgia AFA wrote that "Fierstein is enjoying the work aimed at the younger generation, but his motive is frightening." They then quoted Fierstein as saying, "It would be wonderful to have a generation grow up not frightened of gay people. We can't reach a lot of their parents, but we can reach kids, and if they grow up without being full of hate, we can have hope." The program is scheduled to air in September 1999.

'Trevor' on HBO

Focus on the Family (FOF) denounced "Trevor," an award-winning short film that aired on HBO in August 1998. The film depicts a 13-year-old boy named Trevor who attempts suicide after being rejected by his peers as he comes to terms with his homosexuality. The film's airing coincided with the creation of the Trevor Helpline; its focus is to help gay or questioning teenagers considering suicide. A segment on one of Focus on the Family's radio programs, "Family News in Focus," however, suggested that the film would not be of any help to teenagers, and said that the messages would just confuse young people. "Does it mean that because I am going through adolescence and my parents don't give me enough attention that I am going to be gay? Or, because I don't play sports, am I going to be gay? Those are the messages that are kind of subtly inferred there," said a parent who screened the film for FOF. The organization's youth culture analyst agreed, saying, "The truth is that this film is a propaganda piece for homosexuality."

Unitarian Universalists vs. Boy Scouts

In May, in a letter, the Boy Scouts of America (BSA) asked the Unitarian Universalist Association (UUA) to refrain from issuing Religion in Life badges to Boy Scouts. The badges are issued by national religious organizations to Scouts who have completed a year of study about their own faith. This was the first time any religion had been asked not to award such emblems to its youths. BSA cited the Unitarian position expressed in its Religion and Life manual on atheism and homosexuality as being incongruent with BSA principles regarding religion. In addition, in 1992, the UUA had issued a statement criticizing the BSA for its exclusion of gays as Scouts or Scoutmasters. According to Lawrence Ray Smith, BSA Chair of the Religious Relationships Committee, "Boy Scouts is an ecumenical organization that requires belief in God and acknowledgment of duty to God by its members. The reference to the 'trouble' some Unitarian Universalists may have regarding the duty of God inappropriately incorporates doubt in an award process that is designed to forge a stronger link between a youth's Scouting values and religious life. ...We note with considerable dismay that this version of Religion and Life also includes an official expression of disapproval of Boy Scouts' membership policies relating to known or avowed homosexuals. The Committee believes that this has no place in a Boy Scouting/Exploring youth religious award manual."

> "Cincinnati now stands as an island of intolerance with discrimination built into the city charter."
>
> — The lawyer who challenged Cincinnati's Issue 3, a 1993 initiative that prohibits the city from outlawing anti-gay discrimination, after the Supreme Court declined to review the case.

The Rev. John A. Buehrens, president of the UUA and a former Boy Scout, countered in a letter to the BSA, "Surely the Religious Relationships Committee of the Boy Scouts of America cannot intend to tell a religious group what we may teach in regard to our own religious principles. We teach our youth, as a matter of religious principle, that discrimination against people simply by virtue of their belonging to a particular category of human being is wrong...You risk exposing the BSA to charges of discrimination — not only against a sexual minority, but against entire religious groups."

The BSA has defended its practice of excluding gays by claiming that it is a private organization and therefore, it argues, exempt from civil rights laws prohibiting discrimination in public accommodations. The California Supreme Court ruled in March that the BSA was a private organization, while an appeals court in New Jersey ruled that the organization was public and therefore had to obey the state's public accommodations law forbidding discrimination against gays. In August 1999, that ruling was upheld by the New Jersey Supreme Court.

The UUA responded to the BSA's request by revising its Religion and Life manual. The UUA agreed to issue a new edition that would contain nothing objectionable to the BSA and would include separate materials detailing its stance on "the multiple ways God could be understood" and anti-discrimination of gays. In April 1999, the BSA agreed to the new manual, but then rescinded the approval in May, claiming that material separate to the manual "simply reopens the entire issue of using boys as a venue to air your differences with the policies of the Boy Scouts of America."

Virgin Cola TV ads not aired

Media in at least six major markets refused to air television commercials for Virgin Cola featuring a real same-sex wedding between two men, the first same-sex marriage ever featured in a television commercial. The ads were part of Virgin Cola's "Say Something" advertising campaign, in which real people were invited to stand on a soapbox featuring the product's logo and say "exactly what was on their minds." One station, WJLA in Washington, D.C., reportedly claimed that due to audiences' reactions to same-sex marriage in the past, the station felt the ad was "inappropriate" and "awkward to air." At WCVB in Boston, which also declined to air the ad, the station manager called it unacceptable. He said, "These spots are not like 'Ellen.' Ellen had a plot, these spots are more PR than advertising the product." In the same-sex wedding spot, two gay men were married, exchanged rings, and kissed.

Gore speech at Human Rights Campaign event

When Vice President Al Gore spoke at the Human Rights Campaign annual dinner in Washington D.C. in September, he was quickly denounced by many Religious Right organizations, including Americans for Truth About Homosexuality (AFTH) and Focus on the Family. AFTH said it found his appearance hypocritical for a man who "campaign[s] as a 'pro-family' candidate." Gore told the audience, "We are determined to stand for justice and the American dream being available to all of the people in this great nation of ours." He also urged the Senate to vote on the stalled nomination of James Hormel to serve as ambassador to Luxembourg, and reminded the audience of Clinton's numerous federal appointments of gay men and lesbians. The vice president also called for the passage of the Employment Non-Discrimination Act (ENDA) and of federal hate crimes legislation.

Peter LaBarbera, President of Americans for Truth about Homosexuality, released a statement Sept. 18 criticizing Gore for appearing. "Mr. Gore cannot have it both ways. By celebrating a group — the Human Rights Campaign — that smears faithful Christians and Americans of all faiths who oppose homosexuality as 'extremists,' he has sided with anti-religious bigotry. He has also turned his back on those who offer homosexual men and women the truth: that they can change, with God's help. But worse than that, the vice president has turned his back on the God that made this country great, whom America abandons at its own peril."

Statewide: Parental visitation rights

In March, the Alabama Court of Civil Appeals refused to review a lower court's decision to bar contact between a divorced man's children and his male partner. Dr. Joseph Openshaw, the father of the children, had presented evidence to the trial court judge that his children were performing well in school after his relationship with Kenny White, his partner, was made public. It was also shown that the children had become quite close to White. The trial court judge also heard from a psychologist who testified that gay men and lesbians are as adept at parenting as heterosexuals, while a religious family counselor argued that the children would be irrevocably harmed by their father's lifestyle.

Statewide: Same-sex marriage

In April, after a heated debate in which members grappled on the House floor and hurled accusations of homosexuality at one another, the Alabama House of Representatives passed a bill 71-12 prohibiting the state from recognizing same-sex marriages performed outside Alabama. During the debate, an opponent of the bill, Rep. Alvin Holmes, said, "[Backing this legislation] is a political ploy to get [the bill's supporters'] names in the paper. They are just trying to get some votes." Legislators who voted to adjourn rather than debate the bill were said to be supporters of gay marriage, and all members of the legislature received anonymous fliers in their mailboxes identifying those members who had voted to adjourn, warning them that "We will remember this in the next election." The bill's sponsor, Rep. Phil Crigler Jr. (R), denied that the bill was unfair to gay men and lesbians: "I don't think it in any way insinuates that we are trying to snuff out that lifestyle as it exists." He also remarked that gay men and lesbians "should not expect the rest of society to acknowledge [homosexuality] as legal or acceptable."

The Alabama Senate later passed the bill unanimously on the last day of the session, after a group called, "Save Traditional Marriages" ran full-page ads in Alabama newspapers urging passage of the marriage ban. Gov. Fob James, in the throes of a re-election campaign that he ultimately lost, signed the bill on May 1, making Alabama the 29th state in the union to enact an anti-same-sex marriage law.

Jefferson County: Child custody

In June, the Alabama Supreme Court ruled 7-0 to remove a girl from the custody of her mother, a lesbian, who she had lived with since her parents divorced in 1993. "While the evidence shows that the mother loves the child and has provided her with good care, it also shows that she has chosen to expose the child continuously to a lifestyle that is 'neither legal in this state, nor moral in the eyes of most of its citizens,'" Justice Champ Lyons wrote, quoting an earlier decision. The court claimed that the father, who had since remarried, "...established a two-parent home environment where heterosexual marriage is presented as the moral and socictal norm..." unlike the mother's home, "where their homosexual relationship is openly practiced and presented to the child as the social and moral equivalent of a heterosexual marriage." A spokesman for the Christian Family Association, a Christian fundamentalist organization, praised the ruling: "The Supreme Court has placed the girl with a real family....People can say a family is whatever they want to, but God said a man and a woman would come together to start a family, not two women or two men."

Montgomery: Child custody and visitation

In a 5-2 ruling in March, the Alabama Supreme Court held that two children were better off with their father than with their mother and her female partner, although dissenting Justice Mark Kennedy characterized the father as violent, abusive, and a frequent drunk-driving offender. A lawyer for the mother reported that the father had been cited for driving under the influence with the children in the car while the case was pending. The court also reversed a Court of Civil Appeals decision that had permitted the mother to visit the children along with her partner, and reinstated a circuit judge's decision to allow visitation with the mother only at her own parents' home, and only in their presence. In denying the mother broad visitation rights, Chief Justice Perry Hooper Sr. stated: "Both women are active in the homosexual community. They frequent gay bars and have discussed taking the children to a homosexual church. Although they do not engage in intimate sexual contact in front of the children, they openly display affection in the children's presence."

ALASKA

Statewide: Same-sex marriage

In November, Alaskans voted to amend the state constitution to restrict marriages recognized by the state to those between a man and a woman. The initiative was placed on the ballot in reaction to a February ruling by Superior Court Judge Peter Michalski that threatened to overturn a 1996 Alaska law banning same-sex marriage. The law had been challenged by Jay Brause and Gene Dugan on the ground that it violated the state constitution. Judge Michalski ruled that choosing a partner is a fundamental right, and that any prohibition on same-sex marriage therefore infringed on an important state constitutional right. He wrote, "It is the decision [to marry] itself that is fundamental, whether the decision results in a traditional choice or the nontraditional choice Brause and Dugan seek to have recognized. The same constitution protects both." He also expressed his belief that the court should not "merely assume that marriage is only, and must only be, what we are most familiar with." The court held that the state's prohibition on same-sex marriage could only be upheld if the state could demonstrate a "compelling interest" for the discrimination.

Immediately, state Sen. Loren Leman (R), one of the sponsors of the 1996 law prohibiting same-sex marriage, introduced an amendment to the state constitution to define marriage as a union between one man and one woman. Leman said, "One judge who's unelected and unaccountable to the public should not be the one making social policy." Leman later expanded on that theme: "The court needs to be a reflection of Alaskan society and our values. And if it isn't, then we need to get hold of it." On April 17, the Alaska Senate passed the measure to put the amendment on the November ballot with all 14 Republicans voting for the measure and all 6 Democrats voting against. In the discussion before the vote, one of the bill's supporters, Sen. Jerry Ward (R), said the amendment was designed to answer the question: "Do you believe that one man and one woman should be married, or do you believe a goat and a cow, or two homosexuals should be?" The proposed amendment read: "To be valid or recognized in this State, a marriage must exist only between one man and one woman. No provision of this constitution may be interpreted to require the state to recognize or permit marriage between individuals of the same sex. The legislature may enact additional requirements related to marriage to the extent permitted by the Constitution of the United States and this constitution." On May 11, the Alaska state House passed the measure by a vote of 28-12, although it first deleted the final sentence of the proposed amendment, saying it was unnecessary and could confuse voters. The final stage in amending the constitution was to send the proposed amendment to the voters as a ballot initiative, Proposition 2.

> "Do you believe that one man and one woman should be married, or do you believe a goat and a cow, or two homosexuals should be?"
>
> — Alaska state Sen. Jerry Ward, explaining his support for a state constitutional amendment that defined marriage as between a man and a woman.

Three lawsuits were filed objecting to different aspects of Proposition 2. One case, filed by a group of Republican state legislators, objected to the wording of the summary of the initiative, which would be printed on the ballot, claiming that the summary was designed to generate "No" votes, as it read "This measure would amend the declaration of rights to limit marriage." They claimed that "limit" was an inappropriate term because marriage was currently legal in the United States only between a man and a woman, so no new limitations were being imposed. Another lawsuit was filed by two couples, a Baptist minister and his wife and Brause and Dugan. The suit charged that the proposed amendment would violate the Equal Protection Clause of the U.S. Constitution, and would also infringe on the separation of powers because it directs courts on how to interpret the constitution. The third suit was filed by the Alaska Civil Liberties Union and asserted that because Proposition 2 was specifically designed to discriminate against some Alaskan citizens, it amounted to a change in the foundation of Alaskan government and would revise the constitution, something that could only be done at a Constitutional Convention. This suit also alleged that religious freedom could be infringed, since religious wedding ceremonies performed for same-sex couples could also be made illegal under the proposed amendment. On Aug. 31, Alaska Superior Court Justice Senter Tan ruled against all three challenges to Proposition 2. The Alaska Supreme Court, however, shortened the amendment, ordering the second sentence to be deleted, but approved Proposition 2 for the ballot.

Pro- and anti-Proposition 2 camps, the Alaska Family Coalition and Alaskans for Civil Rights/No on 2, respectively, had been organizing and now launched their campaigns in earnest. The Alaska Family Coalition, a coalition of Religious Right organizations, received start-up money from Gary Bauer's Campaign for Working Families, and up to an additional $25,000 was promised in matching funds. Bauer himself flew to Alaska in August for Proposition 2 fundraising events. There he described the same-sex marriage issue as part of a "very well organized movement" that was engaged in an attack on the American family. Fundraising materials used in a nationwide mailing by the Alaska Family Coalition also warned, "If homosexual 'marriage' is legalized in Alaska, thousands of same-sex couples from the other 49 states will go to Alaska, get married, and then return home to demand that their marriages be recognized under the laws of your state." The Alaska Family Coalition campaign got a huge boost when the Utah-based Mormon church donated $500,000 in September, raising the campaign's total budget to about $600,000 and dwarfing the $108,000 that had been raised by Alaskans for Civil Rights, 94 percent of which was raised from Alaska citizens. In an interview, a spokeswoman for the Alaska Family Coalition said that although there seemed to be nationwide interest in passing the proposed amendment, she did not know of any non-Christian organizations that were involved with the Coalition. On Nov. 3, Proposition 2 was passed by Alaskan voters, 68 percent to 32 percent.

ARIZONA

Statewide: Domestic violence bill

Gays in Arizona were excluded from protections under domestic violence laws in April, after a House provision that would have included same-sex relationships was removed by the Senate Committee on Family Services. Currently, unmarried heterosexual couples who live together are covered by the law, even though the state defines cohabitation as a misdemeanor offense. Sen. David Petersen (R) claimed that gay and lesbian homosexual victims of domestic violence are not entitled to the rights given to heterosexual victims of domestic violence, and he also stopped an amendment that would have legalized cohabitation in the state. "For those of us who are opposed to that type of lifestyle, the mere fact that you start to break down the laws [against sodomy] on the books and say that's OK is a step in the wrong direction."

Statewide: Job discrimination

In May, the Arizona state legislature scrapped an amendment to HB 2392, a civil rights bill, that would have prohibited job discrimination based on the fact or belief that the applicant associates with gay men or lesbians. Sen. John Kaites, R-Glendale, who spearheaded the opposition to the amendment, explained his position: "Many of us don't support giving gays and lesbians any new rights to sue the state." He felt so strongly about this, in fact, that he held up for weeks a pair of bills that would allow the continued enforcement of existing civil rights laws. "I don't think we ought to be legislating special rights," he remarked. The two bills, one preserving the Arizona Civil Rights Advisory Board and one streamlining the process for filing civil rights complaints in some cases, were passed after the amendment was stricken. Sen. Elaine Richardson, D-Tucson, the sponsor of the amendment, pointed out that employment discrimination is already illegal in Arizona if based on sex, race, and other factors. She expressed frustration with the outcome. "What we're saying is that it's OK in the state of Arizona to discriminate against gays and lesbians."

Glendale: College professor attacked

In January, says Batya Hyman, a professor at Arizona State University West's Glendale campus, she found the words "kike" and "dyke" painted on the rear bumper of her car. Later, she asserts, a rock was thrown through a window of her home and that someone attempted to run her car off the road. Despite the fact that she teaches a class titled "Violence Against Vulnerable Populations," she stated that she did not go public with her story out of fear that more drastic actions might be taken against her. Eventually, however, she decided she should let the community know what she had experienced. The campus and the community responded positively — first the university issued a statement condemning the incidents and advocating a diverse campus community. Then in March, ASU West held a rally whose goal was to protest hate crimes, bring together "community allies" and show the perpetrators of hate crimes that they were not going to stop anyone from being true to themselves. Although this was the first hate crime reported at the college in its ten-year history, police say that 220 hate crimes were reported in Phoenix in 1997, an increase of 85 from 1996.

Phoenix: Phelps pickets Goldwater's funeral

Calling the late Senator Barry Goldwater "a supporter of sodomites," Rev. Fred Phelps sent his crew of picketers from Westboro Baptist Church in Topeka, Kansas to Phoenix to picket Sen. Goldwater's funeral. Phelps, notorious for protesting at the funerals of AIDS victims, and for his godhatesfags.com web site, explained Goldwater's "sins" to a local reporter: "When you say it's OK to be gay, then you're saying God is a liar and the Bible is not a reliable guide. You're saying it's OK to sin, because if the Bible is wrong on that weighty matter, then it's not reliable on any matter."

Pima County: Domestic partner benefits

In April, Samuel Morey filed an appeal from a ruling by Judge Allen Minker of Greenlee Superior Court, which had temporarily put to rest a year-long debate on the question of the county's right to extend health and dental benefits to unmarried county employees. Morey contended that to offer the benefits would be unconstitutional because the state considers cohabitation to be a misdemeanor.

In March 1997, the Pima County Board of Supervisors had voted 3-2 to extend health and dental benefits to unmarried domestic partners and dependents of county employees. The couples could be either heterosexual or homosexual and had to sign an affidavit saying, in part, that they lived together, were unmarried, not related by blood, and shared expenses. Out of 97 employees who signed up to receive the benefits, 10 had domestic partners of the same sex. In response to protests by Morey and another citizen, the County Attorney's Office moved to block the measure, which resulted in the benefits for all 97 employees who had signed up being put on hold until the case could be decided. In court one year later, Deputy County Attorney Chris Roads argued that state law did not permit the county to define "dependent" as it was defined in the policy. He did, however, allow that the county "[does] make a very compelling argument as to why it's the right thing to do to provide insurance to domestic partners," adding, "the state law doesn't necessarily support what's the right thing to do."

After Judge Minker ruled that "[t]he Board of Supervisors did act within its authority on this case," Morey filed his own appeal. Rumors began to circulate from sources close to the County Department of Human Resources that benefits would be frozen until the appeal was resolved. Finally, the county announced that it would begin extending domestic partner benefits beginning April 26, 1998. In January, Republican state Rep. Karen Johnson proposed a bill to ban any Arizona municipality from extending such benefits. Taking a cue from Morey, she based her argument on the Arizona law on cohabitation. "That's their free agency to choose if they want to cohabit or not, be it against the law or not. You have the free agency to choose to murder or not, but I certainly wouldn't think it is incumbent upon the state to reward such behavior." In February, the bill was killed in committee.

Tempe: Student newspaper cartoon

In March, Arizona State University's student newspaper, the State Press, ran an anti-gay cartoon portraying an effeminate gay man, complete with earrings, a limp wrist and a purse, who was acting as a troop leader to two apparently terrified Boy Scouts. "OK BOYTH! WHO WANTS TO EARN THEIR 'FIRST-AIDS' MERIT BADGE?!.." he announced. The cartoon, by staff cartoonist Brian Fairrington, was printed in the Opinion section accompanying an article opposing the New Jersey Supreme Court's recent ruling requiring the Boy Scouts to allow gays and lesbians to become troop leaders. The paper quickly heard from the campus community, the majority of whom expressed their rage over the cartoon, sending more than 60 letters to the State Press. The newspaper declined to print an apology, though it did print a large selection of the letters. Coincidentally, the following week, an anti-hate crime rally was scheduled at ASU West in response to a series of attacks on Batya Hyman, a Jewish lesbian who teaches at ASU.

Statewide: Foster parenting ban

In 1998, Arkansas became the second state in the nation, New Hampshire being the first, to prohibit gays and lesbians from being foster parents. When the issue was first raised in June at a meeting of the state's Child Welfare Agency Review Board, board member Robin Woodruff, who spearheaded the issue, announced, "I would like to require foster parents to be heterosexual, married couples." She further stated, "Allowing single foster care...takes away enforcement" of the no-gays restriction because "homosexuals who say they're single with a roommate or a boarder" could slip through the restrictions. Another board member voiced his support for the change: "I think we should never promote homosexuality in any fashion. I know there's a problem getting foster parents, but in my opinion it would be devastating for a child to go into a homosexual home." In 1997, the board was created to set minimum licensing standards for child welfare agencies. The old regulations for both public and private agencies made no mention of sexual orientation or marital status. Assistant Attorney General Karen Wallace warned that enforcing the proposed rules would be difficult: "[Y]ou can regulate what someone does, but not who someone is." She also cautioned that the regulation could be challenged constitutionally if the board attempted to "single people out." Nonetheless, the board asked Wallace to devise language that would exclude unmarried cohabiting couples, singles, and gay men and lesbians from the foster parent pool. The ACLU of Arkansas issued a press release the day after the meeting, objecting to the proposal, saying that it could violate the right to equal protection under the U.S. Constitution.

In July the board voted 6-1 to bar both single individuals and gay men and lesbians from serving as foster parents through private agencies. Wallace recommended that the board keep the current standards and not add the anti-gay restrictions due to concerns about equal protection and discrimination. Because many agencies in Arkansas use single individuals as foster parents, it was suggested that they be able to file for some sort of exemption under the new policy to continue to do so. Woodruff responded by saying that if unmarried people were going to be permitted as foster parents, she wanted a way to ensure that they were not homosexual. Dr. Bob West, the only board member who dissented, said that it was impractical to shrink the pool of parents when Arkansas already has a shortage of foster homes. Gov. Mike Huckabee's liaison on family life issues was also present at the board meeting, and he announced the governor's support for the change. He stated that Huckabee believed "[I]t is not in the best interest of the children for them to be placed in an environment that the legislature has specifically and purposefully removed from legal sanction and recognition." In Arkansas, sodomy, either homosexual or heterosexual, is illegal.

In August, the board met again and was told that it would be illegal to bar single Arkansans from serving as foster parents, especially since the law that created the board itself clearly sanctions single-parenting, defining a foster home as a "private residence of one or more individuals." It also agreed to work on language that would describe exactly what sort of conduct would be banned by the regulations. Joel Landreneau, the attorney for the state Department of Human Services, said that in order to discriminate against gays as foster parents, the board would have to prove that placing a child with homosexual parents is necessarily not "in the best interest of the child." The board agreed to drop the portion of the new regulations that would have barred singles from serving as foster parents but to move ahead with the anti-gay proposal, adjourning to do research into the effects of gay parents on children. Landreneau also expressed concern about enforcement of the policy: "An unscrupulous parent whose rights are being terminated may seek to use this against a foster parent." West remarked, "Short of installing video cameras in people's homes, I don't see how we're going to enforce this." The only other state with such a restriction at the time was New Hampshire, and while that state required foster parents to sign a form stating that they were heterosexual, the law does not provide for any enforcement of the regulation.

> "Short of installing video cameras in people's homes, I don't see how we're going to enforce this."
>
> — Dr. Bob West, a member of Arkansas' Child Welfare Agency Review Board, objecting to a proposal to prohibit gay men and lesbians from serving as foster parents.

In September, a subcommittee collected information from concerned organizations to submit to the board for consideration. Dennis Rainey, executive director of the conservative organization Family Life, called gay families "partners in perversion" and stated his support for the exclusionary measure: "We do not have to condone a way of life that represents the further unraveling of the family and is thus a danger to society." His and other Religious Right groups submitted studies from Paul Cameron, a discredited anti-gay psychologist who was kicked out of the American Psychological Association in 1984 for unethical practices. In January, the board finally voted on the measure itself, passing it with only West dissenting, and without taking comments from the overflow crowd. This began a 30-day public comment period before the new rules could actually go into effect. At the last public hearing, Cameron himself was on hand to argue with the ACLU, who had promised to file a suit if the regulations passed. Cameron criticized APA studies showing that children are not negatively affected by being raised in gay households and are no more likely to be gay than children raised by heterosexual parents, claiming the researchers are often homosexual and lie to support their personal biases. Richard Livingston, a child psychologist and medical director at Charter Hospital, testified in opposition to the new policy, saying that sexual orientation was not a warning sign of bad parenting and that Arkansas should concentrate on "factors that are valid and important and protect foster kids from real danger and risks." Jim Harper, of the Family Treatment Program at the University of Arkansas for Medical Sciences and Arkansas Children's Hospital, said that in a career in which he has treated hundreds of children, "I know of no case in Arkansas in which a foster child was sexually abused by a homosexual parent." This did not persuade the board, however, and the measure was passed. It reads, in part: "No person may serve as a foster parent if any adult member of that person's household is a homosexual."

In April 1999, the ACLU of Arkansas filed a suit in conjunction with the ACLU's National Gay and Lesbian Rights Project seeking to have the policy overturned. They assert that the new regulations are contrary to agency directives and state laws that require the agency to find foster homes that are in the best interest of the children. They are also challenging the policy on constitutional grounds, arguing that it violates their clients' equal protection, privacy, and intimate association rights. They are representing six plaintiffs in all, including a gay minister and his partner, a librarian, who have been together for 14 years and would like to serve as foster parents, and a heterosexual, married couple who are prohibited from becoming foster parents because they have a gay teenage son who lives with them.

Fayetteville: Anti-discrimination ordinance overturned

Gay men and lesbians working for the city of Fayetteville are once again without protection from job discrimination after a ballot initiative overturned a resolution that had added sexual orientation and family status to the city's anti-discrimination policy. The amendment, which made the city the first in the state to protect citizens on the basis of sexual orientation, was first passed by the Fayetteville City Council April 21, after three hours of debate and heavy citizen involvement on both sides of the issue. When Mayor Fred Hanna vetoed the measure, Alderman Randy Zurcher, the sponsor of the resolution, proposed that the council override the veto. More than 300 people attended the city council meeting on May 6, which was also broadcast live on a gospel radio station. The

Northwest Arkansas Christian Coalition led the opposition, and Brent Watson, its chairman, explained his objections to the resolution: "[The Northwest Arkansas Christian Coalition] objects to inclusion of familial status and sexual orientation as a basis for special protection or inclusion and consideration. Sexual orientation includes homosexuality, pedophilia, bestiality, and conceivably any other aberrant and abnormal sexual practices and beliefs. Familial status implies homosexual marriage." Supporters were there as well, wearing T-shirts that read, "There is no fear in love, but perfect love drives out all fear." Hanna was on hand to defend his veto, saying the resolution was unnecessary and would lead to costly litigation for the city. Because of the extraordinary number of attendees, the council did not take public comments. The council overrode the veto in a 6-2 vote, dividing along the same lines it had in the initial vote.

For a few months, the resolution stood. In June, a group of people calling themselves "Citizens Aware" were able to get enough signatures to put another resolution on the Nov. 3 ballot, one that would strike "sexual orientation " and "familial status" from the anti-discrimination policy. Mike Snapp, the group's leader, said the resolution "probes into private behavior not related to job performance, and yet confers special employment recognition on the basis of that behavior." A group dedicated to preserving the existing ordinance, "Campaign for Human Dignity," sprang up in response and began organizing for the November elections. Zurcher, the alderman who had originally proposed changing the policy to include gay men and lesbians, commented, "I'm saddened and a bit embarrassed that a group of community members would go to such trouble to try to deny other community members their basic human rights, and do it as a Christian duty, at that." After a heated campaign, the initiative to overturn the "human dignity" resolution was successful on Nov. 3, winning 58 percent to 42 percent.

Springdale: Mayoral election

In the first debate for the mayoral seat of Springdale, Arkansas, held before the Northwest Arkansas Christian Coalition, all five candidates present appeared to pander to their hosts by making anti-gay statements. Lashing out against the passing of a Human Dignity resolution in nearby Fayetteville that barred job discrimination on the basis of sexual orientation, they all stated that they would oppose the adoption of such a resolution in Springdale. One candidate, Timothy Hill, condemned the Fayetteville resolution with this rebuke: "They have a problem down in Fayetteville — they cannot figure out what's wrong and what's right." He also declared, "Homosexuals are perverts," adding, "this is a Christian nation. To put up with perversion like that, you're willing to put up with anything. They've spread their disease worldwide, and I'll do everything I can to keep them out of Springdale." At the forefront of Hill's goals was the posting of municipal signs: "Welcome to Springdale: Home of God-fearing, armed Christian citizens," and: "No fags in Springdale." He also vowed to enforce a sodomy law inside city limits.

In the end, the race came down to a runoff between Louis McJunkin, who erroneously had claimed in the initial debate that state and federal laws already guaranteed gay men and lesbians protections from discrimination, and a sixth mayoral candidate, Jerre Van Hoose, who had not participated in the Christian Coalition debate. Van Hoose, who was endorsed by outgoing Springdale Mayor Charles McKinney, eventually won the election by 162 votes.

CALIFORNIA

Statewide: Domestic partner benefits

In January, a gay rights bill went down to defeat, 4-2 (four senators abstained or were not present), in the Judiciary Committee of the California Senate. The legislation would have required all government contractors in the state who provide benefits to employees' spouses to also offer them to employees' domestic partners. The sponsor of the bill, Sen. Tom Hayden of Los Angeles, modeled his legislation after the groundbreaking San Francisco Equal Benefits Ordinance. Art Croney, a representative of an advocacy group called the Committee on Moral Concerns opposed the bill. "Domestic partners are adult friends. They are nothing more than that. Domestic partners are not dependent on one another. They are free to find a better job [if a company does not offer benefits]." Sen. Ray Haynes argued that the bill would discriminate against employers who are morally opposed to homosexual relationships. A civil rights attorney who co-authored Hayden's bill defended the legislation: "This law is truly about equal pay for equal work." Hayden agreed, stating, "The bill is obviously about gay issues, but it's also about public policy and health coverage and an economic discrimination that goes very deep...because you're creating a second class of citizens with respect to health care, bereavement, and family leave." The same bill was defeated in 1997 on a 4-3 vote in committee.

Statewide: National Guard

In 1994, Andrew Holmes, who served for eight years and was a decorated First Lieutenant in the National Guard, was discharged from service after he wrote a "coming-out" letter to his commander. In the letter, Holmes wrote, "As a matter of conscience, honesty and pride, I am compelled to inform you that I am gay," which violated the military's new "Don't Ask, Don't Tell" policy. Following his military discharge, Holmes filed separate lawsuits against the U.S. Department of Defense and the state of California. In the former, Holmes argued that his expulsion violated his First Amendment right to free speech, and in the latter he contended that the state National Guard's policy violated California's constitution, which he said prohibits employment discrimination based on sexual orientation. The suit against California was a class-action suit filed on behalf of all gay men and lesbians in the California National Guard who face expulsion if they openly declare their sexual orientation or who had already been discharged from duty on account of their sexual orientation.

The outcomes of the two cases were mixed. Holmes lost his case against the U.S. Department of Defense in 1997 because he did not prove that he would not engage in homosexual acts, something that is considered evidence that a service member acknowledges that he or she is gay. Holmes appealed that decision to the U.S. Supreme Court, which declined to hear the case in January 1999. That was the fifth time the Court has refused to rule on the "Don't Ask, Don't Tell" policy.

However, in June 1998, California Superior Court Judge David Garcia ruled that the state National Guard must open its ranks to gays and lesbians, including those who had been discharged from duty, finding that the National Guard's policy did indeed violate the Equal Protection clause of California's constitution. In addition, the judge ordered that the National Guard cease classifying the discharge of gay men and lesbian as criminal discharges. The state of California and the California Army National Guard appealed Judge Garcia's ruling in December, claiming that it cannot violate federal military policies regarding homosexuals. Holmes has expressed hopes that Democratic Gov. Gray Davis may withdraw the appeal, but as of publication, Davis had not done so.

Statewide: Same-sex marriage

In April, state Sen. Pete Knight (R) began a new campaign to pass a ballot initiative that would prohibit the state from recognizing same-sex marriages, and in March 2000 California voters will decide whether or not he is ultimately successful. Knight has tried three times before to pass legislation expressly barring same-sex marriages, but has never succeeded. The fact that similar initiatives were being voted on in Hawaii and Alaska in November may well have contributed to his fervor. The Defense of Marriage initiative (DOM), as it is called, would change the current California Family Code by adding "Only marriage between a man and a woman is valid or recognized in California."

Using direct mail with lines like: "Believe me, if we don't stand up and fight, we could see a change in our laws allowing widespread adoption by homosexual partners, homosexual curriculum in schools, taxpayer-funded healthcare for gay partners, etc.," Knight attempted to gather 433,269 signatures by June 25 to put the question on the November 1998 ballot. He fell short, but with the help of a web site maintained by the Capital Resource Institute, a conservative non-profit dedicated to preserving "traditional families," along with $500,000 and hundreds of volunteers, Knight was able to gather enough signatures to have DOM put on the March 2000 primary ballot. The California Defense of Marriage initiative also had an effect on November elections, when it was discovered that Republican U.S. Senate candidate Matt Fong, who had been portraying himself as a moderate, had donated $50,000 to a conservative Christian group that was pushing the anti-gay initiative and that once advocated quarantining people with AIDS. Gubernatorial candidates were also quizzed on the issue during a debate. Gray Davis, the Democrat, said "...I do not believe this state is ready for gay marriages or same-gender marriages, and if someone put a bill on my desk today to sign such a measure, I would not sign it." Dan Lungren, the Republican candidate, stated his support for the initiative, and added that if it were not for Davis, who voted against the measure when Knight had brought it up in state legislature, DOM would already be California law.

Statewide: School chief campaign

In September, Gloria Matta Tuchman, a candidate for California schools chief best known for her efforts to eliminate bilingual education, distributed a newsletter designed to elicit anti-gay sentiment to be used against her opponent, incumbent Delaine Eastin. The literature proclaimed, "Look who Eastin proudly lists as endorsers," followed by a list of donors, highlighting openly lesbian politicians and the Alice B. Toklas Gay Lesbian Democratic Club. Eastin replied to the gay-baiting tactics saying, "Language like this only gives comfort to those who practice bigotry and discrimination against the gay community." Eastin went on to defeat Tuchman in November with 53.5 percent of the vote.

Statewide: Senate campaign

Campaigning for a United States Senate seat, California Treasurer Matt Fong said that he agreed with fellow Republican and Senate Majority Leader Trent Lott's assertion that homosexuality is a sin according to the Bible. Fong, who says he is Christian, explained, "What Senator Lott was speaking was in the biblical context, and that was accurate." When pressed as to whether he agrees with alleged anti-homosexual biblical messages, Fong said he did not want to "talk about [his] religious and biblical beliefs." Fong attempted to moderate his statement by saying, "I do not support homosexual behavior, but I don't think there should be discrimination" against gay men and lesbians. Also, Fong said he would support the nomination of openly gay philanthropist James Hormel for ambassador to Luxembourg. Senate Republican leaders, including Lott, had been blocking a Senate confirmation vote on Hormel's nomination for several months.

Ironically, in his primary contest against millionaire entrepreneur Darrell Issa, Fong had been accused of being beholden to the gay lobby. After Fong courted the California chapter of the Log Cabin Republicans, Issa sent out a press release targeted to religious fundamentalist media outlets publicizing that the organization of gay and lesbian Republicans "has mailed out its candidate slate, headlined by none other than U.S. Senate candidate Matt Fong." In November, Fong was defeated by incumbent Sen. Barbara Boxer.

Antioch: Gay youth photo exhibit

"It is a political statement that they're trying to make that the homosexual lifestyle is acceptable and it should be encouraged for our youth. It's not something we want to promote in our community if we care about our youth." That is how Antioch City Councilman Allen Payton described "I Got All My Friends With Me," a photo exhibit of and by gay youth, which was created with the intention of "promot[ing] that gay people aren't strange or weird, that [they're] just people."

The exhibit was scheduled to travel to several cities over a period of a few months. Initially, scheduling conflicts prevented the exhibit from even being considered for space as part of the art exhibits at the council chamber at City Hall. However, the Antioch Civic Arts Commission deemed that the exhibit had artistic merit, and that it would reconsider the application later in the year, when space became available. Immediately, Councilman Payton began to undermine the authority of the Arts Commission, arguing that because the exhibit was controversial and political, the decision to display it on city property needed to be made by the city council, and not the Arts Commission. The Arts Commission later decided that the exhibit should be included in a youth art show at the city's Lynn House gallery. Payton advanced the same objections, however, stating that "Any government building is an endorsement of the political message they are trying to get across."

A local gallery owner offered his space to house the show, saying he had been offended by Payton's objections to the show. Meanwhile, Payton continued his fight to stop the exhibit from appearing in the Lynn House gallery, claiming he was trying to protect the city's youth. "They are being encouraged to pursue a lifestyle that is not natural," Payton said. He pushed the city council to help him overturn the Arts Commission's decision, and a vote was held on the matter in November. The result was a 2-2 deadlock (one member was absent), which meant the show would go on. The exhibit appeared at Lynn House during the summer of 1999.

> "If [the guard] wasn't there, I'm sure somebody would come by and smash it with a baseball bat."
>
> — A student at a Danville high school, where a gay pride display featuring rainbow flags was repeatedly vandalized.

Danville: Gay pride exhibit

Administrators at San Ramon Valley High School took down a gay pride display early after students reacted negatively to it. The display had been developed for Gay Pride Month by the school's Diversity Club and provided information and urged tolerance. It featured a rainbow flag and an explanation of its symbolism, a pink triangle and a description of the treatment of gays by the Nazis, and several small signs identifying famous gay, lesbian and bisexual historical figures. Unfortunately, tolerance was not what the display elicited from many of the students. Just hours after it was completed, some students were trying to deface it, covering it with Confederate flags and other negative symbols. One student was so bothered by the exhibit that he distributed T-shirts that read "I'm Proud to Be Straight" and circulated a petition calling for the exhibit's removal. Another student expressed her support for the exhibit: "If people don't like it, they don't have to look at it. I'm sure there are gay students at this school; I know one. It's gay pride. It's just like celebrating anything else."

Repeated attempts to vandalize the exhibit prompted the school administration to post a school supervisor as guard to keep watch over the display. Unable to attack the display physically, students continued to launch verbal attacks, shouting epithets at the display as they walked down the hall. "If [the guard] wasn't there, I'm sure somebody would come by and smash it with a baseball bat," said one student. A few days later, a student raised a Confederate flag on the school's flagpole, apparently in opposition to the display. Although the principal had been previously quoted as saying the exhibit would remain in place for at least two weeks, the display was taken down four days after it was put up, to the surprise and dismay of the Diversity Club. "I'm surprised [the gay pride display] lasted all week," said one faculty member. "Some kids spat on it. Some kids started yelling obscenities about gays." A district trustee said that administrators should use their discretion to remove distractions that interfere with class activities: "It doesn't have to be specific to gay pride, it can be anything disruptive."

During the week following the removal of the display, two-foot-high anti-gay slogans, "Fags Must Die," "God Hates Fags" and "Fags Will Burn," were painted on a classroom wing of the school. Still wet when discovered, the messages of hate were quickly painted over before school began and were seen by few students. Students and teachers say there is a small white supremacist movement on campus, although they make an effort to teach appreciation of diversity in the classrooms. "I'm not surprised by the reaction or the paintings," commented next year's Diversity Club adviser. "A lot of adolescent identity comes from negative identity. They don't know who they are, so they state what they are not."

> "[A student] said 'I'm going to get you. I'm going to have my parents file a complaint and get you out.'"
>
> — A teacher at San Leandro High School, quoting what a student had told him after another teacher was censured for discussing homophobia in his class.

San Ramon Valley High School has a history of intolerance and hostility to gay-related exhibits. The AIDS Memorial Quilt was defaced with homophobic words while on display two years ago, and at a subsequent rally, students carried Confederate flags. A similar Gay Pride display was quickly taken down two years ago in reaction to student complaints, and in 1981, the tragic suicide of a gay man who had dropped out of another county high school after being ostracized by his peers received national attention. One student, a junior at the high school where the display was removed, attributed the bigotry to the degree to which his fellow students are "sheltered." "So kids just blurt out what they hear at home or what they think is cool. We should have more classes where we learn more about diversity," he said. A member of the Diversity Club that created the controversial display vowed to try again next year. "I'm proud of myself; I'm not going to hide myself. But I do know people who feel like they have to. Regardless of people's reactions to the display this year, I think it's important that we create another one next year to show that there are gays in the community. We need to try and educate people." The local paper also called for the subject of intolerance to be discussed in social studies classes and in assemblies, and suggested that local ministers preach sermons about the "sickness in the schools, and how to heal it." The title of the editorial was "Educate the Uneducated."

East San Diego County: Anti-gay campaign literature

With the candidate's name in letters that appeared to be dripping blood, "A VOTE FOR TOM PAGE IS A VOTE FOR HOMOSEXUAL CURRICULUM!" screamed the bottom of a campaign flier for a special Grossmont Union High School District board recall election in June 1998. The caustic piece, paid for by Friends of Gary Cass, urged constituents to use their web access to find out "what's happening at school — behind your back!" directing them to a website for the PERSON Project, an organization that promotes gay and lesbian awareness to educators. In case recipients lacked a computer or the drive to find out the secret, it is spelled out a few lines later: "The number of homosexual teachers has increased by more than 1/3 (36%) from 1996 to 1997. The political unrest in Grossmont centers on the issue of homosexuality. Gay and lesbian teachers here felt threatened when discovered by pro-family activists and our 'conservative' minded school board majority."

Page eventually defeated Cass 43 percent to 33 percent for the open seat on the La Mesa school district's governing board, which has been plagued in the past by ideological battles. However, Cass, a minister at West Hills Christian Fellowship in Spring Valley, ran again for the board in November, 1998 and won a seat with only 12 percent of the vote amidst a wide field of candidates. He now sits on the board with his old rival, Tom Page.

Hayward: Anti-gay teenager's campaign

In Hayward, an anti-gay University of California at Berkeley student ran for city council under a platform that included abolishing a gay and lesbian prom that he claimed is financed by the city, selling off the city's airport and water systems, and bolstering the police force. Nathaniel Bruno, 19, a self-described conservative Christian, explained his decision to run: "I'm running because I feel as if Hayward is bankrupting itself financially and morally." Prior to the election, the local chapter of the Christian Coalition distributed questionnaires to the candidates to gauge the extent of their conservative values. Questions included whether the candidates supported the city's gay prom and whether they believed council meetings should be opened with a prayer. Most of the eight candidates ignored the surveys, and Mayor Roberta Cooper even said she felt "insulted" and that the questionnaires were "intimidating." Bruno, however, responded energetically: "It is informing voters about candidates who would be most likely to be sympathetic [to Christian fundamentalist causes]."

As a candidate, Bruno lobbied along with other local members of the Religious Right against the funding of a program for crisis intervention and counseling of gay and lesbian youth, and said that the "large Christian and moral segment of our community feels mocked" by homosexuality. At a city council meeting, some speakers said they feared the money would go to the gay prom, although Mayor Cooper insisted that no city funds are spent on the prom, contrary to Bruno's campaign statements that $30,000 of Hayward's finances were spent on the prom annually. Cooper told those who had spoken against funding the program, "You talk about [gays] as if they are some deranged animals we have to get rid of, and I find it appalling."

Bruno placed fifth among the eight city council candidates in the June, 1998, election, but a month later he was appointed by the city council to a position on the city's library commission. The council vote was 5 to 2, with Mayor Cooper casting one of the two no votes. She said of the Bruno appointment, "I think [the council is] going to be really sorry. I think this is a mistake."

Kern County: Human Relations commissioner's comments

In June, prompted by a group of gay citizens who offered to lead an effort to combat local hate crimes, Pastor Douglas Hearn, a Kern County Human Relations commissioner said, "I [am] opposed to having homosexuals lead in the community. Because any man who wants to have sex with another man has a problem. He's really sick and doesn't know it." In an interview, he elaborated, saying he believed "Gays have a right to live, shop and be human beings" that he also felt that "...if they were teaching our youth, I'd be scared they might rape them or something. Homosexuals are biblically way out." The Human Relations Commission was formed in 1990 to investigate discrimination complaints and promote tolerance, among other duties. Kern County First District Supervisor Jon McQuiston invoked those values in Hearn's defense: "The commission promotes respect and tolerance of gender and religious beliefs. Mr. Hearn's opinions are based on his religious beliefs, and he has the right to verbalize his view. In order to have open communication someone can't be asked to refrain their thoughts." The ACLU of Southern California disagreed, however, and sent a letter to the commission calling for Hearn's ouster. "As the United States Supreme Court has long held, when a public official makes statements in his official capacity that are inconsistent with his official duties, those statements are not protected by the First Amendment," the group wrote.

Citing Hearn's intolerant remarks, a retired Methodist minister and former commissioner filed an official complaint against him, asking that he be removed. The commission then was forced to discuss Hearn's future on the commission. In July, in a forum open to the public, Hearn tried to explain that because he was black and had grown up suffering from extreme forms of discrimination, he understood what it was like, and that he did not "hate" homosexuals. He said he did not, however, like their "lifestyle." People backing the effort to remove Hearn as well as Hearn's own supporters came to speak. Based on this session, the Human Relations Commission voted to keep Hearn, but asked him to wear "two hats," respecting the role and the rules of the commission. Immediately after that meeting, Rev. Hearn was asked to express his views again by the media, and he responded that he could not separate his religious convictions from his role: "My faith comes before bylaws. I cannot stop being a preacher."

Kingsburg: United Methodist Church

Symbolic of the opposition to the growing tolerance of gay men and lesbians by many in the religious community, one conservative church, Kingsburg's First United Methodist Church, opted to sever all ties between itself and the Methodist Denomination. On June 28, the congregation voted unanimously to rename itself the Kingsburg Community Church, and to purchase the property on which the church structures lay. The Kingsburg church had been a member of the California-Nevada Annual Conference, a regional Methodist organization of some 375 churches. But Kingsburg's Pastor Ed Ezaki and his congregation had been outraged that the conference did not discipline ministers who performed same-sex marriages, that it promoted a liberal interpretation of biblical passages, and that its leadership did not include enough conservative ministers. Ezaki declared that he and his congregation "can no longer in Christian conscience remain members of the United Methodist Church." Addressing those who believe the Bible's message of love was meant to include gay men and lesbians, Ezaki's church's resolution noted, "We are tired of fighting against those who hold tolerance and Inclusion to be higher values than Scriptural truth."

Los Angeles: Board of Education kills GLEC

In June, Los Angeles gay and lesbian youth lost their top advocate in the city's school district when the Gay and Lesbian Education Commission (GLEC) was terminated. For seven years, GLEC had provided gay youth with information on safer sex, substance abuse, family issues, leaving the gang life, and myriad other issues through a counseling service called Project 10. Bowing to pressure after the 1996 passage of the voter initiative Proposition 209, which prohibited affirmative action in public education and other state-funded institutions, the Los Angeles Board of Education voted unanimously to scrap GLEC and consolidate its services and mission into a new Human Relations Commission. Although Proposition 209 had no direct effect upon the legality of GLEC because the commission serves all genders, races, and ethnicities equally, the board felt that dropping race-based and gender-based commissions while holding on to the gay and lesbian commission would not have "flown politically," said openly gay board member Jeff Horton. Horton is familiar with such politics, having been a target of the Los Angeles Christian Coalition, which attempted to prevent him from being re-elected to the board.

In addition to counseling services, Project 10 also provided continuing education programs for gay and lesbian students and coordinated a Gay Prom. GLEC, which was created in 1991, offered scholarships to needy gay and lesbian students as well as legal support and networking for students who faced anti-gay harassment. Despite the demise of GLEC, Project 10 was still in existence during the 1998-1999 school year. However, as of early March 1999, the Los Angeles Unified School District had yet to form the new Human Relations Commission and had only recently hired a director of operations. This left Project 10 without a defined structure for continuing the extracurricular programs to assist gay and lesbian youth in the L.A. public high schools. Moreover, Project 10 was receiving so little financial or personnel support from the school district that it was forced to rely on private donations to the non-profit Friends of Project 10. Its new program director, Gail Rolf, said that while the school district promised that the Human Relations Commission would eventually fund Project 10, she had no idea how long it would be before the Commission would be operational. In the meantime, she and her team of volunteers were putting in 100-hour weeks trying to keep Project 10 on its feet and serving gay and lesbian teens in L.A. schools.

> "Domestic partners are adult friends. They are nothing more than that. Domestic partners are not dependent on one another."
>
> — Art Croney of the Committee of Moral Concerns, a group opposed to a bill in the California legislature providing domestic partner benefits.

Los Angeles: NARTH conference

In October, the conservative Claremont Institute and NARTH (National Association for Research and Therapy of Homosexuality) held a conference in Los Angeles entitled "Making Sense of Homosexuality." The conference's purpose was to "explain to a wide audience how the homosexual movement has targeted children, the family, and the popular culture in its attempts to increase its numbers and its acceptance in society." Promotional material for the meeting read: "Discussions will include how children are being indoctrinated through homosexual propaganda in school and in the media, the harmful effects of 'counselors' who reinforce homosexual behavior in dysfunctional children, and how families are having their authority undermined through the promotion of homosexuality. Constitutional scholars will discuss why homosexuality is not a civil rights issue and how homosexuals are trying to destroy organizations such as the Boy Scouts, which seek to promote decency and traditional morality."

Conference organizers ran into some major snags, however, including rallies protesting the anti-gay rhetoric, condemnation of the conference by city officials, and the cancellation of their reserved space at the Beverly Hilton after hotel managers received complaints about the tone and content of the forum. The conference was quickly rescheduled for the Regal Biltmore Hotel, which regularly does business with the Claremont Institute and did not inquire as to the nature of the conference. An employee there told a reporter that once the Regal Biltmore had agreed to host NARTH, it could not back out of the deal. The Los Angeles City Council and other elected officials then called a press event to officially denounce the conference. Openly lesbian California Speaker Pro Tempore Sheila Kuehl said that promoting the idea that gay men and lesbians can be "cured" is akin to the belief once held by some Christians that Jews could be "cured" by kissing the cross. "It doesn't take a rocket scientist to understand that when you combine that ideology with dogmatic self-righteousness, you are encouraging the kind of dehumanizing hatred that leads to the extreme, hysterical violence that took Matthew Shepard's life in Laramie less than a month ago."

The day of the conference, protesters at the Regal Biltmore reportedly outnumbered conference participants. Two California elected officials were scheduled to speak, Assemblyman Keith Olberg and Senator Raymond Haynes. Haynes had earlier derided the L.A. officials' condemnation of the conference as "highly inappropriate." Dr. Charles Socarides, the president of NARTH, spoke about the "anti-heterosexual" movement, claiming that two of its objectives are eliminating research into the causes and cures of homosexuality and eliminating therapy options for gays seeking to change their sexual orientation.

Morgan Hill: Student harassment

Alleged unrelenting anti-gay harassment against students in the Morgan Hill Unified School District prompted five current and former high school students to file a lawsuit, *Flores vs. Morgan Hill,* in federal District Court against the school district, the district superintendent, several teachers, and several assistant principals. Represented by the American Civil Liberties Union and the National Center for Lesbian Rights, the students alleged that the school district and the accused district employees refused to take any action to protect the students from harassment or even to discipline students who committed acts of harassment against students perceived to be gay or lesbian. The suit also alleges that the plaintiffs were told by administrators that they "were to blame for their own harassment, because they were or appeared to be lesbian, gay, or bisexual." Plaintiffs also assert that refusal to respond to harassment complaints or to discipline harassers violates of the school district's policy barring harassment based on sexual orientation, a California law guaranteeing students a harassment-free learning environment, and the students' constitutional rights to equal protection. The students are suing for unspecified damages and want the school to take "concrete steps to ensure student safety."

The students say that the vicious harassment against them included epithets such as "faggot" and "dyke" that were repeatedly shouted at students, death threats and physical violence. In one alleged incident, a seventh-grade student was beaten to the point of needing hospitalization for bruised ribs. The incident allegedly was witnessed by a bus driver who the plaintiffs say failed to stop the beating and sought no disciplinary action against the victimizers. One of the claims in the lawsuit was that faculty, staff, and administrators were often entirely negligent in addressing the harassment. Alana Flores, the lead plaintiff and the first female plaintiff in an anti-gay peer harassment case, alleges she found violent pornographic photos and death threats in her locker and that although she reported the incidents to administrators, it took weeks to have epithets that had been scratched into her locker removed, and she was not permitted to change lockers. Other students were reportedly permitted to change lockers simply to be near their friends. As of publication, the students' lawsuit was still pending.

A personal essay by Alana Flores appears on p. 23 of this book.

Palm Springs: Rainbow flags

After a Palm Springs city official fined five different gay-owned businesses for flying rainbow flags, a symbol of gay pride, the business owners, who suspected anti-gay bigotry behind the fines, challenged the flag ordinance. Palm Springs' sign ordinance restricted the types of flags or banners that can be hung in the city to those representing a political subdivision, such as a nation, state, city or county. However, one business owner charged that while he had been fined twice for his rainbow flag, "You go out on the street here and [all the other store owners] put all their crap outside. They hang their plant things, their wind tunnels. Why can't I put a flag outside?" After doing research, the city council admitted that it had found that creating different classes of flags was a practice that had been struck down by courts as unconstitutional. A new ordinance was ordered that would permit any type of flag to fly in the city. The city also agreed to drop the citations filed against the gay businesses under the old ordinance.

Pleasanton: Pastor's ouster sought

Holding signs that said "Unrepentant sodomites risk hell" and "Sodomy is not a family value," 30 protesters caused Josie Martin and Carol Parker to cancel a "friendship blessing" ceremony in May at St. Elizabeth Seton Catholic Church in Pleasanton. Mary Arnold, a protest organizer, said, "To hold this kind of blessing of a homosexual union in the sight of the tabernacle is a complete disgrace." St. Elizabeth Seton is part of St. Augustine Parish, which has held two other ceremonies for same-sex couples in the past three years. "Some people saw it as a gay wedding when it was not that at all; we weren't going to exchange rings or do any traditional things associated with marriages," said Martin. "It's going to take a lot to effect any kind of change, so we just have to be brave and move forward, and we've done that."

The event had repercussions-Arnold and others decided to file a complaint with Oakland Diocese Bishop John Cummins seeking the ouster of Dan Danielson, the St. Augustine Parish pastor, who had sanctioned, but not performed, the same-sex prayer services. Of the 15 people signed onto Arnold's petition, 10 were not in St. Augustine parish. The petition read, in part, "We are aware of the church's constant teaching that 'homosexual acts are acts of grave depravity' and of the pope's clear teaching that such relationships must never be blessed by the church." Arnold also accused Danielson of straying repeatedly from the Roman Catholic Church's teachings. "What I think he's really doing is allowing homosexual marriages, but just not calling it that, which goes completely against church teachings. ... There's been so many things that he's done over the years that don't fall into regular church practices, like holding dissent workshops and dream interpretation workshops." Danielson remarked, "I think we need to remember what it means to be welcoming and that there are all types of people and that we are all sinners. So I don't have a hesitation to continue to hold friendship blessings as appropriate when a gay couple in the parish represents a stable long-term relationship to allow this statement of commitment." The Diocese of Oakland did, however, decide that same-sex blessings are no longer permitted in the church buildings. "The diocese has made no policy prohibiting blessings for same-sex couples, but to have a prayer service for committed gay couples right in the church might send the wrong message to parishioners that the Catholic Church is holding gay marriages, when indeed we are not," explained Danielson. As of publication, Danielson is still remains the pastor of St. Augustine.

Bakersfield: Students transferred from class

Although he was named a "Teacher of the Year" two years ago, James Merrick was deemed unfit to teach by the parents of 15 of his pupils because he is gay. The controversy began in June, when Merrick publicly voiced anger at the comments of a Kern County Human Rights Commissioner who had called gays "sick" and said he was opposed to having them teach or lead in the community. Merrick's outrage sparked a community debate on whether the commissioner, Rev. Douglas Hearn, should be removed from the commission, and also propelled Merrick into the press as a gay rights supporter-which in turn fueled suspicions that he himself was gay. Although Merrick had been open to family and friends about his sexual orientation, he had generally kept his private life private.

In the fall, parents began requesting to have their children removed from Merrick's class-although he was the sole eighth-grade science teacher at Rio Bravo-Greeley Union School in Bakersfield. Students pulled from the class were placed in a study hall. Principal Ernie Unruh reported that the majority of parents objected to the fact that Merrick was gay and to his condemnation of Rev. Hearn. Unruh explained to parents that those were not legitimate reasons to remove the children from Merrick's class, however, the parents persisted. One mother voiced her concerns: "His body movements are different than a normal man teacher....His use of the English language is also just plain weird. When a student talks too loud, he'll tell them, 'Your voice molests me.' In my book, that's inappropriate for any teacher." The school policy has always been to accommodate parents' wishes, so eventually Unruh made other arrangements for the students in question.

Merrick decided to fight the school district's decision. He filed discrimination complaints with both the state Division of Labor Standards Enforcement and the Rio Bravo-Greeley School District. He explained his actions to a local newspaper; "When you pull a child out of my class you defame me. You create fear I will harm your child so you discredit me." Priscilla Winslow, staff attorney for the California Teaching Association, elaborated. "If in the absence of misbehavior or bad treatment, to take kids out of a class because the parents don't want them taught by a gay man is discrimination." Merrick said he appealed to district officials for the sake of his students as well as himself. He also said, "I told them there were a lot of gay kids in junior high school and that by taking kids out of my class, they would send a message that there's something wrong with me and something wrong with them." In a January 1999 meeting that was closed to the public, the Rio Bravo-Greeley Union School District school board voted unanimously to dismiss Merrick's complaint. In the weeks before the decision, another teacher, Gail Schultz, questioned what such a ruling would mean for her own future. "When's it going to stop?....Are they going to start removing our students because parents don't like that we're Jewish or black or that they saw us take a drink at some bar?"

> "I [am] opposed to having homosexuals lead in the community .... if they were teaching our youth, I'd be scared they might rape them or something. "
>
> —Pastor Douglas Hearn, a Kern County human relations commissioner, when a group of gay citizens offered to lead an effort against hate crimes.

The state Labor Commission, however, found that "by granting requests for the removal of students when such requests were based solely upon [Merrick's] perceived sexual orientation, the school district fostered 'different treatment in an aspect of employment' based upon [Merrick's] perceived sexual orientation" in violation of state laws. The agency ordered the district to stop removing students from Merrick's classes and to cease treating employees differently based on their sexual orientation. The agency did not, however, give any specific recommendation on what should be done with the students who had already been transferred out of the class. The school board issued a statement disagreeing with the Labor Commission's ruling, but decided not to challenge the decision and signed an agreement that allows Merrick, who had been on leave since the beginning of 1999, to return to the school in an administrative capacity until the end of the school year. The school board has also agreed to apologize to Merrick and implement a program for staff aimed at helping them appreciate diversity of race, religion, sexual orientation, etc. Mary Ann Ronk, who had pulled her child out of science class to avoid contact with Merrick, reacted to the decision: "I am pleased this man is no longer in the classroom, but I am angered that he could convince the district to rewrite its policy regarding gay teachers. The [former] policy allowed parents to decide who can educate their children and who they don't want them to be around." The lawyer for the parents of the students indicated that he would appeal the ruling. Merrick said he would retire at the end of the year, saying the whole episode had made the climate extremely uncomfortable.

San Diego: Congressman insults Barney Frank

U.S. Rep. Randy "Duke" Cunningham (R-CA) showed gross insensitivity toward both his audience and a fellow congressman in September, when he described a rectal procedure he had undergone to treat cancer as "...just not natural, unless you are Barney Frank." Cunningham was speaking before a convention of prostate cancer survivors in San Diego. Later he made an obscene gesture to an audience member who asked a question. Cunningham issued a public apology for his statement; however, he did not extend a personal apology to Frank. This was not the first time Cunningham had insulted gays in general or Frank, an openly gay congressman from Massachusetts, in particular. Last year, Cunningham came to blows with another representative on the House floor after making an offensive remark about Frank, and in 1994 he said that "the same people who would put homos in the military" were behind the Clean Water Act. The Massachusetts representative's reaction to the incident was casual. "I wouldn't list stability as his strongest characteristic.... The congressman kind of blurts these things out from time to time."

San Diego: Ad pulled from newspaper

The San Diego Union-Tribune refused to run an ad for the film Billy's Hollywood Screen Kiss because it depicted two men on the brink of a kiss. In the ad, which was approved by the MPA for general audiences, the men were fully clothed and are not actually embracing. The same newspaper's movie section ran several ads that week depicting men and women in the act of kissing, and even an ad depicting two men who were each holding two basketballs in a suggestive pose. The Union-Tribune was the only paper to refuse the original ad, saying only that it "did not fall within our guidelines." The paper did agree to run a substitute ad for the film, which included no kissing.

San Francisco: American Legion Post 448

In 1996, San Francisco's Alexander Hamilton Post 448 filed a lawsuit charging that since 1983, the American Legion has systematically discriminated against it. The Post contended that the California Department of the American Legion repeatedly lost the Post's request for a charter after learning that the Post would be predominantly gay, and discouraged veterans from joining the Post once it was established. The Post also accused the Legion's newsletter, the Legionnaire, of refusing to print 448's events or notices even when it offered to pay for the space (posts are routinely given free space in the newsletter) and said the Department called its members "damn queers." The lawsuit also said the Department had distributed anti-gay literature inside its offices, and had sold an anti-gay propaganda video to other Legion Posts and to the public. The battle came to an end in March when the California Department settled, paying the Hamilton Post an undisclosed amount of money. The settlement also stated that the state Legion accepted no responsibility for alleged acts of discrimination, but that it would officially prohibit homophobic actions and statements in its offices and meetings, inform the Legionnaire's editor about the non-discrimination policy and encourage districts to inform members about the Post.

San Francisco: Domestic partner discounts

Shortly after Congress voted 214-212 to withhold federal housing funds from San Francisco to punish the city for its Equal Benefits Ordinance, the city council passed another ordinance expanding recognition of unmarried couples throughout the city. The measure requires businesses in San Francisco to offer the same discounts to domestic partners (such as family memberships) that they offer to married couples. Contrary to claims made by the Religious Right that the measure was an attempt to "force private businesses to recognize same-sex unions and heterosexual cohabitation as equivalent to legal marriage," it was more of a codification in law of a widespread business practice. The sponsor, County Supervisor Mark Leno, said he couldn't name a business in the city that would have to change its practices. The ordinance was also backed by both the Chamber of Commerce and the Small Business Network, evidence that far from "forcing" businesses, it was reinforcing businesses' own profitable decisions.

San Francisco: Jehovah's Witnesses shut down gay site

A complaint by a lawyer for the Jehovah's Witnesses shut down a web site run by an international support group for ex-Jehovah's Witnesses who are gay, lesbian, bisexual or transgendered. The complaint charged that San Francisco-based A Common Bond had violated copyright laws by using an illustration from the religious publication, The Watchtower, on the support group's web site. GeoCities, the site that provides the Internet service, immediately shut it down — but Jim Moon of A Common Bond quickly notified GeoCities that in the United States it is legal for a non-profit group to use copyrighted material for educational purposes. Despite Moon's quick reaction, it took four days for GeoCities to reopen the site, and even then GeoCities said the illustration in question had to be removed—legal or not. Moon was angry: "What [they] did to us is an illustration of the Jehovah's Witnesses' total homophobia." Members of Jehovah's Witnesses can be "disfellowshipped" for being gay, which not only means being punished by the church itself, but that friends and family within the church are forbidden to communicate with them.

San Francisco: Phelps protests

Fred Phelps was on the road again in June, leading a series of protests in San Francisco to denounce the first anniversary of that city's domestic partners law. The first two demonstrations were held in front of Grace Cathedral and the Metropolitan Community Church in the predominantly gay Castro neighborhood, where Phelps and his followers from Westboro Baptist Church in Topeka, Kansas, were reportedly overwhelmed by pro-gay protesters who had gathered at the other end of the street singing "Amazing Grace" and shouting "Bigots go home." The grand finale at San Francisco City Hall featured signs declaring that gays would burn in hell and that AIDS would cure homosexuality. Amos Brown, a San Francisco supervisor who is also a Baptist minister, countered the protesters' slogans, saying, "These people don't have a clue what Jesus was about." Sporting a San Francisco souvenir sweatshirt, Phelps' daughter Shirley Phelps-Roper remarked, "Homosexuals have taken this city hostage." Phelps himself had an even more dire view— when asked why he was coming to the city by the bay, Phelps told a San Francisco Examiner reporter, "You're not only letting the homosexuals take over the Bay Area, but the rest of the country."

San Francisco:
Salvation Army and domestic partner benefits

The Salvation Army was so opposed to complying with San Francisco's domestic partners law that it gave up $3.5 million in city contracts. Salvation Army Lt. Col. Richard Love explained the group's objection to the law: "The ordinance conflicts with our theological position, which recognizes the importance of the traditional family." The law requires that any business that contracts with the city and provides spousal health insurance to married couples must also provide benefits to the unmarried domestic partners of their employees, be they the same or opposite sex. Other groups had contended in the past that the ordinance conflicted with their religious beliefs, but many, like Catholic Charities, eventually agreed to offer the benefits.

San Francisco: United Airlines suit

After refusing to abide by San Francisco's Equal Benefits Ordinance, which requires companies doing business with the city to offer employees the same benefits for domestic partners that they provide for employees' spouses, United Airlines reversed course and proposed a policy that complies with the city's law. In early 1998, United, the largest carrier and employer at San Francisco International Airport, joined a lawsuit that had been brought against the city by the Air Transport Association, a trade association for air carriers, which claims that as a federally regulated industry, they are exempt from the laws of San Francisco. In question are employees who work at the airport, where United maintains both a kitchen and maintenance facilities.

In April, a U.S. District Court ruled that airlines were not obligated to provide health and pension benefits to the partners of San Francisco workers; however, Judge Claudia Wilken did not address the issue of other benefits, such as family medical leave. While other air carriers who were part of the Air Transport Association's suit were satisfied with this ruling, United filed a second lawsuit, denying any obligation to provide these "soft benefits." In August, United requested an injunction in order to continue to operate while refusing to comply with the law. The airline had signed a short-term lease with the city during the implementation of the domestic partners law that stipulated that United would agree to abide by whatever benefits law was in effect as of Aug. 31, 1998, or the lease would be terminated. If it did comply, the city had agreed to extend the lease for another 23 years. United now argued that because the court case to determine whether the carrier was subject to the law was still pending, the carrier should not be forced to comply. Wilken agreed, ruling that although San Francisco was not under obligation to extend the lease, it could not terminate the lease until after the lawsuit had been decided.

> "When's it going to stop? Are they going to start removing our students because parents don't like that we're Jewish or black or that they saw us take a drink at some bar?"
>
> —Gail Schultz, a teacher at a Bakersfield high school, after the school board dismissed another teacher's complaint that students were transferred from his class because he is gay.

In September, Judge Wilken combined United's suit with another one filed by Pat Robertson's legal foundation, the American Center for Law and Justice (ACLJ), which was attempting to overturn the domestic partners law on religious grounds. In December, a San Francisco-based group, Equal Benefits Advocates, announced a boycott, "United Against United," which was supported by members of the San Francisco Board of Supervisors and civil rights groups. Elizabeth Birch, executive director of the Human Rights Campaign, voiced HRC's support of the boycott: "We have rarely seen anything so appalling in over a decade of gay and lesbian workplace organizing. Clearly, United has redefined corporate irresponsibility and they ought to fasten their seatbelts, because they should expect a great deal of turbulence in the upcoming months caused by their unfair treatment of gays and lesbians." In January, United further angered detractors by agreeing to abide by a Living Wage law in Southern California. "United has argued for months that this is not about domestic partners, but about the fact that a national air carrier cannot subject itself to local regulation. United's disingenuous argument has just been eviscerated," remarked San Francisco Supervisor Leslie Katz, a co-sponsor of the Equal Benefits Ordinance. Days later, San Francisco faced United and ACLJ in court as all sides presented their final arguments. In April 1999, Equal Benefits Advocates took to the airwaves with a television commercial supporting the boycott of United. "This campaign will stamp United Airlines and Pat Robertson as leaders in anti-gay discrimination in the minds of gay people across the country. Because United's chosen to be on the same side as religious political extremists like Robertson, by the time this ad campaign is completed, the lesbian and gay market will be lost to the airline forever," explained the commercial's producer.

In July 1999, Judge Wilken ruled that airlines must provide the noneconomic benefits, such as bereavement leave, that had remained in question. United, along with the other airlines, quickly appealed the decision. In August 1999, United unveiled a plan to extend domestic partner benefits to all its gay employees. However, the lawsuit against the city goes on.

San Leandro: Teacher reprimanded

Karl Debro, an English teacher and the adviser of the San Leandro High School Gay/Straight Alliance (G/SA), received a censure in his personnel file charging he "misused class time" when he attempted to discuss homophobia during a class discussion. The controversy began in November 1997, at a school board meeting called to discuss the issue of gay and lesbian students at San Leandro High. Several events had raised the profile of gay and lesbian issues in the school, including the charging of two lesbian students with inappropriate sexual behavior. The two students left the school soon after, citing harassment. In the aftermath, a parent wrote to the local paper, and said he was "appalled to discover the existence of a homosexual club" at the school. "This type of conduct will not be tolerated and the irresponsible teachers and administrators that have supported it need to be fired," he wrote. At the meeting, PIPE, or People Interested In Public Education, a group that had come together to protest discussion of homosexuality in class, explained that the school's academic standing was suffering because teachers were "pushing homosexual issues instead of academic excellence." At the same meeting, Debro said that gay students needed protection from harassment in schools. "We've got to do something about the harassment of gay and lesbian students. This isn't about sex, it's about sexual identity." The next day, students were discussing the board meeting, according to Debro, and he attempted to facilitate a class discussion on intolerance and homophobia. Debro's account of PIPE's actions at the board meeting allegedly upset two students, whose parents, members of PIPE, then filed complaints against Debro.

The two parental complaints that were upheld by Superintendent Tom Himmelberg charged that Debro had "disrespected a student's race and sexual orientation" on one occasion and that he had "misused class time" by discussing the contentious school board meeting. Jeff Godkin, one of the parents who complained about Debro, later said of the G/SA, "They're a bunch of snotty elitists who have contempt for working families and their values." During another school board meeting, one teacher warned that gagging teachers would undermine their authority in the classrooms. "[A student] said 'I'm going to get you. I'm going to have my parents file a complaint and get you out.....You know what happened to Mr. Debro." When other teachers tried to testify on Debro's behalf, they were cut off by the school board, who claimed that public comment was not permitted on the topic in an open meeting. That statement was countered by two reporters who said that it was only the board itself that could not comment on the topic in an open meeting. A disciplinary hearing for Debro was scheduled for April, but was canceled when the parents withdrew their complaint. Debro then said that he wanted to have a hearing so that he could clear his name. "It's all unjust fabrications," he said. "I've worked too long and too earnestly to have this on my record."

In May, a hearing was held before the school board. Debro was represented by the California Teachers Association and the Godkins, one of the families who had filed complaints against Debro, were represented by the right-wing Pacific Research Institute. The Godkins alleged that Debro had humiliated their son and another student, denigrated their religious beliefs, and defamed them. Debro had also allegedly revealed in class that the Godkins had lodged a complaint against Debro. The CTA lawyer made the case that Debro was simply facilitating a class discussion, not imposing his personal views on the students. All seven board members voted to keep the censure in Debro's files. In addition, a new policy was devised that states that undefined "controversial issues" need to be cleared with the principal before they are broached in class. The principal can appeal to a higher authority on a topic if he or she sees fit. Around the same time, the San Leandro School Board voted to implement diversity training that would "address the needs of all students including gay, lesbian, bisexual and transgendered and those who come from homes with gay or lesbian parents." In addition, a policy pledging to "foster a culture of safety and respect" for gay, lesbian, bisexual and transgendered students was finally passed.

In February 1999, Debro filed a lawsuit against the San Leandro Unified School District and Superintendent Himmelberg alleging that the "gag order" placed on him was unconstitutional and that it was done to intimidate other teachers into silence. "What Himmelberg's actions and the school board's actions did was to intimidate people from addressing the horrible treatment gay, lesbian and bisexual students get," he said. As of publication, no action has been taken.

San Marcos: Lutheran minister resigns

After being "outed" by congregation leaders, Rev. James Bischoff resigned his post as pastor of San Marcos Lutheran church in September. Bischoff, a pastor for 22 years, had never told his congregation of his sexual orientation, or that he was in a committed relationship with another man. The president of the church somehow found out that Bischoff was gay, and alerted Murray Finck, the newly installed Lutheran bishop who oversees the region. The Lutheran church has a policy of not ordaining "practicing homosexuals," saying that any sexual relationship outside of marriage is wrong.

When Bischoff realized what had happened, he announced to his congregation that he was gay. His partner, who attended the church, stood by his side. Bischoff also personally called the bishop and discussed the matter with him. Although the bishop gave him time to decide what course to take, some parishioners were already refusing to take communion from Bischoff to show their disapproval, and congregational leaders were pushing him to step down. To complicate matters, some of Bischoff's supporters were leaving the congregation altogether to protest the way he had been treated. Bischoff said he realized that he would never have the same relationship with the San Marcos: "It became pretty obvious that the best thing for the congregation was for me to resign."

Santa Barbara: Domestic partner benefits

In Santa Barbara, hotel owner Rolland Jacks sued the city in an attempt to repeal a city ordinance granting health benefits to employees for their homosexual and heterosexual domestic partners. Jacks, a spokesman for the "pro-family" group Citizens for Accountable Government, said it was a misuse of tax dollars. However, Chris Haskell, a lawyer who donates his services to CAG, said the problem was moral: "You have elected officials saying we think all these other relationships are just as good [as marriage], be it two heterosexuals who are not married or homosexuals or bisexuals....Promoting homosexuality is not something that makes a better Santa Barbara or community."

Jacks was represented in his lawsuit by the conservative "pro-family, pro-life, pro-liberty" American Center for Law and Justice, founded by Pat Robertson. ACLJ charged that the city of Santa Barbara was out of line for granting the benefits, because "The state...has established a clear public policy embodied in law that favors marriage and has furthered this policy by creating legal benefits and obligations for married persons that do not exist for non-marital relationships." In the end, Superior Court Judge Thomas P. Anderle upheld Santa Barbara's policy, stating that it did not violate California law. During the course of the lawsuit, ACLJ also lost another case it had filed against the city of San Francisco, challenging that city's policy requiring companies it does business with to offer domestic partner benefits.

Santa Clara: Alleged job discrimination

Dr. Katherine O'Hanlan, a nationally acclaimed gynecologist who has twice been named one of the Bay Area's best doctors by San Francisco Focus magazine, sued Stanford University for refusing to promote her to a permanent faculty position because she is a lesbian. O'Hanlan, a faculty member at Stanford since 1991, played a leading role in the 1992 campaign to extend Stanford's insurance and other benefits to same-sex domestic partners of campus employees. Her lawsuit, filed in Santa Clara County Superior Court, alleges that medical school administrators blocked her advancement within the faculty because of her sexual orientation and that there has been a pattern of discrimination against her by administrators. O'Hanlan's civil suit cites an alleged comment by one administrator, Dr. Mary Lake Polan, to another faculty member that O'Hanlan "should knock off that lesbian stuff" after she was elected president of the Gay and Lesbian Medical Association. Polan is named along with three other administrators as defendants in the suit. O'Hanlan also contends that school administrators unjustly accused her of having a poor medical billings performance despite, she says, tripling her billings from 1991 to 1997. Furthermore, she alleges that the medical school was trying to fire her for incompetence at the same time that it was honoring her with its prestigious Kaiser Award. O'Hanlan's case is one of several complaints by female faculty and staff members at Stanford University alleging that the university has maintained a consistent pattern of discrimination against its female and minority faculty. In November 1998, the U.S. Labor Department began investigating complaints by 15 female faculty members at Stanford, including O'Hanlan. The Labor Department investigation was still pending as of publication, but Stanford had approached O'Hanlan about a possible settlement.

Petaluma: Veteran Scout ousted

In September, a lifelong Boy Scout and Scout troop leader was ousted from the Texas-based national Boy Scouts of America after he assisted a Scout and his father, also a troop leader, in their effort to end the Boy Scouts' policy of excluding gays from the organization. Dave Rice had been involved with the Boy Scouts for 59 years, and in 1993 he had started his own campaign, "Scouting For All"—which sought to include not only gays, but also atheists and girls. The campaign died out, but was revived when Steven Cozza, a 12-year-old Scout, wrote a letter to the editor protesting the gay ban. The primary focus of the new action was the "Scouting for All" Internet site. The volunteer-run site housed a petition drive that quickly gained more than 20,000 signatures in favor of reversing BSA's gay exclusion policy.

BSA's official reason for expelling Rice was that he used his position of leadership to coerce the young Cozza into joining his anti-discrimination effort, although both father and son said they approached Rice, not vice versa. Rice, who is also an elder in the First Presbyterian Church of Petaluma, was considered an exceptional leader by the Scouts in his troops as well by most of their parents, none of whom called for his removal. He believes he was removed because of an undue amount of Religious Right influence in the leadership of the BSA. " If the people who don't agree with this [anti-gay] policy give up, they'll hand the Boy Scouts movement over to the religious conservatives without a fight," Rice said. Fallout from the nationally publicized battle also cost Cozza's father his position as assistant Scoutmaster. In November, a committee of parents from Petaluma Troop 74 decided not to renew Scott Cozza's contract. "He had his own agenda, which is not necessarily our agenda. That interferes with the running of the troop," stated the chairwoman of the troop committee. Rice and Scott Cozza plan to continue in the crusade alongside Steven, who is now pursuing the rank of Eagle Scout.

Simi Valley: Gay Pride festival

Simi Valley's first gay pride festival encountered stiff opposition from area church leaders and conservatives. "The homosexual agenda is about recruitment and getting people into that kind of lifestyle....That's something we have to work against," said Pastor Dennis Chapman of Calvary Baptist Church in Simi Valley, one of about 30 conservative Christian protesters at the event who warned parents about the "recruitment drives" that awaited children inside. He later stated, "We didn't want our women and kids seeing this. These people are living a perverted lifestyle." The county Board of Supervisors marked the day of the festival, May 31, by declaring it Lesbian and Gay Pride Day. Russ Hopkins, a member of the Simi Valley and Moorpark chapter of the California Republican Assembly (CRA) commented, "It's shameful that our supervisors, who say they speak for all of us, would support this. If they had taken the time to talk to some of the people here, they'd know we're not into this homosexual agenda...." Local chapters of the CRA, a conservative Republican grassroots organization, also released statements that said in part that the "gay lifestyle" is "detrimental to the longevity of those engaged in it and destructive to the quality of life and health of a community." A spokesperson for Supervisor Judy Mikels, who sponsored the county board's proclamation, qualified Mikels' support of the festival. "She was thinking of the taxpayers. If this was shot down, the county could have been left open to a suit" by the festival's organizers. However, the organizers considered the festival an all-around success, with 3,000 people attending from all over the area. One woman who came to the event with her boyfriend said, "With everything I've heard, I thought it was going to be some kind of totally outrageous party with nude men running around everywhere." But the festival changed her mind. "It's nothing like that . . . I've seen a few things that you don't see every day, but mostly everyone here seems pretty normal."

COLORADO

Statewide: Same-sex marriage bill

State Rep. Marilyn Musgrave introduced a bill to prohibit Colorado from recognizing same-sex marriages in January. Gov. Roy Romer had twice before vetoed similar prohibitions on the recognition of same-sex marriages. In March, a commission created by Romer held hearings to help determine what legal and economic rights, responsibilities and benefits were unavailable to gay and lesbian couples because they could not marry. In July, the commission released a report saying that a domestic partners registry should be instituted and maintained by the state so that same-sex couples who registered would be able to have the same rights as married couples under health-care laws, inheritance provisions, and other areas. The commission stopped short of advocating recognition of same-sex marriages, saying instead the "parallel" rights should be instituted, which one gay rights advocate termed "legal apartheid."

Colorado for Family Values (CFV), a Religious Right organization that has pushed for statewide and local anti-gay laws, immediately announced that it would produce a report to counter the commission's. Its report was released in September by a coalition of Religious Right forces, including the Christian Coalition, the American Family Association of Colorado, Concerned Women for America, Exodus-Where Grace Abounds, American Jewish Assembly of Colorado, and Family First in addition to CFV. Calling the gubernatorial commission's report "a declaration of war on the traditional family," the report claimed that the "amoral — or immoral — position of the commission is rejected by faithful Christians and Jews. The empirical, academic, medical and scientific evidence of homosexual behavior being unhealthy and destructive is overwhelming. To dethrone marriage the way the commission proposes is both deceptive and unreasonable." Recommendations from the coalition included passing the Defense of Marriage Act, the same-sex marriage ban proposed by Musgrave. That bill, HB 1248, was withdrawn at the end of the 1998 legislative session, without having ever had a committee hearing.

Aurora: School club

In January, the Homosexual-Heterosexual Alliance Reaching for Tolerance (HHART), a club formed by 25 Denver-area students to promote tolerance, sued the Cherry Creek School District over alleged discriminatory practices. The group, made up of both gay and straight teens, said its activities ranged from a trip to see the AIDS Memorial Quilt to marching in the local Martin Luther King Jr. Day parade. Among the group's list of complaints were exclusion from the school's club and organization lists, the school's failure to grant funds for the group's activities or to pay the group's adviser for her time, censorship of the group's posters, and attempting to replace the club's adviser with a mental health counselor. "...[T]hey didn't ask for a counselor. They don't want anybody to tell them that what they really need is mental health care," explained Julie Tolleson of the Colorado Legal Initiatives Project, the group that filed the case on behalf of HHART. She also said that the group's purpose is "really about the social world in which we live, and tolerance." The school district denied any wrongdoing in the case. A settlement was eventually reached under which HHART pledged not to act as a "support group" for gays, and the school agreed to give the club all of the rights of other student groups

Colorado Springs: 'Anti-discrimination' ordinance

Colorado for Family Values (CFV) outdid itself this year by proposing an "anti-discrimination" ordinance for Colorado Springs for the stated purpose of allowing discrimination against gay men and lesbians. The group is notorious for its sponsorship of Amendment 2, an amendment to the Colorado Constitution that barred the state and local governments from enacting laws to protect gay men and lesbians from discrimination based on their sexual orientation. Amendment 2 was ultimately struck down by the U.S. Supreme Court, but CFV has consistently pursued different strategies to codify discrimination against gays ever since. One plan was to override a Colorado Springs City Council resolution that stated "zero tolerance for any form of discrimination of a racial, ethnic, sexual or religious nature." Although the resolution is not legally binding, and it nowhere lists gays as a category of people who would be protected, CFV became worried that its ambiguous use of the word "sexual" would lead to equal rights for gays.

In order to bring CFV's proposal to overturn the ordinance up for a vote by the citizens, 11,085 signatures had to be collected by the ordinance's supporters by Dec. 14. In an ad placed in the local paper, the group said: "We need your signature now to say no again to preferential treatment of homosexual behavior. The mayor and some members of city council are attempting to elevate sexual behavior of any kind, including homosexual behavior, to the same minority status as race." Rev. Paul Jessen, the Director of CFV, explained, "What we object to is being forced to affirm what we cannot affirm, and that is the homosexual lifestyle." Not enough Colorado Springs citizens agreed with him, however, and CFV fell 783 names short of getting the initiative on the ballot. In addition, the group committed campaign violations by failing to register with the City Clerk's Office and by failing to disclose campaign contributors and expenses. CFV later filed the appropriate paperwork, disclosing that it had spent $6,207 of its own money on the losing campaign. Will Perkins, then-president of CFV, warned that the issue would raise its head again, however: "The forced affirmation of sexual behavior is an issue that just needs to be debated and decided in a democratic manner."

In January 1999, City Councilman Dawson Hubert, who agreed with CFV that the resolution was unclear, faxed the other council members a proposed amendment to the city charter that would specifically prohibit legal protections for gays in Colorado Springs. The amendment would have been placed before voters on the April 6 mayoral ballot. At the next council meeting, Councilwoman Linda Barley voiced her frustration at the relentless attack on the gay community: "I'm saddened that people have questions about this resolution. That indicates that they may think that there are some people they can give sub-standard service to. That indicates they may think there are some people who are not deserving of respect." Hubert backed away from his amendment idea, and suggested amending only the resolution itself to clarify the meaning of the word "sexual." He was thwarted in this, too, however, receiving support from only one other councilman. CFV's Jessen vowed that his group and the Christian Coalition of Colorado would continue the fight, although he was unsure of his next step. Mayor Mary Lou Makepeace, who called CFV's entire campaign against the resolution "mean spirited," decided to put the issue to rest once and for all by having a lawyer give a legal interpretation of the resolution. Makepeace's decision was attacked by the ex-president of CFV, Will Perkins, who was running against her for mayor at the time and claimed it was an attempt to sabotage his campaign. In March, Mary Rouse, the assistant city attorney, said that in the context of the resolution, "sexual" "refers to one's gender, not sexual preference or orientation" but that "[t]he resolution says we don't tolerate discrimination in any form, against any person," and that gays were covered under state and federal anti-discrimination laws. No federal statute of general applicability prohibits discrimination on the basis of sexual orientation.

Colorado Springs: Curriculum proposal

Colorado for Family Values was on the march again in Colorado Springs School District 11, pushing the board to pass a policy that would have required teachers to promote hetero- sexual marriage. The provision was part of a three-pronged agenda CFV had been active- ly campaigning for over a four-month period. (The group's other two issues, promoting abstinence and discouraging promiscuity, were included in the new policy.) In June, the anti-gay policy proposal was defeated in a 5-1 vote. CFV's lone supporter related his opinions on the matter: "The Ten Command- ments say honor thy mother and thy father. Marriage is sacred. It's not a guy with a guy or a girl with a girl. If a marriage isn't between a guy and a girl and God, it won't work."

> "It's not like the race issue, where we can look at her and we can know that... she's different than the white, normal American."
>
> — El Paso County Commissioner Betty Beedy on ABC-TV's "The View," gesturing to a black woman on the set, explaining her belief that gays are not discriminated against the way African-Americans are.

One board member who voted against the proposal explained that he feared that requiring teachers to promote heterosexual marriages would hurt not only gay families, but anyone living in single-parent homes as well. District 11's policy now advises that parents are the chief source of guidance for children in areas of "marriage, procreation, sexuality and individual lifestyle," and that in sex-ed classes students should learn the advantages of raising children in "stable, committed, mature, long-term family relationships." However, who and what constitutes a family is not defined.

El Paso County: Remarks by commissioner

An ambitious Colorado politician has been making a national name for herself by making offensive remarks about gays and other minorities. El Paso County Commissioner Betty Beedy's most publicized comments were aired nationally on the ABC talk show "The View." Beedy claimed that since you cannot "see" sexual orientation, gays cannot be dis- criminated against and therefore do not need legal protections against discrimination. To demonstrate, Beedy gestured to Star Jones, the host, who is African American, and said, "It's not like the race issue where we can look at her and we can know that she's got a dif- ferent, mmm, she's different than the white, normal American."

For these and other public remarks by Beedy, such as referring to single mothers as "sluts," citizens in and around the city of Colorado Springs waged a recall campaign against her. However, the activists, led by groups including the Pikes Peak chapter of the

National Organization for Women, fell about 1,000 signatures short of the required 8,000 by the Sept. 21, 1998 filing deadline. Beedy, who represents a heavily Republican district, was undaunted by those efforts and said of the voters, "I think they appreciate a leader like myself who is willing to openly and publicly talk about where I stand on issues." Since the recall campaign, Tess Powers of the Pikes Peak NOW chapter says she has witnessed a greater degree of caution in Beedy's behavior and comments. Powers noted, "She's not getting people riled up anymore." Powers also said that Beedy is well-financed and may seek higher office.

Fort Collins: Civil rights ordinance

In the city where Matthew Shepard spent his final moments, the Colorado Christian Coalition led a fight that blocked legal protections in housing, public accommodations, and employment for gay men and lesbians. Fort Collins had defeated a similar policy by a wide margin in 1988, but the city's Human Rights Ordinance had been extended to include protections for gay men and lesbians in a unanimous vote by the Fort Collins City Council on March 3, 1998, after months of research and extensive debate. On the very night the City Council voted to protect gays and lesbians, opponents declared their resolve to overturn the measure via a referendum.

The Colorado Christian Coalition quickly became involved. Calling the ordinance a "bizarre and irrational legal theory," their director declared: "We are going to encourage our people to be involved. They cannot be absent or stand on the sidelines with this ordinance." By April, the ordinance's opponents had gathered the 1,783 signatures they needed to force the council to bring the revision of the ordinance up for a public vote. The vote was scheduled for the Nov. 3 general election ballot. The battle became more heated after Shepard was murdered, partly because he was treated in the days before his death at a local hospital. The final vote was 62 percent to 38 percent opposed to expanding the Human Rights Ordinance, leaving gays in Fort Collins without basic legal protections.

Fort Collins: Matthew Shepard float

Fort Collins was the site of a repulsive act of intolerance in October, when a float in Colorado State University's homecoming parade mocked gays in general and Matthew Shepard, who lay dying five miles away in Poudre Valley Hospital, in particular. The float featured a scarecrow with the words "I'm Gay" painted across its face and "Up My Ass" painted on its back. The scarecrow was lashed to a fence — the same way Shepard had been found days earlier after the fatal beating. The float was co-sponsored by a sorority and a fraternity, Alpha Chi Omega and Pi Kappa Alpha. Fraternity members claimed that the scarecrow was intended to wear the uniform of CSU's rival in the homecoming game, but that a few days prior to the parade, someone had vandalized the float, removing the uniform and covering the scarecrow with graffiti.

The homecoming chairman for Pi Kappa Alpha, the fraternity involved, explained, "We weren't gonna use it, but we had a goalpost on the float that broke on the way to the parade. It fell out of the hole it was supposed to be in and someone replaced it with the scarecrow."

In Fort Collins, while Matthew Shepard lay dying a few miles away, a college parade float featured a scarecrow lashed to a fence, painted with the words "I'm gay."

The university was swift to condemn the float, and immediately launched an investigation into who was responsible for it. Both Alpha Chi Omega and Pi Kappa Alpha quickly released statements saying that neither condoned the action, and that they would help in any investigation. After a few days, Alpha Chi Omega sorority surrendered its charter at CSU, and Pi Kappa Alpha's national organization suspended the Fort Collins chapter. Ten days after the incident, the CSU Greek Judicial Board voted unanimously to recommend that CSU withdraw recognition from the two groups, and CSU followed their advice. Revocation of school recognition meant that the groups could not use school facilities or participate in university sanctioned activities — the strongest action the school could have taken. Later, 11 students were given hearings and were individually punished, with penalties ranging from probation to suspension. CSU said the punishments were based on parade violations (rules require all people to be portrayed in appropriate ways that enhance the group the portrayal represents) and misleading statements made by the students following the incident.

Pueblo: Charges against coaches

Five female college basketball players at the University of Southern Colorado in Pueblo filed sexual harassment charges against the head coach, Sherry Winn, and her assistant coach, Lynne Fitzgerald, both of whom are lesbians, for allegedly attempting to turn the players into lesbians. While the charges were eventually found to be baseless, the coaches' reputations were called into question and the two coaches nearly lost their jobs on unrelated charges that arose during the investigation. The players alleged that their coaches were spreading rumors that the players were lesbians, putting the players in "uncomfortable situations," and attempting to promote homosexuality. After an investigation by Greg Sinn, USC's executive director of university relations, this charge was found to be groundless. However, the coaches were found to have mishandled some situations by allegedly not taking adequate steps to prevent or discipline unacceptable behavior by players. Sinn recommended to the university's President Tito Guerrero that the two coaches' contracts not be renewed. However, Guerrero rejected the recommendation and renewed the coaches' contracts for the 1998-1999 season. Two players who levied the sexual harassment charges left the team in protest and they and others who were disappointed by Guerrero's decision said they are considering filing a lawsuit against the coaches and the university.

Bristol: Book censorship attempt

In Bristol, a library patron so objected to the inclusion of a gay relationship depicted in John Banville's "The Untouchable" that he tried to have the book banned from the public library. "I was disgusted by it....a young person could read it and be led astray" by its "tale of homosexuality," he claimed. The book was cited by the Library Journal as one of the year's best novels. The nine-member library board voted 9-0 to keep the book available to the public, although they thanked the complainant for his "concern and interest."

Hartford: Campaign for state representative

Rev. Gabriel Jose Carrera's campaign for state representative for the 4th District in a race against openly bisexual Rep. Evelyn Mantilla included hanging offensive signs throughout the community and posting anti-gay rhetoric on his web site. Carrera said he opposed what he called Mantilla's attempts to teach "anal sex" and "lesbian love" to school children. His web site carried anti-gay rhetoric, personal attacks on Mantilla and links to Religious Right web sites. One of his campaign posters, which depicted a bull's eye with the words "No Metas La Pata" written on top, generated a large amount of controversy. The phrase, which means "don't put your foot [in your mouth]" also carries a second meaning— pata is an extremely vulgar term for lesbian in Spanish. Carrera denied any knowledge of this second meaning, although he did capitalize the word and placed it directly over the bull's eye in his posters, and again on his web site, where he also added the words "En El Districto" which translates to "in the district." His claims to represent the Hispanic community's values led one 75-year-old woman to state at a rally: "I decry that he is from our community, and that the Latin community is anti-gay as if it's passed down by God. We have as many people who are gay as any other community." Mantilla, who publicly announced her bisexuality and proposed marriage to her female partner four months after being elected to the Connecticut House in 1997, largely ignored Carrera's homophobic campaign. "Actually," she said, "I do believe it has been gay-bashing, however, I'm more worried about what this does to a community that really has major needs, a community that we should be paying attention to." Mantilla ended up trouncing Carrera by a 7-1 margin.

Hartford: Diversity poster protested

In July, the "Coalition of Hartford Churches," which included the Christian Coalition, organized a protest and march to oppose Hartford's decision to display a poster promoting cultural diversity, which it claimed was part of a "gay agenda" to recruit children. The offending poster showed children of varied ethnic and racial groups standing under a poem titled "Life's Rainbow." In the center stood two girls, one with her arm around the other. One of the girls was wearing a T-shirt that said "Gay Pride." "I have no problem with the adults being gay, but where does the city of Hartford get their authority to depict a child being gay? Homosexuality has little to do with cultural diversity," said Rev. Gabriel Jose Carrera, chairman of the coalition. The group also started a petition to have the posters taken down and to pass a city resolution to keep any sort of "homosexual influence" out of any city-funded program that could affect children under the age of 17. The petition read, in part, "I am not pleased by the Homosexual influence that has been bombarding our children recently and we demand positive action swiftly and quickly to correct the situation."

Carrera ran into problems, though, when he approached elected officials, who he says told him they believe sexual orientation is something a person is born with, and that they represented all community members, gay or heterosexual. One official, City Council Member Mike McGarry, agreed with Carrera, and urged him to continue to make his case. He said of the poster, "At the very minimum, it's perceived as a political statement by the gay agenda." Carrera also organized a march to protest the "hidden gay agenda" in local schools and libraries. The "Christian March" featured Angel Rocker of Kids First America/Africa, a pro-voucher group affiliated with the National Baptist Convention of America. She voiced her support for the coalition's work to protect children from the "homosexual influence" in elementary schools and pledged to help seek help for the cause from the NBCA.

West Hartford: Family discount excludes gays

Filing discrimination complaints proved fruitless for gay men and lesbians demanding the same membership discount for domestic partners that married couples receive at the city swim center in West Hartford. Same-sex couples first brought complaints because they were excluded from a family rate at the Cornerstone Aquatic Center that was only $50 more than the $345 individual membership, a significant savings for heterosexual, married couples. In June, the town council voted 6-3 not to extend the discount to unmarried couples, although it did decrease the individual rate by $50. Mayor Robert Bouvier, who also serves on the town council, said the intent of the discount was to encourage children to learn to swim. Same-sex couples should not be given the same deal, he says, because then, "[y]ou're putting them on par with traditional families." Mark Melanson, one of the people who had requested the change in policy, remarked, "They just made discrimination more affordable." In mid-July, the matter was brought before the council again with a petition signed by 400 citizens requesting that "family" be extended to include domestic partners. The council declined to act, saying that it would

> "They just made discrimination more affordable."
>
> — West Hartford resident Mark Melanson, after the town council voted against offering discounted memberships for domestic partners to a swim center. Married couples currently receive the discount.

reconsider the policy at a later date. By the end of the month, Barry Amos and Andrew O'Brien, a gay couple who have lived together for four years in West Hartford, filed an official complaint with the state's Commission on Human Rights and Opportunities. Amos and O'Brien had twice tried to register as a "resident family" at the pool, and had been rejected both times. "As residents and taxpayers of this town, they can't understand why services are essentially provided on a discriminatory basis," said their lawyer. In March 1999, the West Hartford Town Council decided to restrict the discount to families with children. The discount would be good only for the parent or guardian of a child, so unmarried parents' partners, gay or straight, would be excluded. Married couples with no children would also be excluded, but childless married couples who are current members will continue to get the "family" rate.

DISTRICT OF COLUMBIA

Access to services discrimination

Tyrone "Tyra" Hunter, a 24-year-old pre-operative transsexual, was involved in a car accident in Southeast Washington when the car she was riding in was struck by another car. Rescue workers who arrived immediately began working on the injured Hunter, who was wearing makeup and women's clothing. However, when firefighter Adrian Williams cut the leg of Hunter's pants, he discovered Hunter had male genitalia. Williams reportedly exclaimed, "This bitch ain't no girl. It's a nigger, he's got a dick," and allegedly halted his rescue work until his supervisor arrived five to seven minutes later and ordered him to resume work. One witness testified she had watched Hunter "turn blue" while the rescue crew stood by, laughing and joking. Hunter died an hour later at D.C. General Hospital when a doctor failed to perform routine medical procedures.

An internal investigation at the Fire Department was halted when Hunter's mother filed a $10 million discrimination and wrongful death suit against the city. No rescue workers were disciplined because of their involvement in the incident. Attorneys for the city initially argued that firefighters were exempt from the 1977 D.C. Human Rights Act because the fire department was not subject to the "public accommodations" provision in the act. They also argued that Williams' derogatory remarks were protected by the First Amendment.

The jury awarded Hunter's mother $2.9 million. The largest portion of the damages—$1.5 million — was awarded for "conscious pain and suffering" from the malpractice the jury found that Hunter experienced at the hospital. Additional amounts were awarded for the "humiliation, embarrassment or indignity" the jury found that Hunter suffered at the hands of the rescue workers. The city has decided to appeal the verdict.

Adoption amendment to spending bill

An amendment to the 1998 D.C. appropriations bill proposed by Rep. Steve Largent (R-OK) would have forbidden unmarried couples from jointly adopting children. Largent said on the floor of the House that his measure "does not single out homosexuals. ... This could be a heterosexual couple that does not have a marriage contract that binds them together. Sure, it might give some gay rights advocates a warm feeling to see gay couples treated just as if they were married. But these are real kids...who have already had a rough start...It is simply wrong to turn them into trophies from the culture war, to exploit them in order to make some political point." The amendment was initially defeated by the House Appropriations Committee but was offered again on the floor by Largent and passed by the House by a vote of 227-192. The amendment was ultimately dropped from the House-Senate conference version of the bill.

Catholic University cancels speech

After receiving a vitriolic letter from an anti-abortion group, Catholic University President Brother Patrick Ellis canceled an appearance by Candace Gingrich, who was scheduled to give a speech on anti-gay discrimination. "I have concluded that the presentation could not be compatible with the Catholic identity of the Catholic University of America," Ellis said. Gingrich had been invited by the Organization for Lesbian and Gay Student Rights (OLGSR), which had already received approval for the speech from the university. Soon afterward, university officials reportedly decided to "review" the organization's charter, a move that could mean the group was in danger of losing its status as an official campus organization.

The letter, sent by Graduates for Life, claimed that Gingrich, who is a Human Rights Campaign spokesperson, was going to promote "the acceptance of homosexual behavior" which the letter called "both self-absorbed and self-destructive, a far cry from the mutual self-gift that God intends in the act of marital love....Homosexual acts are objectively disordered, involving the irrational gratification of one's sexual desires through the abuse of another's body." Furthermore, the letter claimed that allowing a lesbian to speak to the school's students would violate a ruling by the Vatican barring Catholic universities from allowing anyone who would "undermine the teachings of the church" from using school facilities.

Jacob Fabbri, co-president of the Catholic University OLGSR, and Gingrich herself adamantly denied that she was planning to discuss anything pertaining to sexual activity. Both asserted that she intended to address discrimination against gays as well as gay civil rights issues. Gingrich added that she had been planning to quote from the U.S. Council of Bishops' 1997 pastoral letter to parents of gays, which states: "The teaching of the church makes it clear that the fundamental human rights of homosexual persons must be defended and that all of us must strive to eliminate any form of injustice, oppression, or violence against them."

Catholic University punishes group

Catholic University public safety officers required members of the school's Organization for Gay and Lesbian Student Rights to wash off chalked announcements for National Coming Out Day from school sidewalks, then reported them to the student judiciary committee — which sentenced the students to five days of community service for destruction of school property. Melinda Sawyer, the club president, said that the safety officers told her they became involved because the chalked announcements promoted a gay event. Chalked messages included "Equal Rights For All People" and "Happy Coming Out Day." Sawyer asserts that other campus groups regularly advertise activities by chalking the sidewalks without any disciplinary action being taken. Catholic University public affairs representative Ann Smith had no comment, except to say that "the matter has been processed and resolved appropriately."

Church parishioner's complaint

In August, Robert Kimball, a parishioner at St. Matthew's Cathedral, sent a letter addressed to Monsignor W. Ronald Jameson, the church rector, and several other church members in which he charged that the pastor's practice of allowing gay couples to show affection openly in church was unacceptable. Kimball wrote, "I think such overt demonstrations, which have occurred so often in the Cathedral since you came, when they occur within the sight of children as they usually do, already constitute child abuse. ... You and the other priests at St. Matthew's must explain clearly during Sunday Masses that homosexual behavior is always wrong and can never be the basis of any 'genuine affective or sexual complimentary'...." He went on to ask that announcements of " 'Courage' meetings [be printed] in the Cathedral bulletin so that homosexual Catholics can receive help in dealing with this disorder." "Courage" is a Catholic group that encourages gay men and lesbians to be celibate.

This was not the first time Kimball had expressed hostility toward gay couples in the parish. The letter was a reaction to an incident that had occurred the day before, in which Kimball was ejected from the church after allegedly harassing a gay couple

"It might give gay rights advocates a warm feeling to see gay couples treated just as if they were married. But these are real kids."

— U.S. Rep. Steve Largent, who offered an amendment to the D.C. spending bill prohibiting unmarried couples from adopting children.

for holding hands during the service. At the time, he was wearing a shirt that read "Homosexual behavior is wrong" across the back. He defended himself, saying that according to Catholic doctrine, his actions were just. Rev. Jameson stated that Kimball had been abusive to gay parishioners on previous occasions as well, and he asked Kimball not to return.

Ward 1 election

While openly gay Ward 1 City Council candidate Jim Graham campaigned on improved trash collection, better substance abuse programs and stronger crime-fighting efforts, his opponents campaigned on Graham's sexual orientation. The most blatant anti-gay rhetoric came toward the end of the campaign. A flier that was sent to the media and distributed anonymously throughout Ward 1 proclaimed in big, block letters: "Ward One Candidate Jim Graham HAD SEX WITH MEN WHILE MARRIED." The flier insisted that there was a "hidden side" of Graham that voters needed to know about— secrets that included a history of alcoholism, secrets that "kept Mr. Graham in the bedroom of strange men, the side that kept [him] in dirty, filthy and disease infested gay bars in the late nights while his wife and the rest of the world slept."

Graham had been completely up-front about his battle to free himself from alcoholism (he said he had been sober for 21 years, something never mentioned in the flier). He was also open about his failed marriage, his "coming out" to his wife, and his struggle to understand his own sexuality. He had voluntarily disclosed this information years before to the Washington Post, when the Post magazine did a profile on him as the director of the Whitman-Walker clinic, a clinic that Graham had turned into a nationally renowned model for AIDS treatment and prevention. The source of the flier was never discovered. In the end, Graham won the Ward 1 seat with 49 percent of the vote, followed by two other candidates.

Ward 6 election

In the Ward 6 race for City Council, candidate George Stallings' posters were defaced by fliers proclaiming "GEORGE STALLINGS IS A FRAUD!" The fliers went on to say that although Stallings "would have you believe he is an upstanding, moral, competent member of our community. He is a fraud. George Stallings is a known homosexual." Stallings, who left the Catholic Church in 1989 to form his own African-American congregation, was the topic of a newspaper story at that time that suggested he had been sexually involved with altar boys in his congregation. "The Coalition of Concerned Men of Ward 6" paid for the printing and distribution of the fliers. The fliers also implied that Stallings was somehow responsible for the death of a child during a christening at his church and declared that he was not a positive role model for the children of the community. Stallings lost the race to incumbent Sharon Ambrose, who had won the seat 15 months earlier in a special election in which she had beaten Stallings by about 800 votes.

Statewide: Child custody

The non-recognition of same-sex marriages and the prohibition on gay and lesbian adoptions in Florida cost Penny Kazmierazak custody of her daughter Zoey in June. Kazmierazak's former partner, Pamela Query, gave birth to Zoey after being artificially inseminated in 1993. Kazmierazak, who says she is unable to bear children, said she paid for the insemination, selected the donor, and acted as Zoey's primary caregiver. Under Florida law, Kazmierazak could not obtain parental status in relation to Zoey without Query giving up her parental rights. However, the two were able to obtain a "delegation of parental authority" that allowed Kazmierazak to take the child to the doctor and enroll her in day care. Describing her role as a parent, Kazmierazak said, "I stayed up nights feeding her, I read to her, I took her to swimming classes, I took her to library reading every Thursday." After Kazmierazak's and Query's 14-year relationship ended, Kazmierazak filed a lawsuit seeking custody of Zoey. Judge Ben Byron dismissed the case, however, because Kazmierazak was not biologically related to Zoey and because Florida does not recognize same-sex marriages and prohibits adoptions by gay or lesbian partners. Kazmierazak commented, "I would have adopted Zoey in a heartbeat," had she had the legal right to do so.

She appealed the ruling, and stated that she'd hoped to have a trial at which she had intended to introduce such evidence as a letter from Query which reads, in part, "Thank you for having our beautiful little girl with me...You are her mommy and will always be. I will never do anything to change that. I promise you." Query's lawyer characterized Kazmierazak's claims as "child snatching" and said, "I see the case as being a slippery slope. Does someone who loves my child and helps with the care have custody rights?" On June 23, 1999 the appeals court dismissed the case. The court held that a "psychological" parent did not have the same rights as a biological parent, and that lacking a blood or adoptive tie, Kazmierazak did not have the right to seek visitation or custody rights with respect to Zoey.

Statewide: Presbytery rejects ordination of gays

A regional association of Presbyterian churches, the Tropical Florida Presbytery, voted in March to continue to prohibit the ordination of gay ministers. The 165 delegates to the Presbytery, meeting in North Palm Beach, were considering an amendment to church law that would have abandoned the requirement that clergy be either married to heterosexuals or "chaste" and single regardless of sexual orientation. The new rule would have read that clergy must "demonstrate fidelity and integrity in marriage or singleness." The delegates feared that dropping such a requirement would permit the ordination of gay ministers. Marie Gallant, an elder of Sunset Presbyterian Church in Fort Lauderdale, voiced opposition to the amendment when she said before the delegates, "If you take a role of leadership, whether political or religious, you're responsible to children. I respect gays, but I feel that what they're doing is wrong." Mary Alice Pugh, an elder of the Lakeside Presbyterian Church in West Palm Beach, thought ordaining gay men and lesbians would amount to sinning, and she said, "We are not voting on whether we sin; unfortunately, we all do. We are voting on whether we approve of sin. And if we do, we aren't really Christian." Ray Whetstone, an openly gay member of the Second Presbyterian Church of Fort Lauderdale who was seeking reappointment to church office and supported the amendment, said, "If Jesus criticized anyone, it was those who held by the black-and-white letter of the law. The reason this denomination is declining in numbers is not because of a lack of decisiveness, but because of hostility."

> "I stayed up nights feeding her, I read to her, I took her to swimming classes, I took her to library reading every Thursday."
>
> — Penny Kazmierazak, describing life with her 4-year-old daughter Zoey. A court denied Kazmierazak custody and visitation rights because she was not the girl's biological parent.

Whetstone had been "outed" by elder Ron Wier in 1995 as the church elders were debating whether or not to ordain Whetstone as an elder. The only one to vote against ordination in 1995, Wier has been the driving force behind efforts to have Whetstone's ordination overturned. Wier was the only elder who voted against the initial ordination. Under church rules, Whetstone would have been unable to keep his position after openly avowing his sexual orientation, however, in August, his ordination as a church elder was allowed to stand. The debate within the Tropical Florida Presbytery was part of a larger debate over the inclusion of gays and gay ministers by the national Presbyterian Church. In June, the church's annual general assembly concurred with the Tropical Florida Presbytery, as well as most other regional presbyteries, and voted to reject the amendment. A moratorium was placed on discussion of the issue until 1999.

Statewide: Same-sex marriage

The Florida Family Association and the Christian Coalition of Florida waged a statewide campaign opposing adding a "Basic Rights Amendment" to the Florida Constitution out of fear that it could lead to same-sex marriage as well as other gay-friendly legislation. The proposed amendment prohibited discrimination on account of national origin, replaced the term "physical handicap" with "physical disability" in the Declaration of Rights' protection clause, and stated that "All natural persons, male and female alike, are equal before the law." David Caton, executive director of the conservative Florida Family Association, said of the proposed amendment, "The wording appears harmless, but this is going to open the door to a lot of harm. It allows homosexual extremists to claim legal same-sex marriage." Originally, the proposed amendment also included a Christian Coalition-backed "religious freedom" measure that would have strengthened the position of religion in church-state disputes. But proponents of that measure refused to let their clause be associated with the gender equity clause and chose to separate it from the rest of the proposed amendment before the vote for passage by the Constitution Revision Commission. The religious freedom amendment then failed by one vote, while the basic rights amendment was passed and placed on the November 1998 ballot, to be considered by Florida voters. The FFA and the CC of Florida launched an intense campaign to defeat "Revision 9," as it was now called, sending voter guides to churches and e-mail alerts warning about the alleged perils of gender equity and urging people to vote against the proposed amendment. Caton said, "It is dishonest for the Revision 9 sponsor and supporters to claim this amendment is for women's rights when the amendment has such deep gay rights roots and potential for liberal interpretation by the Florida courts." Despite the opposition, Revision 9 passed with 67 percent of the vote.

Statewide: Domestic partner benefits

In December, the Christian Coalition and Gov. Jeb Bush stopped the South Florida Water Management District's attempt to become the first Florida state agency to grant benefits to domestic partners. Miriam Singer, a governing board member of the district who also chairs the district's Human Resources Committee, proposed that unmarried partners of district employees be eligible for coverage under the district's CIGNA HealthCare policy. Then Governor-elect Bush opposed the plan, and his spokesperson Corey Tilley commented, "He's opposed to it in concept. He doesn't support gay marriages, for one thing. Defining a live-in partner of the same sex would be basically a roundabout way of defining them as a spouse." The Christian Coalition, for its part, flooded the water district with e-mails and phone calls voicing opposition to the benefits proposal. Singer reacted to the controversy over the plan: "Unfortunately, something which should be just natural, common sense, let's just move forward, has become politicized. It's just an issue of respect and fairness and equality." The campaign against the proposal worked. Although a date was set for a vote on the measure, the district governing board instead postponed the vote, citing the excessive amount of controversy that had been stirred up. One board member said he feared "throwing away political capital" on the issue. Singer was not reappointed to the board after Bush took office.

Statewide: U-Fla. anti-discrimination policy

The University of Florida's gay and lesbian employees are still not protected by the school's anti-discrimination policy. In November, University of South Florida President Betty Castor proposed adding sexual orientation to the state university system's anti-discrimination policy. As a part of the state university system, South Florida's policies have to be in line with system-wide policies. A University of Florida faculty meeting where the issue was debated was described as hostile by the chair of the Committee for Gay, Lesbian and Bisexual Concerns at UF: "[S]ome of the speakers associated gay people with pedophiles." While the University of Florida Board of Regents professed to support the change in the policy, they were reluctant to take any action on the measure. Dennis Ross, the chairman of the board, said the proposed change would endanger an effort to win state lawmakers' approval for a restructuring of the university system. "By raising the profile of the issue, we could attract opposition that may not be in our best interests right now," Ross said. In the end, Chancellor Adam Herbert said that the Board of Regents could not extend employee protections for the system beyond the limits of the state anti-discrimination policy-which currently does not include protections for gay men and lesbians in the workplace. "We oppose discrimination of any type on our campuses. But I don't second-guess the legislature," said Herbert.

Brevard County: 'Daddy's Roommate'

Coral Lee Craig, a member of the Christian Coalition, used an imaginative strategy to remove the children's book "Daddy's Roommate" from the Brevard County library: she and some friends took turns checking the book out for three weeks at a time, and effectively managed to keep the book out of circulation for over a year. Craig came up with the plan after having been foiled in her attempt to have the book removed from the library collection last year. She claims that the book, which depicts a family situation in which a divorced father who lives with his partner enjoys visits from his son, is inappropriate for children. Craig's efforts to censor the book resulted in a donation of four other gay-friendly children's books to the Brevard County Library. The books "Asha's Mums," "Anna Day and the O Ring," "Families," and "Who's in a Family" were given to the library by Richard Cohen, the associate director of education at the Kohl Children's Museum in Wilmette, Illinois, who heard about the incident and wanted to make a difference. "We tend to hate what we fear and we tend to fear what we don't know. If, as children, we can come to know the diversity of humanity, we can learn not to fear [different people] as adults."

Broward County: Reclaiming America conference

In February, the Center for Reclaiming America — an outreach of Coral Ridge Ministries, which is well known for its work in the "ex-gay" movement — held a conference in Broward County. "Reclaiming America for Christ," as the conference was called, included anti-Clinton and anti-abortion rhetoric in addition to gay-bashing and a great many directives about how to defeat the liberal agenda. Speakers claimed that gays were a threat to America and were working against the Christians of America. One speaker testified about his campaign to stop a local bank in Wisconsin from extending a loan to rebuild a "gay hotel" that had burned down. He picketed the bank, which, he said, withdrew the loan offer a week later. "The hotel wasn't built," he said. Janet Folger, director of the Center for Reclaiming America, urged participants to avoid getting information on current events and issues from the mainstream press, which she said is prejudiced against the Christian viewpoint. She recommended they get their news instead from religious organizations that they could trust, and that they pressure their elected officials and candidates to listen to the Christian perspective on issues. One attendee told a reporter he monitored a gay newsletter to track gay issues and political efforts, and that he planned to return home and organize community members to do battle with gay activists.

Gainesville: Anti-discrimination ordinance

Despite bitter debate and two council members' unwavering opposition, sexual orientation was added to the Gainesville anti-discrimination ordinance on June 1. Gay rights advocates in Alachua County, where Gainesville is located, had watched anti-gay forces overturn a county-wide ordinance protecting gay men and lesbians from discrimination four years earlier by ballot initiative. In 1997, the Gainesville City Commission's Ad Hoc Committee for Human Rights held public information-gathering hearings on the idea of expanding the city's anti-discrimination ordinance to once again include gay men and lesbians. At the Feb. 9 commission meeting, the committee recommended that the ordinance be amended to include sexual orientation and that Gainesville also consider domestic partner benefits for city employees. Two more public hearings were scheduled to debate the issues. From the start, it was clear that two of the city commissioners were wholeheartedly opposed to the change. Commissioner Edward Jennings was the most vocal, claiming the measure would "dilute and diminish" the rights of African-Americans and would overburden local businesses. "The gay community was able to go into the restaurant. I wasn't. They sat in the front of the bus. I had to go to the back. There was no question black folks needed protection. [Homosexuals] already had these privileges. ... We will be giving these people a hammer to beat the business community with." The other commissioner who strongly opposed the measure was Paula DeLaney, who claimed that because there was no "institutional pattern of discrimination" against gay men and lesbians, the protections were unnecessary.

At the first public hearing, about 50 anti-gay protesters gathered outside City Hall. At the hearing, citizens who spoke on the issue were divided fairly evenly for and against the change. Steve Summerlin, who had led the fight to overturn the county's anti-discrimination ordinance, said, "It's not about gay-bashing. It's about a law that legitimizes immoral behavior." Commissioner Jennings said, "If you pass a law about choice, an alcoholic will be asking for the same rights." Proponents of the change told stories documenting the existence of anti-gay discrimination in Gainesville and stressed that neither the city nor local businesses would incur great costs as a result of the amendment.

The second public hearing produced a change in the amendment: an exemption for "religious institutions, organizations, corporations, associations or societies." This came after a representative of the Gainesville Christian Academy testified that the school would continue to discriminate based on sexual orientation, as it was written into the school's "faith charter" to do so. He wanted to know if there was a way around the proposed ordinance for the school. Because the second meeting was not advertised properly, the final vote on the amendment had to be postponed until June. At the final hearing, with opponent Paula DeLaney absent, the measure passed 3-1. In her closing remarks, City Commissioner Pegeen Hanrahan, who had long been a supporter of the measure, told about an incident that had proved to her that there was a need for the change in the anti-discrimination ordinance. She said she had been riding with a police officer who repeatedly used the term "fag" to refer to the victim of a robbery. She said the officer later awakened the victim in the middle of the night out of sheer malice, simply because he believed that the victim was gay.

Gainesville: 'Hell House'

A family wails over the coffin holding their dead son. "Out of the closet, all right," says a scary hooded figure, pointing at the crowd of terrified, or maybe just disgusted, onlookers. This was the scene in Gainesville at the First Assembly of God Church's "Hell House" in October. The haunted house is designed to scare people into following the church's beliefs on homosexuality, abortion, and a host of other sins. After going through a maze dramatizing the terrible consequences of sin, guests entered "heaven" complete with a "Jesus" and gold lame crosses. Visitors could not only travel to heaven from hell, but also see a host of real-live picketers outside First Assembly of God Church with slogans like "Don't buy the hate!" "All we want to do is to let people know that this is intolerant, this is judgmental, and not everyone has to feel this way," said one protester. Rev. Dr. Arnold Lastinger, Hell House host, stood behind his $10,000 investment: "We wanted to do a first-class act."

Groveland: Ad for gay-dating service

A teen at South Lake High School in Groveland was "outed" to his parents, had his web site shut down and was put in counseling after he placed an ad for a gay and lesbian dating service in his school newspaper. The controversy began after other students' parents saw the ad in The Talon, South Lake's student paper, in October and called the school to complain. The ad had been reviewed and approved by a journalism teacher who had been the paper's adviser for the past two years. Although the school termed approval of the ad "an oversight," the adviser disagreed, saying the ad was tastefully done. "It was something I really thought about. I didn't think it would upset that many people. I just didn't know enough about the community I live in." The South Lake Gay, Lesbian and Bisexual Match Making Service web site was created and run by the student from his home on his own computer. The ad listed an Internet address for the site where students could sign up for free to review "a full list of student profiles" so they could "meet each other and build relationships." One parent said she objected to the site because "As impressionable as kids are, things like this don't need to slip through the cracks." The boy who placed the $20 ad had his web site shut down by his parents, who had not known of his sexual orientation. They then placed him in counseling. School officials said he had not violated any rules and that he would not be punished.

Hernando County: School anti-discrimination policy

"They sent a clear message to [gay students] to continue to hide." That is how Gerri Jenkins described the Hernando County School Board's decision not to include "sexual orientation" in the school's anti-discrimination policy. Jenkins, who says her son suffered from anti-gay harassment when he attended Central High School, was one of more than 150 people who attended the school board meeting Aug. 18 to support or oppose adding specific wording to protect gay and lesbian students from harassment. One of the opponents was David Caton, the president of the Florida Family Association, a Religious Right organization that is "devoted to educating citizens on what they can do to defend, protect and promote traditional biblical values." Caton, who has led many other anti-gay crusades, had come with bused-in followers to explain why gay and lesbian students did not deserve protections. On the other side of the debate were Equality Florida, a gay rights organization, and local chapters of NOW (National Organization for Women) and PFLAG (Parents, Families and Friends of Lesbians and Gays) supporting the right of gay and lesbian students to feel safe in their schools.

The decision to leave gay students out of the policy came after a promising July vote on the measure, in which the board voted unanimously to add sexual orientation to existing anti-discrimination and anti-harassment policies. The Religious Right quickly got wind of the vote and organized 30 protesters to attend the next meeting. The outcry led the school board to delay passage of the measure, and to seek legal counsel. Lawyers suggested that by adding sexual orientation to the policy, the school would invite lawsuits. However, specific wording in the policies has not played a significant role in other anti-gay harassment suits involving schools. While the board reversed itself, unanimously voting not to expand the policy the second time around, only three board members stated that they personally opposed adding the words "sexual orientation." The other two deemed the vote an unfortunate compromise, saying that while the current broad policy should be ample protection for all students, they favored adding "sexual orientation" but wanted to avoid lawsuits. After the board's vote, Caton stated, "It's a victory in the sense that sexual orientation has no legal implication of a minority status in the School Board's discrimination policy."

Largo: Gay and Straight Alliance opposed

The Florida Family Association (FFA) deluged Pinellas County School Board members' home mailboxes with hundreds of postcards and letters to protest the county's first high school Gay and Straight Alliance (GASA). School Board Chair Lucille Casey received more than a thousand cards. FFA President David Caton said that the purpose of the mail campaign was not only to shut down Largo High School's GASA, but also to deter other area schools from attempting to start new clubs. "If there's no objection to this, other schools might jump in," he explained. Two students started the GASA in 1997, and at the time of the FFA attack had a regular attendance of about 35 students, both gay and straight. Caton kicked off the mass mailing by including a story about the GASA in his March newsletter, which is distributed to 10,000 people across the state. The newsletter also instructed readers to write a letter of complaint to the school board members. In addition, he sent out a second mailing to 3,500 homes in Pinellas County, urging recipients to oppose the student group. Caton said the FFA had objected to the group because it costs the school money to pay the counselor that oversees the group and because he says it gives gay and lesian students "special rights." In fact, the counselor, who facilitates other groups at the school as well, is paid through a federal grant under the Safe and Drug Free Schools program and the "special rights" are nothing but encouraging the students to report harassment they encounter so that a counselor can talk to harassers in an effort to head off more serious trouble. The controversy did not seem to faze GASA co-president Matt Popiolek, who said, "Basically, he can say whatever he wants, but we're not going to shut up and sit down."

> "The reason this denomination is declining in numbers is not because of a lack of decisiveness, but because of hostility."
>
> — Presbyterian Rev. Ray Whetstone, when the Tropical Florida Presbytery voted to continue forbidding the ordination of gay ministers.

Miami-Dade County: Anti-discrimination ordinance

The Christian Coalition of Florida fought tooth and nail to prevent adding "sexual orientation" to Miami-Dade County's anti-discrimination ordinance, a battle they lost in a referendum vote. They responded by waging a campaign to overturn it. Miami-Dade County is infamous for the 1977 battle over what at the time was a very progressive human rights ordinance that included protections for gay men and lesbians. It was overturned after a vitriolic campaign spearheaded by former beauty queen Anita Bryant that demonized gay men and lesbians.

In 1997, an attempt to return anti-discrimination protections for gay men and lesbians to the ordinance was voted down by the County Commission 7-5. In November, 1998, when the next attempt was made, Miami-Dade was the only county in southern Florida without such protections for gays. Safeguarding American Values for Everyone, or SAVE, had been working to garner support for the proposition for over a year. The Catholic Archdiocese, which had opposed the measure in the past, had said it would not object this time around after an exemption for religious organizations and affiliated groups was added.

When the County Commission voted Nov. 5 to consider the matter, hundreds of people were there from both sides, shouting, chanting, picketing and praying. Some commissioners had already staked out their position, such as Commissioner Javier Souto, who said he feared giving gays "special powers." Others said they had not made up their minds. One wanted to consult with clergy, and another said she could not be sure anti-gay discrimination existed. Public hearings on the proposed amendment to the ordinance were then held in various cities, including one where an opponent claimed that the expansion of the ordinance would protect pedophiles and rapists. Supporters offered testimonial from gays and lesbians who had been the targets of discrimination as proof of the need to expand the ordinance. On Dec. 1, after four hours of public hearings, the Miami-Dade commission passed the amendment by a vote of 7-6. The vote itself was a surprise. Commissioner Dennis Moss, who had voted against even considering the measure in November, switched sides and voted in favor of the amendment. "The bottom line," he said, "is that I do know gays face discrimination," and he felt it was his duty to "put protections in place." The Christian Coalition and its allies vowed to regroup for another battle. A rally was held at the Orange Bowl to protest the commission's decision. Trumpeted as "Family Indignation Saturday at the Orange Bowl," the event drew about 2,000 people to express "discontent with the new law and the county officials who supported it." Evangelist Oscar Aguero, who organized the rally, claimed that God had asked him to rent the stadium. The Christian Coalition was not involved in planning the event, but attended. Anthony Verdugo, head of the Christian Coalition of Miami, declared, "Whatever we can do to defeat or repeal this ordinance we will do."

In February 1999, the Christian Coalition began mailing requests for volunteers to help gather signatures to trigger a referendum on the issue. Under the name Christians United for Change, a letter on Christian Coalition letterhead was sent out claiming that "[e]very Christian should be so motivated by this outbreak of sodomy that they would do everything in their power to reverse this Gay Rights ordinance," and that "[t]he African American Clergy of Miami-Dade County must become visible in this effort to fight off this effort by Satan aimed at our families." The mailing included a so-called "Gay Manifesto" that was full of blatant falsehoods. It read, in part: "Homosexuality must be spoken in your churches and synagogues as an honest estate. ...We will in all likelihood expunge a number of passages from your Scripture and rewrite others, eliminating preferential treatment of heterosexual marriages...If all of these things do not come to pass quickly, we will subject Orthodox Jews and Christians to the most sustained hatred and vilification in recent memory." The Christian Coalition and its allies filed with the state as the "Miami-Dade Human Rights Coalition" for the repeal campaign, and must collect 33,000 valid voters' signatures to qualify the measure for referendum. As of publication, they had not yet reached that goal.

Miami Shores: Anti-discrimination ordinance

In January 1998, the Miami Shores City Council rejected Vice-Mayor Mike Broyle's proposal to urge Miami-Dade County to add sexual orientation to the county's Human Rights Ordinance. Miami Shores Mayor Mary Ross Agosta and two city council members defeated the resolution in a 3-2 vote. Cesar Sastre, who voted against the measure, compared homosexuality to alcoholism and said, "Why should gay people be treated different than me? What is sexual orientation? Where do we draw the line?" Josue Morales, a minister from the House of Praise, explained his opposition to the resolution at a city council meeting: "I feel I would be forced to hire homosexuals if they are the best-qualified." The chairwoman of the Dade County Christian Coalition, Sara Leon, called the proposal "destructive."

In response to such comments, Yates Fulbright, a Miami Shores resident who says he has been a victim of workplace discrimination because he is gay, stated, "The bottom line is that if you are discriminated against, you have no recourse." Later he said, "To compare being gay to being an alcoholic . . . I find that demeaning and insulting." Sastre defended his comments by claiming that he is a recovering alcoholic who wants gay men and lesbians to "recover" from their sexual orientation. In a letter to a local paper, he stated, "My comparison stemmed solely from my opinion that gay people are not born that way and they, like alcoholics, can choose to leave the lifestyle they are in if they so desire, and are willing to go to any length to leave that lifestyle." He also said, "We shouldn't bring up issues like gay rights, abortion, affirmative action. They serve to divide the community, council, and city. I'm concerned about more neutral issues-like annexation."

Orlando: Gay Day at Disney World

Operation Rescue, an organization usually known for its anti-abortion activities, expanded its activities this year to include anti-gay protests. They appeared in June at Walt Disney World in Orlando to protest annual Gay Day festivities. OR objected to Disney's extending benefits to domestic partners of its gay employees and producing the first network television series with an openly gay leading character, "Ellen." Flip Benham, OR's national director, explained his group's rationale for targeting gays and lesbians in addition to reproductive service providers: "It is incumbent on us to move into enemy territory. We're going to go as families and we're going to make a stand for Jesus. We won't be riding rides." Disney officials prepared extra security arrangements in the face of the OR protest, but only seven protesters actually showed up inside the theme park. Outside the park more than one hundred protesters waved banners with inscriptions such as, "What Would Walt Say," to passing motorists. The OR members inside the park attempted to deliver their message to gay men and lesbians enjoying the park, and gays were also videotaped to create future anti-gay propaganda, according to protesters. One protester confronted a gay park visitor and said, "You come and parade your sexual perversion in front of everyone. How do we explain that to our kids?" Although church groups often participate in Operation Rescue's abortion clinic protests, there were none on hand for the Gay Day picket. While in town, OR members also picketed Barnes and Noble for selling what protesters called "child pornography" and continued their traditional clinic protests. Later in June, when wildfires scorched central Florida, Benham said he considered it divine retribution for Orlando. "A city that protects child killers, those who peddle child pornography, and those who promote the homosexual lifestyle, should not be surprised that the judgment of God would fall."

Orlando: Pride flags

Pat Robertson threatened the city with the wrath of God and anti-gay activists protested when 300 rainbow-colored flags were flown from the top of Orlando's light posts to celebrate National Gay Pride Month. Orlando's policy permits groups to fly flags atop city light posts as long as the groups pay for both the flags and the labor of city workers to raise them, and as long as the flags do not advertise an event that is not free to the public. Though Watermark, the gay and lesbian group sponsoring the project, clearly adhered to these regulations, there was nonetheless an uproar from anti-gay groups and activists when the project was proposed. A local radio and television evangelist, John Butler Book, militantly opposed the flags and urged

> "I feel I would be forced to hire homosexuals if they are the best-qualified."
>
> — Miami Shores minister Josue Morales, explaining why he opposed a proposal to include sexual orientation in the city's Human Rights Ordinance.

his followers to wear black armbands of protest when they attended a city council at which the vote on whether or not to approve Watermark's plans would be held. The Rev. Randolph Bracey, the pastor of the New Covenant Baptist Church, cited the Bible as the reason the city should violate its policy and reject the project, saying, "[Homosexuality] is debauchery, plain and simple." The night of the council meeting, 300 people packed the city hall and about 30 proponents and opponents vociferously argued their positions, while members of Operation Rescue protested the plan outside city hall. One proponent of the plan said of the anti-gay opposition, "This is really about hate."

Pat Robertson used the forum of his "700 Club" television program to rail against the flying of rainbow flags in Orlando: "[A] condition like this will bring about the destruction of Your nation. It'll bring about terrorist bombs. It'll bring earthquakes, tornadoes, and possibly a meteor." Brendan McGarity, an Orlando teenager was caught by police after he tore down and threw 25 of the rainbow flags, valued at $800, into a lake. His sister said McGarity was inspired by the Robertson telecast and had never before expressed animosity towards gays. Jay Sekulow, chief counsel for Robertson's American Center for Law and Justice, later used the rainbow flags for fodder in a fundraising letter. He wrote, "What I saw in Orlando made me realize just how far our nation has fallen."

Tallahassee: University funding for student union

The Florida State University Student Senate voted to drastically reduce the funding of and downgrade the Lesbian-Gay-Bisexual Student Union (LGBSU). By a vote of 17 to 14 with 4 abstentions, the Student Senate adopted a resolution to reduce the LGBSU's status from an "agency" of the student government to an independent "organization." As an agency, LGBSU received $12,000 in funding in 1998 (other agencies receive an average of $21,000 per year, according to a student senator). Independent organizations, however, receive less than $500 per year on average. Senate President Russell Hellein, who sponsored the resolution, had not expected it to pass because the Student Supreme Court had already defeated another of his proposals that would have placed a referendum on the student election ballot asking whether students wanted their activities fees to fund the LGBSU. Senator Dave Collins, a supporter of the motion to reclassify LGBSU, said, "I feel my sexuality is a private, personal matter. I do not think we should be forced to fund it as an executive agency." The resolution then moved to the University Vice President, who signed it into effect. The attacks on the LGBSU have continued into 1999. In March, the Student Senate considered a bill that would prohibit student groups that have a membership based on sexual orientation. And when the LGBSU attempted to add the letter "T," for transgender, to its name, the senate protested strongly, although the senate has never before objected to minor name changes.

GEORGIA

Statewide: Anti-gay multicultural newsletter

A University of Georgia (UGA) newsletter, "Multicultural Perspectives," debuted with an issue calling homosexuality "evil" and Judaism "an unusual religion." The newsletter was started by two UGA College of Education staffers who had received a $1,555 grant from the school to explore multicultural issues. For the premiere issue, they focused on a variety of religions, including Baptist, Islam, and Unitarian Universalism. In the same edition were several paragraphs on "Homosexuality. Gays. Lesbians." It read, in part, "Let's see what the word of God has to say about homosexuals. GOD DECLARES JUDGMENT ON THE HOMOSEXUAL * THE BIBLE SAYS HOMOSEXUALITY IS EVIL, AND AGAINST GOD'S NATURAL PLAN FOR SEXUALITY* [emphasis in original] God wants to turn the homosexual to the straight." In a separate section, author Marcy Nejat wrote that Jews refused to accept Jesus as their Messiah "For the same reason that the Pharisees of His time sought to kill Him and nullify His claims, multiplied by 2000 years. They were, and still are, offended by his teachings." Campus Jewish and gay rights groups condemned the newsletter, and UGA quickly demanded a refund of the grant it had given the two staffers. UGA also said that the newsletter would no longer be published. UGA Spokesman Tom Jackson said, "It's offensive to everyone — to the Jewish religion, to multiculturalists in general, and to homosexuals in specific. It does not reflect the positions of the University of Georgia and the project has been discontinued and the grant money has been returned."

Statewide: Georgia Baptist Convention

In November, the Georgia Baptist Convention voted to expel any church "which knowingly takes, or has taken, any action to affirm, approve, or endorse homosexual behavior." The measure had been paired with another proposal that called for the expulsion of "charismatic" churches that practiced speaking in tongues and other "reckless emotionalism." That proposed measure failed, while the resolution to ban gays passed in a show of hands by an overwhelming majority. It was the first time the convention had imposed rules on its membership beyond mandatory financial contributions and "friendly cooperation with general purposes of the convention." Proponents of excluding gay-affirming churches cited a paper adopted by the convention in 1997. It reads, in part: "Practicing homosexuals are living in sin, and therefore, must not be ordained to the ministry. Homosexual unions or marriages must never be hallowed or sanctioned," and calls homosexuality "unnatural and a rebellion against God."

Rev. Gerald Harris, chair of the committee that suggested the new requirements, said, "Our committee is not here to throw stones, but to lift up a standard of righteousness." Rev. Walker K. Knight, also a leader among Georgia Baptists, disagreed. "Sadly, the Georgia Baptist Convention Executive Committee continues in its history of being reactionary, acting in this instance in a similar way to its leaders who earlier supported slavery, and others who refused to acknowledge God's call to women." Harris introduced the resolution, and said he was not endorsing hatred of homosexuals. "The unanimous verdict of the Scripture is that homosexuality is a sin. However, homosexuals are included among neighbors we are commanded to love." He later said, "Love...must not compromise the church's allegiance to Scripture." Rev. Bill Self voiced his dissent and asked executive committee member Rev. Frank Page, "I want to ask one simple question: this year the homosexual — who's next? Churches that receive African-Americans?" Page was curt in his reply: "Anyone who desires and follows a direction directly opposed to the word of God — they are next."

Statewide: United Methodist Church conference

In June, the North Georgia Conference of the United Methodist Church voted to continue barring homosexuals from the ministry and disallowing same-sex marriages or commitment ceremonies "in a Methodist church or by a Methodist pastor." The NGC resolution also stated that homosexuality is wrong, but homosexuals are accepted as "persons for whom Christ died and whom God loves." This follows the official United Methodist stand on the issue, which was elevated from a guideline to church canon in August. The canon states that same-sex marriages cannot be performed by Methodist ministers and that ministers who perform such ceremonies can be defrocked. This goes against a trend of acceptance within the Methodist community, evidenced by the more than 360 United Methodist pastors who have signed a petition urging compassion toward gays within the Methodist church as well as the sanctioning of same-sex marriages. One retired Methodist minister from Sharpsburg, Harold Murphree, explained his opposition to changing official church policy, saying that a trend toward accepting same-sex marriages is a "devil sickness" contrary to God's will because "Adam and Steve cannot bear children."

Carrollton: Student forced out of school

Although the Georgian Country Day School's handbook extols the values of "diversity in opinion, culture, ideas, behavioral characteristics, attributes or challenges," school authorities still kicked out 15-year-old Alex McLendon, a boy, for dressing in girl's clothing. Alex, who says he is "95 percent girl" but not homosexual, first began dressing in girl's clothing and wearing makeup two years ago. He enrolled at the private school in Carrollton in September because he wanted a better education. Most of the other kids could not tell he was biologically male, and the rest did not seem to care. When Alex was pointed out to classmate Patrick Nelson as the cross-dresser everyone was talking about, Nelson says his reaction was, "No way, that's too weird! Then I thought about it and I said, 'So what's so weird about that?' " Meayghan Denkers, a friend of Alex's, said, "Alex wasn't causing any problems. She was getting along with everybody. She wasn't trying to change anybody to be like her or anything." Alex stressed that he had not done anything wrong. "I just look like a girl, and I dress like a girl. It wasn't flamboyant, not sequins or anything."

> "I hate you because God hates you."
>
> — The Rev. Amos D. Moore's answer when a gay protester asked him, "How can you call yourself a man of God and preach hate?" Moore led an effort to stop gays from moving into his Kirkwood neighborhood.

Alex and his father were called in to meet with school officials after the school received phone calls from parents who objected to Alex's cross-dressing. One mother said, "I believe in sexual standards in society, and I want my child in a school that holds the same sexual ethics that I do." Meayghan's mother tried to explain the town's reaction. "Alex represents something that's way beyond the experience and the comfort zone of the very conservative people we live with." School officials told Alex that he would have to dress like a boy in the future. Alex refused, and his father backed him up, which led to a special school board meeting to consider Alex's fate. After the meeting, Alex was given an ultimatum: Leave the school, or be expelled. As a private school, they had the right to take this course of action, whereas a public school would have to first prove that Alex was disrupting education or undermining safety. School authorities cited his tongue ring as the reason for the extreme action, and have declined to speak to the press about the matter. Students of both sexes donned hair bows to protest Alex's forced withdrawal from the school but were ordered to remove them by the principal.

Cobb County: Gay-baiting in primary runoff

In Cobb County, incumbent County Commissioner Gordon Wysong attempted to hold on to his seat by emphasizing his support of the 1993 "Cobb County Commission Anti-Gay Lifestyle Resolution." He mailed out campaign literature claiming his opponent, Sam Olens, advocated "special rights" for gay men and lesbians. Olens responded, "They ought to be treated as people on this earth. If that's special to Gordon...it must be indicative of his homophobia." The two were competing in the Republican primary runoff for the District 3 seat on the Commission, an area that includes some of metro Atlanta's most prestigious neighborhoods. In an election year with no Democratic challengers, the winner of the runoff became the de facto victor. Wysong's reliance on anti-gay propaganda backfired at the polls, and Olens is now serving his first term as County Commissioner.

Kirkwood: Community divided

Gay men and lesbians faced extreme hostility over the summer after a Kirkwood minister started a campaign to "[P]ut an end to the homosexual and lesbian takeover of our neighborhood." Friction in the community had been slowly mounting in recent years due to the gentrification of some areas, which some residents feared would drive up their taxes. In addition, the Rev. Amos D. Moore of New Mt. Sinai Baptist Church strongly supported a woman who was sued by a gay couple who said she ran a crack house in the neighborhood; Moore claimed that the case was a racially motivated fabrication. Trouble erupted again when Rev. Moore organized a community meeting to address how to stem the influx of whites and gays into the neighborhood. Moore's community group, Concerned Black Neighbors of Kirkwood, passed out fliers announcing the May 19 meeting and its purpose, which spurred concerned citizens to call police, and eventually resulted in the cancellation of Concerned Black Neighbors' space at the community center. A meeting of sorts was held nonetheless, with protesters from the gay community and Moore's supporters rallying at the community center, essentially drowning each other out.

After the crowd dispersed, Moore explained his objections to having gays in Kirkwood, and his belief that 95 to 98 percent of the whites in Kirkwood were, in fact, gay. "Homosexuality is wrong in any neighborhood. It is an abomination unto the Lord. If they want to come into a heterosexual neighborhood, they need to go back into the closet. Then our children will not be exposed to seeing men walking down the street holding hands and kissing, and women doing the same thing. In teaching our children, hopefully we will be able to keep them from falling into that pit of life. Homosexuality is not acceptable in any society. If God doesn't like it, why should we have to put up with it?"

A town meeting convened at City Hall Tower on June 22 to try to bridge the gaps in the community. Outside the meeting, a gay African American asked, "How can you call yourself a man of God and preach hate?" Moore replied, "I hate you because God hates you. I don't have to condemn you, because God condemns you." Apparently, things did not go much better inside City Hall, because on July 4, some residents awoke to find a flier illustrated with pornography, with certain lines of the text highlighted, such as "the wages of sin is death," on their car windshields. Moore denied responsibility for the flier, and even his detractors doubted he was behind the handout. One man who had found the July 4 handout on his truck explained, "We can't blame this on Amos Moore directly, but had Amos Moore not started all this crap, we wouldn't be having this." Although Moore told reporters that he planned to hold a huge march from one end of Kirkwood to the other to protest homosexuality, the march never materialized, and as of publication, the tension seems to have abated.

HAWAII

Statewide: Same-sex marriage initiative

In November, Hawaii voters passed an amendment to the state constitution giving the state legislature the power to restrict marriage to opposite-sex couples. The ballot initiative was designed to preempt a possible decision by the Supreme Court of Hawaii in *Baehr v. Miike,* affirming Circuit Judge Kevin Chang's ruling that denying marriage licenses to same-sex couples violated the state constitution. This decision also effectively rendered unconstitutional a 1994 law that said Hawaii's marriage laws only apply to same sex couples.

National Religious Right organizations such as Focus on the Family and the Christian Coalition led the campaign to pass the restrictive amendment with the Christian Coalition's web site reporting its goal of raising $1.5 million for the campaign. The local Focus on the Family affiliate, the Hawaii Family Forum, and the Hawaii Christian Coalition joined forces with another local group, Save Traditional Marriage (STM). STM, an organization supported by fundamentalist Christians, Catholics and the Church of Jesus Christ of Latter-day Saints, ran a series of television commercials supporting the initiative. In one, a young boy is reading from the book "Daddy's Wedding," looking at an illustration of two men kissing. The ad asks, "If you don't think homosexual marriage will affect you, how do you think it will affect your children?" A second commercial portrayed a man and woman in wedding attire running toward each other. The man, however, runs past the bride into the arms of another man. That ad said that only a yes vote would stop same-sex marriage. The Hawaii Family Forum ran radio ads claiming that a "no" vote on the initiative would "redefine marriage to include homosexual couples." The Hawaii Christian Coalition (HCC) printed 200,000 voter guides for distribution to churches and asked

Hawaii clergy members to "stand up in their pulpits and denounce the evils of homosexuality." However, HCC President Dan McGivern cautioned that "Pastors need to show some guts and tell people how they are personally voting, without telling their flocks how to vote, since that is illegal." One of HCC's fundraising appeals that appeared on its website claimed that "[S]ome, but not all, homosexuals are pedophiles, preying on children and wanting the age of consent laws for sex removed all over the world. Just as they call gay marriages a 'civil right,' some-again, not all-say children are being deprived of their 'civil right' to have sex....God destroyed Sodom for sodomy.... Let's not incur God's wrath all over the world for what could happen in Hawaii, before this Christmas."

In the final stretch, Alliance for Traditional Marriage, a Religious Right organization that splintered off from STM, began airing vicious ads equating same-sex marriage with incest and bestiality. On Nov. 3, voters passed the amendment, 68.2 percent to 31.8 percent. Jay Sekulow, head of Pat Robertson's American Center for Law and Justice, reacted to the victory: "To have that go overwhelmingly in our favor shows that the Lord was clearly at work. With the vote in Alaska and Hawaii, conservative lawmakers can be pro-family without being labeled as extremists."

> "Just as they call gay marriages a 'civil right,' some ... say children are being deprived of their 'civil right' to have sex."
>
> From the website of the Hawaii Christian Coalition, which successfully pushed a state constitutional amendment targeting same-sex marriage.

After the elections, Gov. Ben Cayetano said that while he did not support same-sex marriage, he believed that gay men and lesbians should have the financial benefits afforded to married couples. In 1997, the legislature had passed a "reciprocal beneficiaries" law that ostensibly granted same-sex couples certain legal rights commensurate with those of married couples. However, health care and other provisions were eventually removed from the legislation, rendering it only minimally beneficial to the gay community. Cayetano now proposed new domestic partners legislation and pledged to push the legislature to act on it. The head of ATM, Mike Gabbard, who was also active in STM, called the proposal a euphemism for same-sex marriage. "While we tolerate homosexuals, the people of Hawaii do not want to grant social approval to homosexual unions by allowing them to marry, even if it's called by a different name: domestic partnerships," said Gabbard. He also announced a $5,000 advertising campaign criticizing those trying "to make a mockery out of marriage." The ad began by saying, "Governor Cayetano says he will fight to legalize homosexual marriage, but instead of calling it marriage, he'll disguise it as domestic partnership." The state Senate president announced Dec. 14 that the incoming Senate might not even consider social issues, including domestic partnerships, in the next session, so that it could focus instead on the state's economy. He suggested that after the turmoil surrounding the recent elections, the state needed time to "heal a bit."

On Dec. 23, Hawaii Attorney General Margery Bronster's office filed a brief in the Hawaii Supreme Court arguing that the court would need to reevaluate the *Baehr v. Miike* case in light of the change in the constitution. The brief contended that the 1994 marriage statute was now constitutionally protected, and should be enforced. Dan Foley, one of the lawyers for the three couples in Baehr who had sued the state, argued that the legislature would need to pass a new law, as it was never stated that the constitutional amendment could be retroactive. In addition, he charged that the question over equal rights and benefits was not settled. John Hoag of STM hailed the state's filing, but said he might begin lobbying with another organization to prevent domestic partnership legislation: "I would be opposed to domestic partnerships if they involve adoption and parental rights. I think that's the hot button for a lot of people." In March 1999, Cayetano's domestic partnership legislation, which contained economic benefits but did not extend adoption or parental rights to same-sex couples, was declared dead for the year.

IDAHO

Boise: Ad rejected by student newspaper

Meridian School District's Eagle High School's student newspaper, the Stampede, rejected an ad submitted by a student for a GLBT youth support group in Boise. Travis Riggs, the Eagle senior who proposed the ad, says that the ad for the group, Your Family, Friends and Neighbors, Inc., was rejected because it included objectionable language. He says he substituted "non-heterosexual" for the words "gay, lesbian, and bisexual," so that the ad read, in part, "an open, safe place for all non-heterosexual youth to meet." He contends that the newspaper was unhappy with the language, but he felt he had changed all he could. "If I took 'non-heterosexual' out too, the ad would lose its message," he explained. A spokeswoman for the school district claimed that Riggs had never resubmitted the ad after he was asked to alter the language, and the newspaper adviser later said that the ad had been rejected by a student editor. After the ad was rejected, Riggs contacted the ACLU of Idaho to ask them to look into the case. The ACLU then asked him if he would be willing to talk to the media about the incident, which he agreed to do. Reporters asked him what he had been trying to accomplish. He says he told them, he "was trying to send a message that being gay is OK and there is help if you need it." After his story appeared in the press, he says, a petition was started anonymously at the high school. It read, "We the undersigned believe that the Stampede should allow any and all advertising. We also feel that discrimination is a problem at Eagle High School and we support the current anti-discrimination efforts." Over 400 students signed the petition.

Chicago: Employment discrimination

Fawn Houck was hired at the Inner City Horticultural Foundation on April 1, 1997, to work with children from the Chicago Housing Authority's Cabrini Green apartments. Houck says that she sensed that her supervisor, Daniel Underwood, was uncomfortable with gays and lesbians and that she therefore felt obligated to inform him of her sexual orientation after the hire. According to Houck, Underwood then told her that he was afraid to have her working with children since he did not trust her. She also claims that he expressed fears about Houck's "influence" on the children she was to accompany on a trip scheduled for late April. Underwood fired Houck before that trip.

Houck filed a complaint with the Chicago Commission on Human Relations (CCHR). Underwood did not refute the charge that he had fired Houck because of her sexual orientation; he instead ordered that doing so was justified because it would be inappropriate for a lesbian to work with children. On Nov. 6, 1998, the agency found that the Inner City Horticultural Foundation had violated Cook County's Human Rights Ordinance when it fired Houck for being gay. In its decision, the CCHR wrote that the foundation had made "stereotypical and untrue assumptions about the ability of gay individuals to work with children" and ordered the foundation to pay Houck $13,221 in damages.

Chicago: Minister suspended for same-sex unions

In March 1999, Rev. Gregory Dell of the Broadway United Methodist Church (UMC) in the Lakeview neighborhood of Chicago was found guilty by a jury of 13 Methodist ministers of disobeying church law and was subsequently suspended for performing a union between two gay men in his church. The only way in which Rev. Dell may return to his duties would be to pledge not to perform same-sex unions in the future, which he has said he will not do. "If I can't be a pastor, full to all the people I am appointed," said Dell, "you don't want me as a pastor. You really don't." He continued to act as consultant to the interim minister at Broadway, however, where about a third of the congregation is gay or lesbian.

In August 1998, the United Methodist Church's judicial council ruled that a church directive prohibiting the use of Methodist churches and/or the participation of Methodist ministers in same-sex marriages would be binding church law. This vote was taken after the narrow acquittal of Rev. Jimmy Creech, also a Methodist minister, who had been tried for performing a marriage ceremony for two women and who defended himself on the grounds that the directive was not compulsory. Rev. Dell is the first Methodist minister to be punished under the new church law. He has been a minister for 30 years, and is now the director of In All Things Charity, a support network of UMC members and clergy who advocate welcoming gay men, lesbians and bisexuals into all areas of church life. Dell has appealed his conviction, but as of publication, no action had been taken.

Chicago: Phelps protest

The Rev. Fred Phelps of Topeka, Kansas, known for his rabid attacks on the gay community, came to Chicago on Nov. 22 to protest against Rev. Gregory Dell for performing a same-sex marriage in September. The protest was to take place at the Broadway United Methodist Church, where Dell was pastor and where the gay marriage took place.

When Phelps showed up with his family, they were not the only ones outside the church. About 1,500 hundred members of the Lakeview community were there to show support for the church and Rev. Dell. About 800 of the church supporters surrounded the building to "protect" it from Phelps' clan. The rest staged a counter protest. Phelps' group spent about 90 minutes huddled behind 20 police officers, holding signs with messages including, "God hates fags," "Matt Shepard is in hell," and "Fags die, God laughs." Phelps said, "I'm preaching God's line. They need to hear there is a hell waiting for them."

Phelps' group returned to Chicago to protest against the church again on Dec. 6.

Chicago: Puerto Rican Day parade

The National Latina/o Lesbian, Gay, Bisexual & Transgender Organization (LLEGO) was the target of anti-gay discrimination when it participated in the Puerto Rican Day Parade in Chicago. When the group initially registered its float, it was assigned slot number 44 in the procession. Llego members say that when a parade committee representative discovered LLEGO was a gay organization, the group was contacted and told that the parade committee "did not want anyone to be naked," and "that they did not want any men dressed as women." Allegedly, they were also told that this was not a gay parade and that no gay symbols or rainbow flags were to be displayed.

LLEGO Director Martin Ornelas-Quintero requested and was granted a meeting with parade committee president Ruben Rosado. Ornelas-Quintero says that during the meeting, Rosado said there was no problem with flying the rainbow flag, and that he only expected LLEGO to use good judgment on matters of safety. On the way out of the meeting, Ornelas-Quintero says he was told by Rosado's secretary that a mistake had been made and LLEGO's proper position in the parade would be at the very end, in slot number 129. LLEGO complained about the placement and was told that it would have its original spot returned. When LLEGO members arrived to join the parade on June 13, they were sent to the rear. Despite the placement, those on the LLEGO float decided to reclaim their initial slot on their own, which they did. "There were no boos, and lots of cheers," said Ornelas-Quintero.

Cook County: Employment discrimination

A Lincolnwood Red Lobster restaurant was found in violation of the Cook County Human Rights Ordinance prohibiting job discrimination based on sexual orientation when it fired gay employee Dale Hall in 1996. The Cook County Human Rights Commission's hearing officer, David Lee, determined, based on testimony from other employees, that Hall's termination was a result of discrimination on the part of his supervisor, who would ridicule Hall in meetings and state to other employees, "I've got to get rid of this faggot." In June, Lee recommended to the Cook County Human Rights Commission that Red Lobster be ordered to reinstate Hall to his former position of assistant manager and pay him for damages and lost wages.

Rather than comply with such an order, Red Lobster's parent company, Darden Restaurants (also owner of the Olive Garden, China Coast and Bahama Breeze chains), asked that the Cook County Human Rights Commission declare the ordinance unconstitutional on the grounds that the ordinance exceeds the scope and power of home rule permitted under the state's constitution. The gay and lesbian community publicized Darden Restaurants' efforts, and before long the corporation was inundated with angry e-mails, letters and calls. Possibly fearing a public boycott, the corporation abandoned its legal strategy, claimed that it maintains a strict policy against discrimination of all kinds-including on the basis of sexual orientation-issued an apology to the gay and lesbian community and claimed the furor over its earlier challenge was the result of a "misunderstanding." The corporation then contended that Hall was fired for performance-based reasons and refused to return him to his position — despite the fact that Hall had received many glowing performance reviews throughout his nine-year tenure at Red Lobster.

> "If I can't be a pastor, full to all the people I am appointed, you don't want me as a pastor."
>
> — Rev. Gregory Dell, who was punished after a trial by the Methodist Church but told he could return to his post if he pledged not to perform same-sex unions. Dell refused.

On Sept. 11, the Cook County Human Rights Commission issued a final decision ordering Red Lobster to pay Hall $45,000 in back pay and $50,000 in damages (five times the amount initially recommended by Lee) along with lost benefits and interest. Red Lobster was also ordered to reinstate Hall to his former position of assistant manager and to set up diversity training programs within all Cook County branches.

Statewide: Adoption/foster care

A well-publicized adoption by a gay man led conservative members of the Indiana General Assembly to take action. In September, state Reps. Jack Lutz and Woody Burton announced that they would introduce legislation at the start of the next legislative session to make Indiana, along with Florida and New Hampshire, the only states that ban adoptions and foster parenting by gay men and lesbians. The Republican lawmakers were spurred on by the well-publicized 1998 decision of the Madison County Child Protection Services to grant adoption of a foster child to a gay Indianapolis man. U.S. Rep. David McIntosh, who endorsed the Burton legislation, called the agency's decision "egregious and morally unacceptable." Burton's supporters, which include the Religious Right organizations Advance America and the Indiana Family Institute (a Focus on the Family Affiliate), claimed that their legislation's intent was to protect adopted children from the discrimination and abuse homosexuals face. However, Burton also commented on adoptive parenting, "The nature aspect of it dictates that a man be with a woman and a woman be with a man." And he added, "I've got friends that I believe are homosexuals-good people. That's their business. But they're not out there trying to adopt children or change government."

Burton's allies sponsored a similar bill in the Indiana Senate. That bill was not considered during the 1999 session, although a bill that would have placed extreme restrictions on the ability of persons not living in an "intact marriage" to adopt children passed the Senate Judiciary Committee on a 5-4 vote. When its sponsor said he would alter the bill's wording to specifically bar adoptions by gay men and lesbians, the bill was killed by a voice vote. Burton had no more success in the House. After his original bill was killed in committee, he moved a compromise bill similar to the Senate bill that sought to give married couples preference in adoption and foster parenting. Once it reached the floor, Burton and his supporters filed amendments to reinsert the starkly anti-gay language of his original bill. The compromise bill and each of the amendments failed. Marla Stevens of the LGBT Fairness gay adoption rights advocacy group said she felt encouraged by the lobbying against Burton's bill. However, she cautiously noted, "I will not be surprised if they do this again next year."

Statewide: Congressional campaign

Incumbent Republican Congressman John Hostettler aired an anti-gay radio campaign ad attacking the record of his opponent, Democratic challenger Gail Riecken. The ad criticized Riecken's support of the Employment Non-Discrimination Act (ENDA), a federal bill that would prohibit employment discrimination based on sexual orientation. During her campaign, Riecken claimed to favor ENDA personally, but she vowed not to support such a law because her constituents would oppose it. Nonetheless, Hostettler's campaign ran attack ads in which a male voice says, "Gail Riecken is an outright liberal... The gay and lesbian lobbyists have her vote already... Well, forcing churches and schools to hire homosexuals just won't fly in Southwestern Indiana." Riecken wrote a letter to Hostettler urging him to pull the ad, but Hostettler responded to Riecken's criticism of the ad by saying, "It's where she stands on these issues." The station manager of a Daviess County radio station called the ads "the worst thing I've ever heard."

Anderson: Adoption

An Anderson couple, Butch and Sandy Kimmerling, sought permanent custody of an 8-year-old foster daughter when they learned that a gay man from Indianapolis wanted to adopt her. "Being Christians, we thought [the adoptive home] would be a traditional setting," said Butch Kimmerling. "It was a gay couple and we do not believe in that." The Kimmerlings, who have served as foster parents to over 50 children, had never before sought to adopt a foster child. The man seeking to adopt the child was also adopting her three brothers, who had been placed in a separate foster home. The Kimmerlings said that they did not pursue custody of the girl's brothers because they have developmental disabilities. It is Indiana adoption policy to ensure that, whenever possible, siblings are not separated. Anderson Mayor J. Mark Lawler wrote to the state Division of Family and Social Services and to the judge presiding over the case, urging them to deny the gay man custody, stating that "it is inconceivable to me that any agency would grant an adoption to a gay couple that seeks to raise children under such controversial circumstances." The case also received considerable media attention, and the governor's office placed pressure on the Division of Family and Social Services and the Madison County Child Protective Services to keep the girl in the custody of the Kimmerlings. Her brothers, however, have been in the custody of the Indianapolis man and his partner since October, and are reportedly doing well. Marla Stevens of LGBT Fairness, an Indiana gay and lesbian rights advocacy group, calls the Indianapolis couple, both of whom have chosen to remain anonymous, "amazingly wonderful parents." This battle has also spurred the Indiana Family Institute, an affiliate of James Dobson's Focus on the Family, to initiate an effort to pass a state law that would block adoptions by gay men and lesbians.

> "I've got friends that I believe are homosexuals — good people.... But they're not out there trying to adopt children or change government."
>
> — Indiana state Rep. Woody Burton, sponsor of a bill to prevent gay men and lesbians from becoming foster parents or adopting.

Boone County: Child custody

During divorce proceedings, Boone County Judge Ora Kincaid denied Chris Burgess, a gay man, custody of his 4-year-old son. Burgess contends that his homosexuality was the deciding factor. Custody of the son was awarded to the boy's mother, Patricia Burgess, despite the fact that she is addicted to painkillers. Chris Burgess' lawyer, Sean Lemieux of the Indiana Civil Liberties Union, said, "The judge gave custody to the mother despite her drug addiction, in fact refused to consider the effect of the drug addiction on the child, just because Chris is gay." Chris Burgess' trial witnesses included a doctor and a family counselor who testified that his homosexuality in no way impairs his ability to provide and care for his son. Burgess' lawyer also established that the son would have stability living with his father, as Chris Burgess lived with his partner of three years and the partner's two daughters. Comparing Chris's sexual orientation to Patricia's drug problem as equally "negative," the judge wrote that the two factors "cancel each other out." Chris Burgess and the ICLU appealed the judge's ruling. The appellate court upheld the trial court's ruling, and Chris's lawyers have asked the appellate court to reconsider its decision. No further action had been taken as of publication.

Chesterton: Phelps protest

The Rev. Fred Phelps of the Westboro Baptist Church (WBC) in Topeka, Kansas, led an anti-gay protest against the Duneland School Board in Chesterton for allowing a high school teacher to display a gay awareness poster in her classroom. Phelps is well known for his anti-gay picketing everywhere from Matthew Shepard's funeral to gay-friendly churches. The WBC picketed at the school district's administration center, as well as Chesterton High School. According to Jan Bergeson, principal of Chesterton High School, local police ensured that Phelps and his supporters had a place to hold their protest at a safe distance from the school. The school responded to the protest by making sure the students stayed well within the school grounds so that there was no contact between the student body and the picketers. Phelps also protested at the office of the Post-Tribune newspaper for its allegedly biased coverage of Phelps and his supporters and staged a fourth rally across the street from Valparaiso University where students had been attempting to pass a nondiscrimination policy regarding sexual orientation.

Evansville: Anti-discrimination

In June, the Evansville City Council refused to consider an ordinance to prohibit discrimination based on sexual orientation. The city's Human Relations Commission had recommended that such an ordinance be passed, but Evansville City Attorney Toby Shaw notified the city council that it would face serious legal challenges. Shaw argued that neither the federal nor state constitution bans anti-gay discrimination. He also cited home rule laws that prohibit cities from passing anti-discrimination ordinances that the state legislature could pass. However, Wally Paynter of the Tri-State Alliance of Gays and Lesbians argued that three Indiana cities — Bloomington, Lafayette and West Lafayette — already have sexual orientation discrimination ordinances. Vanderburgh County Commissioner Richard Mourdock supported Shaw's opposition to the ordinance and said the county would follow Evansville's lead regarding legal protections for gays and lesbians. In a November letter to the Tri-State Alliance, the city's Human Relations Commission noted that "We are committed to seeing legislation passed at the state level that will provide the enabling legislation necessary to adopt a local ordinance prohibiting discrimination based on sexual orientations."

Lafayette: Anti-gay threats to teachers

Several teachers in Lafayette received anonymous phone calls and hate mail threatening to expose them as gay and oust them from their jobs. Similar letters were also sent to Lafayette newspapers. One letter claimed that an unidentified group paid a private investigator for surveillance of teachers to prove they were homosexual, and another stated that "it is time to rid our schools of immoral people." Lafayette School Corporation Superintendent Ed Eiler, who called the hate mail and phone calls an "orchestrated smear campaign" and "a clear campaign of hate," said that he had received threats that he would be forced to resign unless he fired suspected gay teachers. In July, the Lafayette School Board passed a resolution to condemn the "hate campaign" against the school employees and to request community support to find those responsible. Concerned citizens held meetings to help bring the harassment to an end. One teacher, who is also a member of the City Council, reflected, "You would think it would be divisive. But it really has sort of galvanized the community in support of diversity. It's just been wonderful to see."

South Bend: Priest resigns from Notre Dame

Rev. David Garrick, a Roman Catholic priest and assistant professor of communications and theater at the University of Notre Dame, resigned his faculty post in March to protest the university's treatment of gay men and lesbians and its failure to adopt a policy to prohibit anti-gay discrimination. In 1996, Father Garrick was the unofficial faculty adviser of a gay and lesbian student group that university administrators prohibited from meeting in the campus counseling center. In 1997, after student protests in support of gay rights, the university offered a "statement of inclusion" toward gay men and lesbians that condemned harassment of gay faculty and students. However, administrators still refused to include a sexual orientation clause in the university's non-discrimination policy. Soon after Father Garrick's 1996 announcement that he is gay and celibate, invitations to say Mass and hear confessions at the university's Basilica of the Sacred Heart stopped coming. In November 1997, he learned that he had been forbidden from taking part in any official sacramental duties in any official way. Father Garrick explained his decision to resign by saying, "It is my intention that this resignation shall serve as a heartfelt protest against the refusal of the officers of the university to make a legal provision for the equal rights for gay persons at Notre Dame." In February 1999, the university's Board of Fellows voted to continue excluding sexual orientation discrimination from its anti-discrimination policy.

Tippecanoe County: Human relations ordinance

The Tippecanoe County Commission was not able to pass a proposed human relations ordinance to provide protection from discrimination, apparently because it would have included protections for gay men and lesbians. A Tippecanoe County councilman, David Koltick, sponsored a resolution urging the county commission not to pass the human relations ordinance. Council members were outraged that Koltick affixed the council's name to the resolution even though he did not have the support of the council and because the council's jurisdiction is limited to fiscal matters. The county commission ultimately decided to put off voting on the proposed ordinance and instead considered a broad resolution condemning discrimination without mentioning sexual orientation. In December, a vote on this resolution was postponed as well. According to the Journal & Courier, the controversy leading to the deferral came from people who believed the ordinance would give homosexuals "special rights."

Valparaiso: Anti-gay radio skit

Valparaiso University radio station WVUR ran an on-air skit performed by campus radio disc jockeys who used homosexual slurs and specifically mocked another student. Immediately following the broadcast, the disc jockeys took calls from students who used abusive and homophobic language. The WVUR disc jockeys were dismissed from their unpaid positions, and the station played music and pre-approved taped programming for two days while its other employees underwent a sensitivity training program. In response to this incident and others, Valparaiso's Student Senate passed a resolution to add sexual orientation to the school policy on sexual harassment. Students who lobbied for the new policy cited the on-air comments as evidence that Valparaiso needed such protections for gay and lesbian students. An advocate for the policy change noted, "It's absolutely terrible that these people used WVUR as a medium for hate." Another said that gay and lesbian students are "probably one of the most harassed groups on campus," and added, "Now students can point to a policy within the handbook that explicitly states we will not be tolerant of sexual harassment on the basis of sexual orientation." A previous attempt to add sexual orientation to the school's anti-discrimination policy failed in 1996.

Valparaiso: Coming Out Week chalkings defaced

Chalked announcements for National Coming Out week were defaced at Valparaiso University in October. Students belonging to the gay and lesbian group Alliance chalked announcements for National Coming Out week on the sidewalks around campus. Before they could finish, three students began throwing water on some of the drawings to wash them away. Later, other drawings and announcements were obliterated, defaced or altered by anti-gay graffiti artists. "Death to Fags" was scrawled in one location; elsewhere that message was echoed by a chalk body outline. The offensive remarks were soon washed away by maintenance workers. To protest the anti-gay graffiti, a rally was held a day later in front of the student union. The rally drew about 200 students and was led by members of Alliance. "These slogans on our walkways are not what we are about," said Rev. David Kehret, associate Dean of the Chapel of Resurrection. The incident occurred months after Valparaiso amended its harassment policy to prohibit "unwanted discussion and teasing based on someone's homosexuality or suspected homosexuality."

Statewide: Anti-discrimination

A bill introduced by State Sen. Robert Dvorsky that would have extended the state's anti-discrimination protections to gay men and lesbians died in committee in January. The bill covered discrimination based on "actual or perceived heterosexuality, homosexuality, or bisexuality." The bill was sent to the State Government Committee, where chairman Sheldon Rittmer opposed the bill, saying he was concerned about excessive lawsuits based on the change. "Someone who is gay can be my best friend; they're free to be whoever they want. However, if you keep putting people in separate categories, and every time you do that, you kind of have that question: Are there lawsuits just based on that?" The bill moved from the State Government Committee to a subcommittee, where it died.

Statewide: Same-sex marriage ban

In April, Iowa became the 26th state in the nation to bar same-sex marriages. In February, bills were proposed in both the state House and state Senate to limit civil marriage in Iowa to heterosexual couples, and to refuse to recognize same-sex marriages performed outside the state (not that any other state recognizes such marriages). Rep. Dan Boddicker, claimed that the majority of the people of Iowa "view homosexuality as deviant behavior" and he only wanted to reflect Iowan's values in the law. Bill Crews, a gay man who has served as mayor of Melbourne, Iowa, for the past 14 years, was angered by the bill. "We're hard-working, tax-paying, law-abiding citizens, but yet we have to struggle to have our families and to have other people value our families," Crews said. The House passed the bill 89-10, with the opponents calling the bill discriminatory and unnecessary. One dissenter, Rep. Minnette Doderer, charged, "It's being used as a tool to defeat people in the next election." In the Senate, the bill was introduced by Sen. Larry McKibben, who stated that same-sex marriages could potentially lead to polygamy and incestuous marriages. The Senate passed the bill, 40-9. On April 15, Gov. Terry Branstad signed the bill into law, declining to comment on it.

Ames: Phelps picket

Rev. Fred Phelps of Westboro Baptist Church in Topeka, Kansas, picketed Iowa State University twice in 1998, once in May and then again in October. Both pickets were to oppose "university-sanctioned sodomy," or, in other words, having the Lesbian Gay Bisexual Transgender Ally Alliance (LGBTAA) on campus. When Phelps and his followers, who are notorious for picketing the funerals of AIDS victims, as well as the funeral of Matthew Shepard, first came to Ames in May to picket ISU's graduation, they carried signs that read, "ISU FAGS." The wording appeared over a likeness of "Cy" the cyclone, ISU's logo. The University was urged by some to sue the church over trademark infringement, but the director of University Legal Services said, "We just determined that it would not be worthwhile to get into a lawsuit with Mr. Phelps." ISU's second encounter with Phelps was actually in Kansas, at the ISU vs. Kansas State football game. The fax Phelps sent out to announce the picket said, "The thousands of Iowans coming to Manhattan, Kansas — as well as Kansans and visitors from other states — need to be warned that Iowa State Univ. is a seething hotbed of militant homosexual activity, sanctioned at the highest levels."

Des Moines: Human rights ordinance

In May, the Des Moines City Council voted to continue to exclude gay men and lesbians from protection under the city's human rights ordinance. After five years of debate, the Des Moines Human Rights Commission, voted 6-2 in February to recommend to the city council that "sexual orientation" be added to the list of protected categories under the Des Moines human rights ordinance. Those who objected to the change cited religious reservations and fears about the "gay rights agenda" and pedophilia gaining a foothold in Des Moines. Public commentary on the matter seemed to favor leaving homosexuals unprotected. "If I am forced by an amendment that says I must rent to a gay or lesbian person, I would think I would be the one discriminated against," said one man.

> "The Bible makes us bigoted."
>
> — Bill Horn, president of the Religious Right group Straight from the Heart, when Des Moines voted not to include gays in its human rights ordinance.

A month after the measure was sent to the city council, a rally in opposition to the proposed amendment to the ordinance drew 600 people. Among the attendees was Alveda King, niece of Martin Luther King Jr., who told the crowd that gays do not face real discrimination. She said, "Say no to any legislation that says you need a special category of law to make [homosexuals] feel right." Also in attendance was Bill Horn, the president of the religious conservative organization Straight from the Heart and the founder and president of the Iowa Family Policy Center, which is associated with Focus on the Family and Family Research Council. Horn had waged war on "the homosexual influence" in schools two years earlier, and had written a column in the Des Moines Register opposing the inclusion of "sexual orientation" in the civil rights ordinance. He stated that he had never heard of any anti-gay discrimination occurring in Des Moines and that sexual orientation was a choice and therefore did not deserve protection. Horn later teamed up with California multimillionaire Edward Atsinger III, who co-founded the California Independent business PAC (formerly the Allied Business PAC) which donated $4 million to right-wing state assembly candidates from 1992-8, facilitating the conservative Republican takeover of the California Legislature. Atsinger also co-owns Salem Communications, which runs one of the largest Christian radio networks in the country. Together, Atsinger and Horn urged Iowa ministers to preach against homosexuality in the pulpit and to get Christians to the polls in 2000. At the rally, Horn declared, "The Bible makes us bigoted." More than two months later, the city council defeated the proposed change, 4-3. Afterward, one council member who had voted against the addition moved to add wording denouncing anti-gay discrimination to the city's personnel manual. That measure failed, 5-2.

Grand Rapids: Minister ousted

On May 22, the 279,000-member Christian Reformed Church's Classis Grand Rapids East, a group of 16 churches, voted to oust Rev. Jim Lucas, a self-proclaimed celibate gay man, for his views on same-sex unions. Lucas had been without a congregation for nine years, and had been hoping to be assigned as a chaplain to an ecumenical support group for gay men and lesbians. The church had been annually extending his credentials since 1991, but last year he announced his support of gay and lesbian unions if the individuals involved did not believe they could remain celibate. The unions are condemned by Christian Reformed Church policy. Rev. Carl Kammeraad, a member of the classis, said, "You've put me, as a delegate, in a real bind. By your affirmation of same-sex unions, you have departed from what we as a denomination believe." Lucas replied, "I feel like I've been in a bind my whole life. I didn't choose to be gay." After the vote to defrock him, Lucas said, "It feels like a death-a death of a relationship with a church I have served faithfully for many years," but urged gay and lesbian members of the church not to give up on God or the church.

Iowa City: Housing assistance

Although Iowa City has had a domestic partners registry since 1994 and prohibits discrimination based on sexual orientation, it took a fight to get the city council to pass a measure ensuring that gay and lesbian families could receive the same housing aid from the city as heterosexual families. When the resolution was proposed by the city Department of Housing and Urban Development, Councilor Karen Kubby thought it would pass easily. "It's not a very controversial issue in my mind. This is the next step to make the definition of families consistent with our Human Rights Law," she said. However, Councilor Mike O'Donnell saw the issue differently: "I'm not comfortable with the fact that domestic partners are competing for assistance as a couple with kids. That's not my definition of family, I support the traditional view of family." Another councilor felt that passing the measure would conflict with the state law prohibiting same-sex marriage. On May 12, the resolution was passed 4-3. Kubby remarked, "I'm somewhat dismayed at the split vote.... I'm happy though, I'll take 4 to 3 any day."

Sioux City: Anti-discrimination ordinance

In front of a crowd of 150, the Sioux City Council defeated a measure in March to add sexual orientation to the city's anti-discrimination ordinance. The change was initially proposed by the Sioux City Human Rights Commission, and would have protected gay men and lesbians from discrimination in the areas of housing, employment and public accommodations. After listening to heated testimony and receiving several phone calls and letters both for and against the change, the city council agreed to hold a vote on the matter. Mayor Tom Padgett indicated he would sign the ordinance if it passed, although he said he realized that many citizens disagreed with it. "The overwhelming number of people I've talked to want to retain the right to discriminate. I think that's unfortunate."

At a public hearing on the issue, those opposing extending civil rights to gays cited religious reasons and predicted that Sioux City residents would soon be forced to hire and accept gay men and lesbians against their will. Eugene Dallas, a senior pastor at the Billy Sunday Memorial Church, testified that sometimes discrimination is necessary. "When it comes to morality, we must be discriminatory or we fail to protect society from all sorts of evil." Thirty-seven religious leaders on the other side of the debate signed a petition calling on the city council to expand the anti-discrimination ordinance. Rev. Bill Skinner, a retired councilman and mayor, remarked, "People are using Scripture to run interference for bigotry. I find that offensive." On March 16, the proposal was defeated in a 3-2 vote. Erma Zimmerman, who said her gay son left Sioux City 12 years earlier because he felt unwelcome, shared her disappointment: "If we want to be a community of bigots, I guess we're going to be a community of bigots. It's real sad."

KANSAS

Statewide: Phelps for governor

Rev. Fred Phelps, the notorious pastor of the Westboro Baptist Church in Topeka who preaches that "God hates fags," took his anti-gay rhetoric on the campaign trail this year, declaring himself a Democratic candidate for governor in March. Announcing his candidacy, he criticized Republican Gov. Bill Graves for permitting "seminars taught by militant homosexual activists spreading gay propaganda" at state universities. Phelps said he was running because the mainstream Democratic candidates had lost touch with the values of Kansas citizens, and that he would make enforcement of the state's sodomy law a priority of his administration. He also advocated cutting sex education classes from the public school curriculum and providing private school tuition vouchers for parents who wanted to shield their children from the "social agenda," such as tolerance for homosexuality, that he says is taught in public schools. Phelps was not the only candidate to express homophobic views. Gov. Graves, who had signed a ban on same-sex marriage into law, called homosexuality unnatural. David Miller — a conservative candidate whom James Dobson, head of the Religious Right organization Focus on the Family, campaigned for — accused Graves of being soft on gays and said he (Miller) supported laws banning gays from adopting children and receiving domestic partner benefits. Phelps, who has run for governor, U.S. senator and mayor of Topeka in the past without success, was defeated in the Democratic primary by Democrat Tom Sawyer, 85 percent to 15 percent. Graves was re-elected in November.

Emporia: University revokes protections

The president of Emporia State University in Emporia removed "sexual orientation" from the school's non-discrimination policy during the summer of 1998. Gay and lesbian students, faculty and staff at the school began the fall semester believing they were protected from dismissal or discrimination under the school's Equal Opportunity statement, as they had been since 1992. It was only when students noticed the language missing and complained that the change was noticed. The amendment had been passed in 1990 by the Associated Student Government, approved by the Faculty Senate and signed by then-President Robert Glennen. Current ESU president Kay Shallenkamp claimed that the language was only included in some of the school's handbooks and policies, and "that protection was never officially there in the first place" because it did not have the approval of a governance body and that "some well-meaning individual" had inserted it without authorization. Shallenkamp singled out protection of gays for review by the university's lawyers, who advised her that because the state and federal laws do not protect gay men and lesbians from discrimination, Emporia was not obligated to do

"If queers spend all their time fighting [Rev. Fred Phelps], then a lot of little stuff gets ignored."

— University of Kansas-Lawrence student Katie Shay, president of the campus group Queers and Allies

so. Although the protections had not produced any negative effects up to that point, other school officials claimed they were concerned about excessive litigation due to gay and lesbian discrimination claims. A representative from the University of Kansas, a school that prohibits discrimination on the basis of sexual orientation, argued that it was beneficial to the school to extend protections, saying "If there is any institutional policy where sexual orientation is absent, the university puts themselves at risk." In April 1999, Shallenkamp approved an Equal Opportunity statement that did not give sexual orientation protected status. However, she did issue a separate statement, which is not legally binding, saying that Emporia would not tolerate discrimination on the basis of sexual orientation.

Lawrence: Phelps protest

Westboro Baptist Church, home of Rev. Fred Phelps and his traveling anti-gay picketers, showed up at the University of Kansas in April to protest Gay Pride Week. "We heard there's a dyke over there and she's part of what they call Gay Pride Week. The sodomite agenda is not something that should be forwarded at taxpayer-funded universities," said Phelps. The president of the campus group Queers and Allies, Katie Shay, dismissed the protest, saying Phelps would protest anything for publicity. He first gained notoriety by picketing at the funerals of AIDS victims, and has since raised his profile by picketing the funerals of such people as Frank Sinatra and Matthew Shepard, as well as by picketing gay-friendly churches and schools. Shay says she believes Phelps can do real damage to the gay and lesbian community. "It's horrible because people look at him, and say that he is so homophobic. So when they look at themselves they say, 'I'm not like that, so I must not be homophobic,' and it allows people to get away with stuff. If queers spend all their time fighting him, then a lot of little stuff gets ignored."

Shawnee County: Phone tax service

In Shawnee County, a pay-by-phone plan for local taxes was canceled because BA Merchant Services, the company that would have handled credit card authorization and payment, is an affiliate of BankAmerica Corp., a San Francisco-based company that provides domestic partner benefits for its employees. The county treasurer contended that such policies violate Kansas' sodomy laws. The issue arose when County Treasurer Rita Cline, who also helped defeat a proposed gay-rights plank to the Kansas Democratic Party's platform, was informed of BankAmerica's policies by Rev. Fred Phelps. Phelps is a notorious anti-gay preacher who travels throughout the country picketing gay-friendly businesses, schools and churches and picketing the funerals of AIDS victims and gay-friendly individuals. Cline immediately investigated, writing a letter to the company marketing the tax payment system informing them that she could not do business "with a corporation which is engaged in violation of Kansas criminal law." She said she believed that providing the benefits was essentially recognizing same-sex couples as married couples, which condones sodomy. Upon being informed that BankAmerica does provide domestic partner benefits to its employees, Cline broke off negotiations for the service. In her letter to BankAmerica and to others who had criticized her, Cline wrote, "In my opinion, written policies nor laws enacted by man should overcome the Bible, which is God's word. In that respect, please find enclosed reasons to believe the Bible," referring to a one-page document that was attached entitled "Why should anyone believe the Bible?" Some who received the letters felt the biblical references were not appropriate, given Cline's position as an elected officer. Cline defended her letters by saying, "When I took my oath of office, I said, 'so help me God.' "

Topeka: Human Relations Commission

The Topeka City Council tried to abolish and eventually weakened and restructured the city's Human Relations Commission (HRC) in June to assure that anti-discrimination protections for gay men and lesbians would not be passed. In March, a gay man and a lesbian who had been appointed to the HRC by Mayor Joan Wagnon proposed adding "sexual orientation" to the city's list of protected categories. This move was tabled, but it was accepted that the commission would study the existence of discrimination against gay men and lesbians in Topeka. This sparked an immediate backlash; in April, five of the nine members of the city council made a proposal to abolish the commission, which they said was unnecessary, claiming the HRC had only handled 13 cases in the past year. The commission had actually dealt with 700 claims and requests for information in 1997. Rev. K.E. Hill, a member of the HRC and the head of the local chapter of the NAACP, supported keeping the commission intact, but wanted to prevent gay and lesbian citizens from using the commission to protect their own civil rights. Hill wrote an editorial in a local paper claiming that the mayor, who had appointed a gay man and a lesbian to the HRC, "has arrogantly used her office to usher in gay rights to the Human Rights Commission, further demonstrating how devious she is capable of being and disrespectfully infringing on the protected right of blacks and other minorities." He went on to suggest that the mayor be personally sued if she continued to show support for Topeka's gay community.

The proposal to disband the HRC met with heavy opposition from the minority community and the four city council members who had not moved to abolish it. Instead of eliminating the HRC, the city council voted to strip the commission of the power to investigate discrimination and, Rev. Hill joined with anti-gay protester Rev. Fred Phelps in asking that the commission not study any gay and lesbian issues whatsoever. Finally, the city council voted unanimously to strip the mayor of her power to appoint human relations commissioners. Instead, each city council member now appoints one member to the HRC board.

Statewide: Same-sex marriage

Fearing a Hawaii Supreme Court ruling to legalize same-sex marriage in that state, conservative Kentucky state legislators worked to prohibit the state from recognizing same-sex marriages performed in other states. Democratic House Floor Leader Greg Stumbo attempted to kill the bill by steering it into an unfriendly committee, but the full House voted 67-20 to override Stumbo's move. Stumbo then denounced Rep. Sheldon Baugh, who sponsored the bill, and his supporters for pushing the marriage ban. "What happens when the rights of people are just thrown to the wind and cast aside because of political aspersions?" he asked, adding, "The Lord created all of His children. He loves them all. He doesn't cast them aside because of their color or their creed or even their sexual prefer-ence." A Republican proponent of the bill retorted that if Stumbo believes that gay men and lesbians are loved by God, "he should pick up the phone at his desk and dial the city of Sodom and see if anybody answers the phone." Stumbo could have used his rank to prevent the bill from reaching the floor, but instead he allowed Democrats, the majority party, to vote whether or not to hear the bill on the floor, and they chose to do so. The House then passed the bill overwhelmingly on a 84-9 vote. Stumbo stated, "When you start trampling on the rights of others, you have taken the first step in destroying America." The Senate passed the bill 13-2, and it was signed into law by Gov. Paul Patton on April 2.

Bowling Green: 'Hell House'

"Homosexual Lies...Violent Rape...Medical Murder...Business is Booming in Southern Kentucky! If You Can't Take the Heat, Stay Out of Hell!" screamed the fliers promoting the Halloween-themed "Hell House" display at a Bowling Green shopping mall in October. The display was intended to scare people into salvation, through scenes depicting the "sins" that Victory Hill Ministries, a non-denominational Kentucky church, claimed will land peo-ple in hell. One such scene depicted a gay teen dying of AIDS. The guide, who is supposed to be Satan, intoned, "We told him he was born that way. Now he is in hell with all the other twisted, perverted souls." The Hell House also included an abortion scene and a teenage suicide. Victory Hill pastor Nathan Oakes said of the display, "This is an outreach for us to get the truth of God's word out. We know that certainly we are not going to win a popularity contest...and we're sure that some are going to be offended." Victory Hill Ministries modeled its display after a similar "Hell House" first staged in 1995 in Colorado by Keenan Roberts. Roberts now has a business selling "kits" with which to stage "Hell House" displays. Roberts says the "Hell House" is "a Bible message, but a very aggressive sight-and-sound communication tool. It's a tool that gets the attention of the MTV gener-ation." The opening day of the Bowling Green display brought out more than 200 protest-ers, many from Western Kentucky University. Matthew Leffler, president of WKU's Lambda Society, a group that organized students to picket the display, said, "A lot of impression-able people are going to go to this thinking it's a haunted house for fun. Instead, they are going to get a political statement from some very warp-minded fundamentalists."

Bowling Green: Preacher at WKU

A traveling Christian fundamentalist preacher, Brother George "Jed" Stock, harassed stu-dents at Western Kentucky University with vicious offensive sermons in November. Stock and his companion, Brother Chuck, targeted women, African-Americans, and gay men and lesbians for their "preaching." The itinerant preachers' sojourn at WKU lasted three days. On the first day, Stock said that male students in fraternities should not pay for sex with prostitutes because "freshman girls give it up" and he claimed that African-Americans have a propensity to sin. On the following day, Stock accosted Matthew Leffler, the leader of WKU Lambda, a gay and lesbian student group, using hand gestures to show Leffler how to have heterosexual sex. Brother Chuck accused Leffler of being a child molester and spreading AIDS. An outraged crowd of approximately 100 students, most of who were not gay or lesbian, denounced the preachers, whom police had to escort off the campus. The preachers were undeterred and returned to WKU the following day and offended another crowd of students by calling them "whores" and "homos." Leffler attempted to approach the preachers and have a civil conversation with them, only to be told by Brother Chuck, "Oh, it's the homo." And when Leffler walked away from the men, the men yelled at him, "Run, homo, afraid of the Lord's word." Angered students forced the preachers to get into their car and leave campus. Afterward, Leffler was encouraged that the preachers' hate had aroused such a student backlash, remarking, "All in all, they have actually helped us."

Bowling Green: WKU gay and lesbian group

While the rugby team and environmental groups may freely chalk school grounds in Bowling Green, when the Western Kentucky University Lambda Society, a campus gay and lesbian student group, chalked a message advertising an upcoming group meeting near the Downing University Center, the center's building director demanded that Lambda members remove the messages or pay the university to remove them. He also banned Lambda from meeting in the University Center until the signs were removed or erased. Matthew Leffler, president of WKU Lambda, surmised that the university had received complaints about Lambda's chalking but no such complaint about any other group's. "One individual walks past an announcement for an environmental club and thinks that's interesting. Four steps later they see a sign announcing a 'gay,les,bi,str8' club meeting and think it's graffiti." While the University Center's Policy and Procedures Manual contains no school policy explicitly banning or even regulating chalking by student groups, the University Center's building director cited another manual that outlaws defacing school property, which he said he interprets to include chalk messages. The university and the Lambda Society did reach a compromise in which the group was allowed to meet and to hang its banner in the student center lobby between the banners of the Campus Crusade for Christ and the Christian Fellowship. Both groups promptly removed their banners.

Highland Heights: NKU athlete files suit

In Highland Heights, a player on the Northern Kentucky University women's basketball team filed a lawsuit against the team's coach and the school's athletic director for kicking her off the team allegedly because she is a lesbian and was having a relationship with another player on the team. Jaime Garner, who received a full scholarship to play basketball at NKU, claims that she was confronted by her coach, Nancy Winstel, about her sexual orientation. According to Garner, Winstel asked her if she was a lesbian and if she was having a relationship with a teammate. Garner says she refused to answer her coach's question and later told reporters, "I didn't answer her . . . because it was none of her business." Garner says Winstel then told her she did not want lesbians on her team. Winstel claimed Garner was cut from the team because she was ruining the team's chemistry, and the university released a statement supporting Winstel's decision. However, the university permitted Garner to retain her basketball scholarship if she did not transfer to another university, and Garner chose to stay at NKU. In her suit, Garner sought unspecified damages and reinstatement to the NKU team. Garner's lawyer, Lisa Meeks, told the Cincinnati Enquirer that her client, who was the second-leading scorer on the team during her junior year, needed to play basketball her senior year because it was crucial to her plans to play professional basketball. Garner later denied being a lesbian and said her relationship to the teammate was merely close friendship. Meeks said, "If her coach perceived her as gay, it has the same effect." In November, a U.S. district judge denied relief, claiming that Garner's return to the team would cause irreparable damage to the team and the university. In February 1999, Garner decided to withdraw her lawsuit. Meeks said Garner's reasons for doing so were confidential, and said that Meeks was legally prohibited from disclosing them.

> "We know that certainly we are not going to win a popularity contest ...and we're sure that some are going to be offended."
>
> — Victory Hill Ministries Pastor Nathan Oakes, on a "Hell House" his church built in Bowling Green, Ky., that featured scenes of a gay teen dying of AIDS, an abortion and a teen suicide.

Louisville: Aldermanic campaign

A direct-mail fundraising appeal to benefit Michael Dickerson's failed campaign for Ward 12 Alderman in Louisville attacked gay men and lesbians with charges that the Letter, a gay Kentucky newspaper, ran personal ads from adults seeking sex with minors. The mailing also attacked an anti-discrimination measure that would protect gays as a push for "Special Rights" and warned that "...if Special Rights passes, there will be overt homosexual activists in ALL Jefferson County Schools." The appeal, printed on Dickerson's letterhead, stated that in the Letter, "Homosexuals are advertising for sex with children." Enclosed with the letter were unauthorized reproductions of personal ads from the newspaper that included homosexual slang terms such as "boy toy" and "baby dyke." Some of these terms were circled in the direct mailing, obscuring the age range the individuals were seeking. For instance, one ad reads "28-38," but is marred by the circle and appears to read "8-38." Dickerson claimed that he knew nothing of the mailing. Dickerson does have close ties to anti-gay activist Dr. Frank Simon of the American Family Association of Kentucky, who has used the personal ads and special rights language for years to advance his anti-gay agenda. The closing of the fundraising appeal, "Your Servant in Christ," was identical to the closing in Simon's mailings. The Letter filed a lawsuit charging Dickerson, Dickerson's campaign manager, Simon, and two of Simon's organizations-the American Family Association of Kentucky and Freedom's Heritage Forum-with libel and copyright infringement. In response to pre-trial discovery questions posed to Dickerson about the case, he admitted that the anti-gay letters did originate in Simon's offices. The case is scheduled to go to trial at the end of 1999 or early 2000.

Louisville: Woman fired from children's facility

Alicia Pedreira was fired from her job as a therapist at the Kentucky Baptist Homes for Children in Louisville in October because her "admitted homosexual lifestyle is contrary to the Kentucky Baptist Homes for Children core values." When interviewing for the job eight months earlier, Pedreira states that she had informed Jack Cox, the clinic's director, that she was gay and said she did not want to take the job if she was going to be fired later on because she was a lesbian. According to Pedreira, Cox assured her that her orientation would not be a problem, although he did recommend she avoid talking about it at work. Pedreira says she replied that as a professional, she does not discuss her private life at work, anyway, and accepted the job. Pedreira's six-month evaluation was full of praise:"[Pedreira] shows exceptional skills, works well with the staff, and is a valuable part of the treatment program." In August, Pedreira and her partner went on vacation. When they returned, they discovered that in their absence, a photo of them had been entered in a contest at the Kentucky State Fair and that Pedreira's job was now on the line. The photo had been taken by an amateur photographer at the Louisville AIDS Walk the previous year, and the two women had no idea that it would be displayed at the fair. It showed Goodman standing behind Pedreira, with her arm around her. Pedreira's shirt read "Isle of Lesbos." About a week later, KBHC administrators asked her to resign. She refused, and in return was offered a desk job until KBHC could find her a new position elsewhere. She still refused, and said she was paid to do virtually nothing for the next three weeks, until KBHC finally fired her. Pedreira asked her employer to put in writing that she was being fired solely because of her sexual orientation. The agency complied, and then released a statement saying "Homosexuality is a lifestyle that goes against the values of the Kentucky Baptist Homes for Children." KBHC also repeatedly stated that the termination was in accordance with state law, which does not prohibit businesses from firing someone due to sexual orientation.

Pedreira's dismissal caused ripples throughout the city. Five KBHC staff members resigned, including Cox. He remarked, "I feel like discrimination in any form, it promotes hate crimes and promotes violence and ignorance in the community and the churches. For me to be a part of that, it felt like I was promoting that. I don't want my kids to think that's okay." Two schools, Spalding University and the University of Louisville, withdrew their students who were training in KBHC homes and said they would not place their graduates at KBHC in the future, due to KBHC's discriminatory practices. Pedreira's minister, Father

Joe Stoltz of St. William Church in Louisville, wrote a letter to the local paper calling Pedreira a "faithful parishioner" and expressing his outrage at the firing, urging the city to "see the beauty that each person holds inside and cease being threatened by those who are different from us." A rally was held in November in front of the building that houses Cabinet for Community-Based Services, the agency responsible for dispensing state money to KBHC, to protest Pedreira's firing, to urge the governor to cut off funding for agencies that discriminate, and to push the state General Assembly to pass a bill prohibiting discrimination based on sex or gender orientation. However, the most dramatic repercussion from the incident was the passage of the "Fairness Amendment," which protects gay men, lesbians, and transgendered people from workplace discrimination in Louisville. The amendment had been defeated three times before; the most recent vote, in 1997, was 7 to 3 against the amendment, with two abstentions. In January, it finally passed by a 7-5 vote. Aldermanic President Steve Magre, who had resolutely opposed the amendment in the past but voted for it this time, said he had never before believed that there was a need for legislation protecting gays from workplace discrimination, but that the stories he had heard made him realize that anti-gay discrimination was a real problem. Ironically, the Fairness Amendment would not have been able to save Pedreira's job, as it was revised before passage to exempt religious organizations like the KBHC in order to ensure its passage.

A personal essay by Alicia Pedreira appears on p. 29.

Spencer County: Student harassment

The U.S. District Court in Louisville ruled that the Spencer County school district acted with "deliberate indifference" toward the pleas of Alma McGowan, who was the target of a prolonged pattern of sexual harassment that included homophobic taunts. Alma McGowan entered the Spencer County public school system when she moved into the area with her German-born mother at the age of 11. For the next four years, she remained in Spencer County schools and was repeatedly harassed in front of faculty by classmates who called her "lezzie" and "that German gay girl." At one point, a male student forced McGowan against a wall, began removing his pants, and said he was going to rape her. Another boy interceded to help McGowan, but when she reported the incident, she was only made to restate the accusation in front of the harasser, who she today believes was never punished. She ultimately left the school system without completing high school when a boy told her he was a member of the Ku Klux Klan and would burn her house down and kill her family. McGowan filed a federal lawsuit in 1996 along with Steven Vance, an autistic man who also stated he was sexually harassed in Spencer County schools. The lawsuit contended that their civil rights had been violated by the school district. Under a June 1999 ruling by the U.S. Supreme Court, they had to prove that the school had acted with "deliberate indifference" toward the complaints and that no punitive action was taken against the perpetrators. In the first McGowan, now 17, was awarded $220,000 for her suffering by a federal jury, but the judge dismissed Vance's case in part because he never reported his harassment to school authorities.

New Orleans: Medical conference

The Gay and Lesbian Medical Association (GLMA) was barred from participating in the annual conference of the American College of Obstetricians and Gynecologists (ACOG), held in May in New Orleans. With 2,000 members, the GLMA is the largest group of gay and lesbian doctors in the country, and had asked to attend the convention to share information unique to dealing with the lesbian community. Although the GLMA had participated in both the American Academy of Family Physicians' and the American Psychiatric Association's conferences earlier in the year, ACOG stated that the GLMA's "service would not benefit or be of interest to the majority of our membership" based on their belief that the GLMA was primarily a "special issue advocacy group" interested in recruiting new members. GLMA asked the College to reconsider its request to attend, stating that "ACOG's statement reflects homophobia by effectively discounting the specific medical needs of lesbian patients." After reviewing the GLMA's request, the ACOG reversed its decision and allowed them to attend the conference.

Statewide: Anti-discrimination law repealed

On Feb. 10, a special referendum made Maine the first state to nullify previously enacted statewide provisions barring discrimination against gay men and lesbians in employment, housing, public accommodations and credit. The Christian Civic League of Maine and the Christian Coalition of Maine began the campaign to overturn the gay rights measure in October 1997, just after it was passed by the Maine legislature and signed by Gov. Angus King. The two groups announced that they had formed a political action committee to overturn the new statute. The committee, deceptively named "Vote Yes for Equal Rights," was the backbone of a Christian-right effort to have the civil rights measure repealed. One fundraising appeal, written by Michael Heath, executive director of the Maine Christian Civic League, made clear the group's position. "We believe that it IS appropriate to discriminate against people if they are wrong....IF a Maine businessman or landlord wants to discriminate against a person because of their sexual orientation, they should be able to do so."

The repeal effort also featured nationally prominent figures such as Alveda King, niece of slain civil rights leader Martin Luther King Jr., who spoke to gay rights opponents gathered at the State House in Augusta shortly before the vote on the ballot initiative. Randy Tate, executive director of the national Christian Coalition, tried to join Ms. King at the State House, but had to cancel because of the weather. Prior to his scheduled visit, Tate commented on the referendum, "The issue of special rights for homosexuals now defines American liberalism as it moves into the 21st century." The national and state offices of the Christian Coalition produced 240,000 "voter guides" that were distributed to more than 900 churches. The pamphlets posed several questions to readers that promoted a "vote yes" strategy to stir voter concern about the alleged effect that a gay-rights law would have on children, and on a person's right to object to homosexuality. Paul Volle, executive Director of the Christian Coalition of Maine, said that the current law "confers special rights to homosexuals" and compromises the rights of "people of faith." "Our core is motivated because they are loving people who are dedicated to the Lord Jesus Christ as lord and savior. They want to teach others of their beliefs, and they don't want legislation in place that inhibits that and encourages a lifestyle in our society and our schools that is not a lifestyle, but a deathstyle."

> "I don't think I have ever seen a homeless gay person. I don't think I have ever seen a [malnourished] gay person. We do not discriminate against gays."
>
> — A Kennebunk resident, objecting to a proposal that would have restored protections against anti-gay discrimination in the city after the repeal of a similar statewide law.

The effort to support the Maine civil rights legislation was led in large measure by Gov. King. During the referendum campaign, he was featured prominently in television ads pledging a vote against the proposed repeal of the statute. "Maine is a big small town," the governor declared in a commercial. "We know each other, we care about each other and we're neighbors in the best sense. And some of those neighbors are gay. But they're part of our community as well and deserve the same basic rights as you and me."

On Feb. 10, the law was repealed, 52 to 48 percent. Gov. King indicated that the fight was not over, however. "I think it's unfortunate," King said. "But we'll move forward. I think this is an evolutionary process." In the wake of the repeal, several municipalities attempted to pass local anti-discrimination protections for gay men and lesbians. Seven towns-Bar Harbor, Long Island, Sorrento, Orono, Falmouth, Portland and South Portland-were successful. However, gay rights activists vowed in November to push to get another anti-discrimination measure before the legislature quickly, while they still had the votes to pass it. Gov. King has indicated he will only sign a new bill this time if it contains a provision stating that the bill would take effect only if a referendum affirmed the legislation. The next opportunity for a referendum would be in November 2000. Maine Lesbian and Gay Political Alliance Vice President David Garrity says he believes that would benefit supporters of the law, as core anti-gay voters would make up a smaller part of total voters than in the single-issue referendum in February.

Kennebunk: Anti-discrimination ordinance

Kennebunk's Board of Selectmen rejected a proposed citywide referendum on anti-discrimination protections for its gay citizens in August. In February, the town had voted nearly 2-1 in favor of retaining the statewide anti-discrimination protections for gay men and lesbians. However, in March, when Selectman Rachel Phipps raised the idea of passing a citywide ordinance to restore civil rights protections to Kennebunk's gay and lesbian community, the meeting room overflowed with people eager to argue both for and against the ordinance. One objector said he did not believe gays suffered discrimination: "I don't think I have ever seen a homeless gay person. I don't think I have ever seen a [malnourished] gay person. We do not discriminate against gays — it's the lifestyle that's wrong." Other objectors cited religious beliefs as the source of their opposition to the proposal. Supporters argued that all of the city's citizens should be treated fairly. The selectmen ended the meeting promising to look into legal issues that might be involved. The Christian Coalition (CC) of Maine had recently challenged Portland's anti-discrimination ordinance, which covers gay men and lesbians, claiming it violated the state constitution. CC Executive Director Paul Volle said, "When you elevate [the church's anti-gay stance] to a hate crime and you say that you can only discriminate within the four walls of the church, it's like saying you can gather all the news within the newsroom and write it up, but you can't publish it."

In July, Phipps proposed that public hearings be held on the proposed ordinance. The Board of Selectmen has no jurisdiction to pass such an ordinance; it could only vote to put the issue on the ballot. The Aug. 24 hearing was dominated by those opposing the ordinance, primarily on religious grounds. Afterward, the board voted 3-2 against placing the measure on the ballot in November, citing the lopsided testimony during the hearing as evidence that Kennebunk citizens did not want to prohibit discrimination on the basis of sexual orientation.

Ogunquit: Anti-discrimination ordinance

Ogunquit voters rejected proposed citywide discrimination protections for gay men and lesbians by nine votes out of 757 cast in November. The issue had been debated by the Ogunquit Board of Selectmen in June as a reaction to the February repeal of a statewide anti-discrimination measure that had provided civil rights protections for gay men and lesbians, which Ogunquit voters had favored keeping by a 2-1 margin. In June, the board backed away from passing an ordinance, and instead adopted a non-binding proclamation endorsing statewide protections for gay men and lesbians. In September, gay rights supporters again approached the board, asking that protections be codified. They also asked selectmen to call for a recall vote on board chairman John Miller, who had angered the gay community over the summer by objecting to a hotel owner flying a rainbow flag, saying that "public displays" of homosexuality are immoral. Miller's detractors had gathered almost three times the number of signatures necessary to force a recall vote. Two weeks later the board voted to remove John Miller from his position as chair and to put both the anti-discrimination measure and the recall measure on the Nov. 3 ballot. With 65 percent of the city's eligible voters going to the polls, the final vote on anti-discrimination was extremely close, with 374 voting for the ordinance and 383 against. The recall vote was also unsuccessful, with 473 voting to retain Miller and only 304 voting to remove him.

South Portland: Anti-discrimination ordinance

In a last-minute effort to stop passage of a South Portland ordinance that would add sexual orientation to the city's anti-discrimination law, the Christian Coalition of Maine created a political action committee called the "No Special Rights Committee." On Oct. 28, an insert was distributed in the Portland Press Herald. Published by Paul Volle, head of the Westbrook-based Christian Coalition of Maine, and others "concerned" about the South Portland vote, the insert was labeled "The Gay Agenda."

One article called "Who Are the Gays? The Image and the Reality," caught the attention of those who supported the proposed gay rights ordinance. In that article Volle wrote, "It is easy to lose perspective on public policy issues, when looking only at the carefully crafted image of the 'modern homosexuals' culture, without looking very carefully at the hard realities lurking behind the seemingly innocent facade." He also wrote, "Once these homosexuals bridge the natural reluctance to come into contact with human waste, a significant number of homosexuals go further and further. Many times to the point of ingesting the urine and fecal matter of their partners....Admittedly, the homosexuals do not have a monopoly on bizarre sexual practices, but their initial attraction to unnatural acts seems to draw them in disproportionate numbers to more widely known practices like masochism and sadism.... They are also known to practice other forms of deviant sexual behavior that is unacceptable to the preponderance of society."

The insert infuriated many Portland residents. The Portland Press Herald received so many complaints that it published an official apology the next day. In it, the paper apologized for the insert that "rightfully offended readers in South Portland and Falmouth, where the editions carrying the insert were distributed, and violated the trust our newspaper has with its community. For that we are deeply sorry.... It was wrong to lend the Portland Press Herald's good offices to the distribution of the publication under any circumstances. It was doubly wrong because the tabloid carried no clear, prominent identification as being a political advertisement." In addition, on Nov. 2, the paper editorialized in favor of passage of the ordinance.

On Nov. 3, the vote was close, with 54 percent voting for, and 46 percent against, the ordinance. Eve Raimon, a spokeswoman for South Portland Citizens for Justice, the organization that was most vocal in its support of the ordinance, was very pleased. "We're elated.

We're just very happy and we're very proud of South Portland for turning away from hatred and turning towards inclusion and fairness and equal rights for everybody." Volle's only response was, "too bad." Raimon also said that she believes that "The Gay Agenda" actually helped get the ordinance passed because it showed undecided voters the ugly reality of discrimination. "We have Paul Volle and the Christian Coalition to thank for this victory," she said.

MARYLAND

Statewide: Anti-discrimination

For the seventh year in a row, the House Judiciary Committee killed a bill that would have added "sexual orientation" to the state's existing anti-discrimination law. Del. Sheila E. Hixson, who had sponsored the bill for seven years introduced the bill again, pre-filing it for the 1998 legislative session. At hearings on the bill in March before the Judiciary Committee, supporters of the bill included clergy and civil rights organizations in addition to gay rights groups who gave testimony about discrimination they had experienced. The opposition to the bill came primarily from the organized Religious Right. Many "ex-gay" organizations, including Parents and Friends of Ex-Gays (P-FOX), testified that being homosexual is a "lifestyle choice," and therefore should not be a protected category under the law. Robert Knight of the Family Research Council also testified. Referring to earlier testimony from Parents, Families and Friends of Lesbians and Gays (PFLAG), he said, "I'm struck by PFLAG's heartfelt stories, but you don't have to accept homosexuality to love the child. By accepting it you will perpetuate the behavior. The answer is to enforce the rules of civility." In the end, the committee defeated the bill by one vote.

Statewide: Same-sex marriage

Although Maryland already bars recognition of same-sex marriages, state Sens. Larry E. Haines and Richard F. Colburn co-sponsored a bill to deny recognition of same-sex marriages performed in the state and recognition of same-sex unions performed in other states. Haines claimed the "Same-Sex Marriage-Foreign Marriage-Invalidity" bill was necessary to pre-empt lawsuits against the state by homosexual couples who want to wed. "It makes it clear in the Bible that [homosexuality] is an abomination. I believe that homosexuality is a behavior problem and it is learned. By permitting same-sex married couples to adopt children, they could teach children to adopt that lifestyle." The Senate passed the bill in a 28-18 vote. A pro-gay marriage bill designed to lift the state's ban on same-sex unions, which had been introduced in the House of Delegates by Del. Sharon Grosfeld, was defeated in the House Judiciary Committee 3-14. Shortly after, the anti-gay marriage bill was also killed in the same committee, 7-11.

Baltimore: Goucher College

At Goucher College in Baltimore, one reaction to Matthew Shepard's murder was scrawled on paper and tacked up in a student dormitory: "That faggot deserved to die." This message and other anti-gay slogans were found on doors and bulletin boards on campus in September and October, and ultimately sparked a strong response from the Goucher community. A 200-person rally and march were held October to protest the messages and show support for the gay community and student safety. In addition to the Oct. 22 events, students and faculty denounced the homophobic rhetoric and Bisexuals, Gays, Lesbians and Straights for Diversity, a student organization, gave out "Safe Zone" and "End Hate Crimes" signs in conjunction with the student government association. Sarah Pinsker, an organizer of the rally who reports that she had an anti-gay statement scrawled on her door earlier in the year stated, "I've been absolutely thrilled with all the support we received since the anti-gay incidents at Goucher."

Baltimore: Notre Dame student harassment

A lesbian student at the College of Notre Dame in Baltimore reports that she was the object of unrelenting anti-gay harassment for a period of nine months by students, their guests and their parents. At the beginning of the school year, as a demonstration of lesbian pride, sophomore Josette Rodriguez says she placed a sign with the word "Butch" on the door of her dormitory room. She believes that this set in motion a prolonged pattern of abuse during the 1997 to 1998 academic year. On the message board next to the sign, students allegedly wrote comments including, "Dyke go home," "Bulldagger," "Get God in your life," and "I will pray for you." Someone also reportedly altered the word "Butch" to read "Bitch." Rodriguez says she returned from a weekend away to learn from a resident assistant that during her absence a pair of women's underwear smeared with ketchup was attached to her door. In another instance the mother of a student in the residence hall allegedly approached Rodriguez and expressed disgust that her daughter was living near Rodriguez. According to Rodriguez, she brought the harassment to the attention of college officials on numerous occasions, but they neither took her claims seriously nor made a serious effort to punish the perpetrators. Rodriguez said that one housing official asked her whether she was "an in-your-face activist," while another ignored her complaints, questioned her about her "sexually ambiguous behavior," and asked her to remove the "Butch" sign. Rodriguez says she refused, and continued to report the harassment to ensure it would be documented.

Rodriguez reports that the most threatening incidents occurred when a group of men, guests of another student, began banging on Rodriguez's door and shouting, "Come out, butch!" When she opened the door, they allegedly continued to assault her verbally as she attempted to alert the resident assistant. The men reportedly ran off when they realized they would soon be caught. The punishment for the student who had invited the men into the dorm was to have her guest privileges revoked for two weeks, although only one week remained in the semester. Finally, college officials brought the harassment before the Judicial Review Board as a case of honor code violation. However, the board found that none of the incidents violated the code, and no further action was taken.

College Park: Column in student newpaper

The Diamondback, the University of Maryland's campus newspaper, printed a virulently anti-gay guest column in October from an unknown individual. The author of the column maintained that homosexuality was a "genetically defective state" and pledged to "devote every ounce of my time and money to making sure that the gay community will never convince society that it is OK to chop off their genitals or that two males being together in life is a productive bond." The column bore the byline "Carter Clark;" however, it was subsequently discovered that no such student exists at the school. The commentary editor of the paper, Joshua Kross, admitted that he never verified the author's identity prior to running the column, as is called for under the Diamondback's procedures. Kross resigned from the paper, although he defended his decision to run the column: "Guest columns are just letters to the editor that run longer. People need to know that kind of hate is out there." A massive backlash against the column included a 200-student rally at the university's College Park campus to denounce the column and the newspaper for running it. Many argued that the column should have been restricted to the "Letters to the Editor" section.

Millington: Pride parade

In response to plans for a gay pride parade, town officials in Millington passed an ordinance requiring groups desiring to hold a parade to secure $2 million of insurance. Millington, a conservative town of 450 people, has hosted other parades over the years, but has never had any insurance requirement. When 21-year-old Ricky Everett proposed holding a pride parade, however, city officials, apparently anticipating controversy, set to work to create some rules. One local minister canceled Wednesday night worship services so that he and his congregation could attend the meetings on the parade. He said his opposition to the parade rests on moral grounds. "If God doesn't accept it, then we shouldn't either," he said.

Mayor R. Dennis Hager said the rules were not designed to prevent anyone from marching, but were necessary to protect those who live along the parade route. The new ordinance requires the planners to give two weeks' notice, clean up after themselves, and obtain insurance. The last requirement is the one that created a controversy. The American Civil Liberties Union (ACLU) said that the ordinance is unconstitutional, and after telephone negotiations, Millington officials agreed to rewrite the policy.

A spokesman for the ACLU explained, "The $2 million insurance [requirement] is a major burden put on people's constitutional right to assembly."

MASSACHUSETTS

Allston: Transgendered person's murder

On Nov. 28 in the Boston suburb of Allston, Rita Hester, a transgendered person, was found viciously stabbed to death in her apartment. Police classified the attack as a hate crime due to the approximately 20 stab wounds to Hester's chest and the fact that nothing in the apartment had been stolen or damaged. At a vigil organized by Hester's sister, she and others said they believed that the crime was motivated by race, gender, and sexual orientation.

In the aftermath of the tragedy, family, friends, and sympathizers protested the media's lack of respect toward Hester by referring to her as a "he" in stories about the murder. The Boston Globe, Boston Herald, and a local gay paper, Bay Windows, referred to Hester as a male in the stories, and were blamed for contributing to a climate of hate and misunderstanding of the lives of transgendered people. The Boston Herald's deputy editor for news, Jim MacLaughlin, defended their use of the word "he" in the following statement: "It was our understanding that since Mr. Hester was still anatomically a 'he,' we would refer to him as such. It has to come down to something. We can't just let anybody who calls say 'refer to me as a woman or as a man'...and [the person's anatomy] seems to the obvious determination, and that is what we went with."

Over the next few weeks, the coverage of the murder sparked an angry reaction from the Boston gay, lesbian, bisexual and transgendered community toward both queer and mainstream media sources. On Dec. 11, a protest that began in front of the Boston Globe also led to the doors of the gay publication Bay Windows. Armed with signs that pointed out that the transgendered community is widely ignored by the media, the protesters called their "Queer Revolt" a "Truth Rally." They carried signs with slogans such as "Cover our Lives, Not Just Our Deaths" and "Transgendered people shouldn't have to die to be in Bay Windows."

Boston: Domestic partner benefits

A long battle over domestic partnership health benefits for Boston city employees ended in defeat for civil rights advocates when the Massachusetts Supreme Court overturned the mayor's executive order in July 1999.

The bill to allow Boston to extend spousal health benefits to the registered domestic partners of its employees was first presented in February. In March, House Speaker Thomas M. Finneran promised that if the Supreme Judicial Court decided that the bill was constitutional, then he would allow the House to vote on it. The legal controversy was over jurisdiction and home rule-the state's high court had to decide whether cities and towns in Massachusetts have authority to offer health benefits to domestic partners of municipal workers. The bill languished until June, when the Massachusetts Supreme Judicial Court affirmed the city's right to define "domestic partner." The bill then moved to the floor the legislature.

One of the principal opponents to the bill was Finneran, who saw the bill as "overt discrimination" against heterosexual city workers. The bill ultimately remained unamended, although Finneran did attach a non-binding resolution asking the city to extend the benefits to relatives of all city employees.

On July 29, two days before the state legislature was to go into recess, the bill passed unanimously in the House and by a voice vote in the Senate. The same day, acting Gov. Paul Cellucci (R) said he would sign the bill, but the next day he said he had changed his mind. This came as a shock to observers, as Cellucci was considered to be a supporter of the gay and lesbian rights movement. Cellucci vetoed the bill in August, saying, "The legislation before me made this available to heterosexual couples. I think that undermines marriage, I think it contributes to fatherlessness, and that's why I vetoed it." Cellucci also said he would sign a bill whose beneficiaries were restricted to same-sex couples only. However, some advocates said

> "Transgendered people shouldn't have to die to be in Bay Windows."
>
> — Sign at a "Truth Rally" outside Bay Windows, Boston's gay newspaper. Marchers criticized the Boston media for identifying a transgendered murder victim as a man, and for generally ignoring the transgendered community.

amending the bill in that manner would make it unconstitutional under state law, which prohibits discrimination on the basis of sexual orientation, and would also make it unconstitutional under the U.S. Constitution, which requires equal treatment under the law.

On Aug. 4, Boston Mayor Thomas Menino bypassed the governor and issued an executive order that would extend health insurance benefits to domestic partners and dependents of Boston city employees beginning Nov. 1. Only those couples who are officially registered with the city as domestic partners would be eligible for the benefits; Boston has had city-recognized domestic partnership registration since 1993.

One day after the domestic partner benefits began, the American Center for Law and Justice, founded by Pat Robertson, and the Catholic Action League filed a lawsuit on behalf of 12 Boston residents, challenging the executive order and accusing the city of "overstepping its authority and attempts to define marriage. The law is both legally and morally wrong." Collectively, the petitioners objected to what they saw as the city's use of tax dollars to fund immoral lifestyles. The Menino administration countered by claiming that the taxpayers and two organizations did not have legal standing to use the courts to undo an order issued by the mayor. The hearing began in early December, and Superior Court Judge Charles Grabau issued a preliminary injunction against the operation of Menino's executive order. The couples who were receiving the benefits were not to be cut off immediately, although suspension of the benefits would take place at an unspecified time. On July 8, 1999, the Massachusetts

Supreme Court ruled that the state constitution "home rule" provision prohibited Menino's executive order. According to the court, under the "home rule" provision, only the powers specifically extended by the state to a city or county may be exercised. Since the state had existing regulations for the health care coverage of the "dependents" of municipal employees that did not include domestic partners, the court held that Boston did not have the power to create its own definition of "dependent." The court recognized that the current state guidelines could be outdated, but said that change would have to come from the legislature.

Statewide: Hate crimes bill

The Michigan Senate shelved a hate crime bill in December that would have added sexual orientation to the state's law on hate crimes, the ethnic-intimidation statute. The statute, which passed the state House in November, was originally passed a decade ago and increases penalties for crimes based on race, religion, ethnicity and gender. The bill died when the Senate rejected a proposal to rush it to the floor for a vote before the legislative session ended by a vote of 20-18. "I think it sends the wrong message in Michigan, when 22 other states have passed similar votes," state Sen. Gary Peters (D) said after the vote. "If it got to the floor I'm confident it would pass."

> "I made this company tons of money. I was ranked in the top 5 percent of general managers in the whole company."
>
> — Jon Trimmer, who was fired by the Olive Garden in Grand Rapids. His picture had appeared in the media when he was shot with a blow dart at a gay pride parade.

There were no arguments in favor of delaying action on the bill, but the majority party, the GOP, said it had not intended to take it up. State Sen. William Van Regenmorter (R), chairman of the Senate Judiciary Committee, said he opposed the bill because it did not define sexual orientation.

Since the motion to delay action was passed, the bill will have to be considered in 1999. Rep. Lynne Martinez (D), who first introduced the bill in the House, said she would be pleased to reintroduce it. She feels it is necessary because violent crimes against gays are on the rise and a call for continuous attention is needed. "Changing attitudes takes time. We simply can't allow the hatred to continue. Sooner or later, even the senators will see that." Jeff Montgomery, director of the Triangle Foundation, a Detroit gay rights group, called the political process that killed the bill "unconscionable." "It is very sad but very clear that the Senate leadership failed to step up to the opportunity to save lives and prevent crimes," he said.

A personal essay by Jeff Montgomery appears on p. 41.

Statewide: Domestic partner benefits

In January, the Michigan Senate voted 28-10 to prohibit the use of public money to pay for health benefits for the domestic partners of unmarried public employees. Sen. George McManus, R-Traverse City, said of the bill, "Let our motto be: 'Taxes for legitimate purposes, not for illegitimacy.' " The bill's sponsor, Sen. Bill Schuette, R-Midland, said, "This is a fiscal management issue. Taxpayers should be only paying for benefits of married partners."

Opponents of the bill argued that such a proposal was not only unfair, but, if passed, would violate the Michigan Constitution, which guarantees public universities the authority to manage their own affairs. The state Attorney General, Frank Kelley, confirmed that universities would be exempt, although he did say that community colleges were vulnerable to the regulation. At the time the vote was held, three University of Michigan campuses, as well as Wayne State University and Michigan State University, already provided benefits for unmarried partners of employees. The bill failed in the House, but Republican legislators managed to slip language into the community college budget, which was passed by both houses, placing a prohibition on the use of state funds for domestic partner benefits at those institutions.

Detroit: TV station uses hidden cameras

WDIV-TV (Channel 4), a Detroit area television station, placed hidden cameras in the bathrooms of shopping malls and libraries in an effort to catch gay sexual encounters during the May sweeps season. Channel 4 news director Deborah Collura says the station was exposing "a growing problem that people and parents need to know about." When asked to comment on whether she had anything to say to the innocent users of the rest rooms who did not know that they were being filmed, she replied: "I'm not going to comment on that. Obviously we did this story because this was something the public needed to know. Children were endangered." In none of the stories, which ran May 14-15 with a follow-up the next week, did any children appear.

According to a San Francisco gay activist, about 20 stations across the country did the same story, locally, during the sweeps-week period.

Grand Rapids: Restaurant fires gay employee

Jon Trimmer was fired from his job as general manager of the Grand Rapids Olive Garden restaurant after being outed as a gay man when he became the victim of a well-publicized hate crime. Trimmer appears to have been an exceptional manager for the restaurant, saying of his performance: "I made this company tons of money. I was ranked in the top 5 percent of general managers in the whole company. I was a phenomenal general manager for this company." The entire staff of 50 employees at his restaurant signed a letter to the company management citing Trimmer's excellent performance and protesting his dismissal.

During Lansing's gay pride parade, Trimmer had been shot with a blow dart by one of two men who were subsequently convicted of the crime. During the trial and sentencing, Trimmer's picture was shown in local news media. After the first assailant pleaded guilty, a new Olive Garden regional senior vice president of operations and a newly-hired director showed up at Trimmer's restaurant for an unannounced inspection. "They spent 10 hours on that property just looking for something wrong," Trimmer said, "that amount of time is very unusual, especially for a property ranked as highly as this one." During the inspection, the company representatives found a bag of money in the store safe, earmarked for employee rewards distributed for wait-staff who successfully promote specialty products to customers. Although it was standard practice to employ such rewards programs — the success of which had won Trimmer praise from his former director and which, according to Trimmer, had been previously endorsed by the new director — he was fired for inappropriate use of company funds. "I don't understand," said Trimmer, "we had done nothing against company policy." Trimmer reports that he received no written reason for his dismissal nor did he receive back vacation pay or a bonus he says he was due.

Darden Restaurants, the Orlando, Fla.-based corporate owner of the Olive Garden chain, also owns Red Lobster, which had recently been found in violation of a Chicago (Cook County) job discrimination ordinance when it fired a gay man. No such law exists in Grand Rapids or the state of Michigan.

Kalamazoo: YMCA membership

Todd Parent, his partner, son and daughter had their family membership at the Kalamazoo YMCA revoked when the facility discovered that theirs was a gay family. Parent had obtained the membership after being turned down by the YMCA in the adjacent town of Portage. A gay friend of Parent's then sought a membership at that YMCA for his family under Parent's advice. When the friend was turned down, Parent suggested he try again and mention Parent's situation. He did, and Parent's family lost their membership.

The executive director of the Kalamazoo YMCA said it was his board's policy not to recognize same-sex couples until the state does. He said he didn't know how the Parent family obtained the membership and that it "caught [him] by surprise." He said, "When we discovered it, we realized we needed to contact some folks." The director of media relations for YMCA USA, a resource center for YMCAs in the United States, indicated that each YMCA sets its own policies. "Each Y is representing the morals and mores of each individual community," he said.

MINNESOTA

Statewide: 4-H discrimination amendment

In February, the Minnesota House of Representatives passed a bill requiring the University of Minnesota to permit agricultural organizations like 4-H to discriminate against gay men and lesbians. Republican Rep. Tony Kielkucki of Lester Prairie said that if the amendment was not passed, the university would be denied $38.5 million in appropriations. Students who participate in student groups, like 4-H, that are sponsored by the university had been required to sign non-discrimination statements that included a sexual orientation clause. Some people objected to this clause, saying it conflicted with their religious faith. When the bill was in conference committee, Kielkucki agreed to a compromise in which 4-H forms would still carry a sexual orientation non-discrimination clause, but the clause would be relegated to small print below the individual's signature. The new forms would be accompanied by a statement notifying students that they did not have to sign any document attesting to their personal religious or political beliefs. Kielkucki said, "This means a person can conscientiously object to homosexuality and still be a leader." The Minnesota Family Council was opposed to the compromise because the forms still retain anti-discrimination language, but the University of Minnesota accepted the deal.

Blaine: Transgendered teacher resigns

The hiring of a transgendered music teacher in Blaine resulted in protests and threats of legal action by parents and local religious leaders that eventually drove the teacher to resign. Alyssa Williams, a male who planned to undergo gender reassignment surgery, was living as a woman when she interviewed for the teaching position at Roosevelt Middle School in August. She had already had all her vital statistics changed on her personal documents, such as driver's license, teaching records and Social Security card, to reflect her new identity as a woman. Because Minnesota's 1993 Human Rights Act forbids employment discrimination against gay men, lesbians, bisexuals and transgendered persons, Williams was not required to disclose her biological gender during the interview. Minnesota is the only state that affords such legal protection to transgendered people. Williams says that the first few weeks of the 1998 school year, she enjoyed her new job. However, after an open house for parents at Roosevelt, one parent asked the school principal about Williams' gender. The principal then contacted Williams, and upon learning that she was transgendered, immediately placed her on two months' administrative leave while school officials devised a way for her to "come out" to parents, students, and school staff. In November, the school held a meeting for Williams and school administrators to meet with teachers and a handful of parents and explain the process Williams was undergoing.

A second meeting drew 400 parents. Some parents excoriated the school for permitting a transgendered teacher to work with children, while others objected to the intolerant vilification of Williams. One parent said, "It's a sin against God. As a Christian family, we teach our children that this is wrong. I can deal with it at work if there's someone there like that, but this is in the school. When do we get to say, 'No'?" Many parents were concerned that middle school-aged children would have difficulty comprehending transgender and sexuality issues. However, one mother noted that she had already talked to her kids, who were unfazed by the news. "My 10-year-old said, 'So?' and my 11-year-old said, 'What's the big deal?' And to me it's no big deal," she said. Soon, local clergy weighed in on the matter. They claimed that Williams's presence in the classroom would be offensive to Christians and amounted to "religious harassment." Parents formed an organization, Parents in Touch, that worked with conservative clergy members worked to have Williams fired or transferred to a position where she would have no contact with children. They received support from televangelist Pat Robertson's American Center for Law and Justice (ACLJ), which threatened to file suit against the school district for discriminating against the civil rights of Christian students by holding the informational sessions, which the ACLJ called an "indoctrination session" to promote transgenderism.

> "What many of us face every day is not so blatant as that, but hate wrapped up in the face of Minnesota Nice."
>
> — State Sen. Allan Spear at a Minneapolis rally protesting Rev. Fred Phelps, referring to Phelps' "God Hates Fags" signs.

ACLJ never filed its suit because Williams resigned in February 1999, citing pressure from a parents' group working with the ACLJ and local clergy. The Religious Right groups Minnesota Family Council, an affiliate of Focus on the Family, and the Minnesota Christian Coalition have attempted to use this controversy as a catalyst for their campaign to repeal Minnesota's Human Rights Act protections for gay men, lesbians, bisexuals and transgendered persons.

Duluth: Mayor refuses to commend students

Duluth Mayor Gary Doty refused to sign a certificate of appreciation for a University of Minnesota student group that held a vigil in honor of slain University of Wyoming student Matthew Shepard. In October 1998, the University of Minnesota at Duluth Lesbian, Gay, and Bisexual Alliance held a vigil for Shepard and invited several noted local citizens, including the president of the Duluth chapter of the NAACP, a minister of the University United Methodist Church, and the University's coordinator for Hispanic/Latino/Chicana student services. The Duluth Human Rights Commission, an official city commission that promotes the elimination of hate, prejudice, and discrimination and educates the community on issues of discrimination and diversity, adopted a certificate of appreciation to the students who organized the vigil. However, when asked to sign the certificate, Mayor

Doty declined, stating that he opposes homosexual activity. He said of his decision, "The purpose of that vigil, in my mind, was to decry hate, which I certainly do. But part of the certificate included a thank you for helping us celebrate diversity. I will not celebrate somebody's sexual practices, and I won't sign something that thanks somebody for celebrating their sexual practices." In response, the chairman of the Human Rights Commission, Bob Jansen, said, "Celebrating diversity is part of our mission statement."

Duluth: Phelps protest

The Rev. Fred Phelps, a Baptist minister from Topeka, Kansas, who preaches that "God hates fags," brought his message of hate and intolerance to Duluth in May. Phelps' purpose was to protest the city's hiring of Darrell Lewis, an openly gay man, as city planner. Lewis had previously turned down a job offer to be Topeka's city planner due to Phelps' presence. Phelps' press release said he was coming to the "sodomite leper colonies of pagan Minnesota" which included Duluth and the Twin Cities. Residents of Duluth were largely united in their opposition to Phelps' hate campaign. Duluth Mayor Gary Doty, who said he does not "endorse the gay lifestyle," also stated, "[Citizens of Duluth] may have differences on certain things, but our message to him is that you're not going to bring a hate message to Duluth and get away with it." Phelps had postponed a December protest to wait for bigger crowds at the North Star Expo, a logging equipment convention, held in Duluth in July. However, the Timber Producers Association said he would not be welcome. While Phelps did not make the trip himself, his son led a troupe of 15 picketers at the Duluth City Hall and at a number of churches in Duluth and the Twin Cities. Lewis, the man who had initially been the target of the protests, had by this time moved to Pasadena, California, and Phelps has said he will stage a future protest there. While there was general disdain for the intolerance that Phelps and his supporters propagate, the city government disappointed the civil rights community by removing and destroying pink triangles that had been placed throughout the city to show support for the city's gay men and lesbians.

Minneapolis-St. Paul: Job discrimination

An openly gay academic counselor for University of Minnesota athletes sued the university alleging discrimination based on his sexual orientation. Rick Marsden had been working as a counselor with various athletes since 1984. The university forbade him from rooming with anyone when he traveled with the teams on road trips, and it forbade him from participating in athletes' academic meetings held in school locker rooms, both of which he contends were discriminatory measures. In his lawsuit, Marsden contends he was denied fair pay and subjected to working in a hostile environment because of his sexual orientation, and his suit alleges that "homophobic attitudes of administrators at Minnesota deprived him of advancement." Moreover, Marsden alleges that the university did not want to encourage gay athletes to attend the school, and he believes that gay athletes who were considering "coming out" were directed to speak with him because the university thought he would advise them against it. According to Marsden, "I was asked to serve as a bridge for gay athletes because they were worried Minnesota would be a magnet for gay athletes and that that would hurt recruiting." Marsden asserts that he repeatedly asked to be transferred to another position within the university, but his requests were always denied. Marsden has been on leave from his job since the winter of 1998, when doctors determined he was unable to work following a mental breakdown. As of publication, Marsden's lawsuit was at an impasse. His lawyer alleges that the delay is connected to the fact that Marsden is also a key witness in a case of academic fraud against the school's basketball team. The university has moved to dismiss Marsden's case.

Minneapolis-St. Paul: Phelps protest

Members of the Westboro Baptist Church (WBC) in Topeka, Kansas, best known for its pastor, the anti-gay crusader Rev. Fred Phelps, traveled to Minneapolis and St. Paul to protest a St. Paul correctional facility that offers what Phelps calls "vile pro-gay workshops" and five churches that have gay and lesbian members or clergy. Phelps himself did not make the trip to Minnesota and was said to be picketing in Alabama. Four of the five churches that WBC targeted have mostly heterosexual congregations but express openness to gay men and lesbians, and these churches reportedly planned to do little in response to WBC's protest. However, the congregation of All God's Children Metropolitan Community Church is about 90 percent gay and lesbian, and its pastor, Rev. Paul Graetz, held a special church service and rally as a counter-protest. Graetz said, "We're thrilled he's coming, because it gives us the chance to turn this into a very positive moment of affirmation that God's love is for everyone." A large group of counter-protesters met 15 of Phelps' supporters at the sidewalk in front of All God's Children Church. And in contrast to the Phelps group's hateful signs that read, "AIDS Cures Fags," "God Hates Fags," and "Fag Church," the defenders of Graetz's church held signs that read, "God Loves Gays," "The Christian Right is Neither," and "Rev. Phelps, we'd like to convert you to Christianity." Five hundred of the counter-protesters stayed for the church service at which several Democratic-Farmer-Labor Party gubernatorial candidates appeared to oppose the Phelps protest. Among the speakers was openly gay state Sen. Allan Spear, who said, "What many of us face every day is not so blatant as that, but hate wrapped up in the face of Minnesota Nice. They don't say, 'God hates fags,' but they say, 'No special rights,' or 'Love the sinner, but hate the sin.' Those words are thinly veneered hate too."

Minneapolis: Transgendered librarian

The Minnesota Christian Coalition and the Minnesota Family Council waged war on school officials at Southwest High School after they allowed a transgendered librarian to remain on the job after "coming out." Erika Roland, the executive director of the Minnesota Christian Coalition, said, "Schools were once in the business of teaching academics, character and citizenship, but now are promoting a radical sexual agenda that continues to undermine the traditional family. We should call them the 'trysexual movement' — they will try any and every form of sexual behavior except traditional marriage." Debra Davis, formerly David Nielsen, had lived for years as a woman yet maintained a male identity on the job. The groundbreaking Minnesota Human Rights Act of 1993, which made Minnesota the first state in the nation to protect transgendered people under the law, gave Davis the courage to express her true identity at work, becoming the first openly transgendered high school educator in the country. Davis, 52, received support from her co-workers at Southwest High when she announced to faculty and staff in May that she would come to work every day as a woman. She does not plan on undergoing gender-reassignment surgery. Principal Robert McCauley said, "We support Debra 100 percent. People have responded very well to the strength and courage that she's showing. We recognize her right to respect, and we want to be supportive and sensitive of that..." Davis recognized

> "My 10-year-old said, 'So?' and my 11-year-old said, 'What's the big deal?' "
>
> — A Blaine parent, after speaking with her children about their school's transgendered music teacher. The teacher eventually quit under pressure from parents and a Religious Right group.

that people might be uncomfortable with her identity, but noted, "All I can ask is that people treat me as a human being and understand that I'm just expressing who I really am."

Religious Right groups in Minnesota are using Davis and a transgendered music teacher in Blaine to rally support for a campaign to repeal the Human Rights Act's protections for the gay, lesbian, bisexual and transgender community. Tom Prichard, the president of the Minnesota Family Council, a "pro-family" activist group affiliated with Focus on the Family, said, "I'm dismayed that school officials are using this man's 'coming out' to indoctrinate children with their politically correct agenda. Parents deserve better than to have their local school district undermine the moral and religious teachings they are providing their children at home."

Minneapolis-St. Paul: Student fees lawsuit

In February, the Northstar Legal Center, an affiliate of the conservative Minnesota Family Council, filed a lawsuit on behalf of a group of University of Minnesota (UM) students against the regents of UM for requiring all students to pay activities fees, some of which go to fund groups they oppose on religious and/or ideological grounds. Northstar argues this is a breach of the students' constitutional rights. Matthew Curry, a UM student and one of five student plaintiffs, told reporters at a press conference, "Students should not be forced to support groups that promote ideological and political positions which are contrary to their own. In our case, we object to being forced to support, through mandatory student services fees, groups that embrace the abortion movement, champion the homosexual lifestyle, and support the Communist regime in Cuba." The student groups cited in the lawsuit are University-Young Women, which is a women's group affiliated with the YWCA, the Queer Student Cultural Center, and the La Raza Student Cultural Center. Nearly all student groups, including those cited in the lawsuit, are forbidden by the university from political advocacy as a condition for receiving student fees. The lead Northstar attorney on the case is Jordan Lorence, who has a similar lawsuit pending against the University of Wisconsin.

In 1998, UM students each paid $160 per quarter in student services fees, which was then divided among the school's many student groups. Per-student funding of the groups in question ranges from 24 to 48 cents. Curry, who was once a member of the committee that dispenses funding to student groups, alleges that the committee is biased against conservative Christians like himself. He said, "I was just shocked by what I saw on the committee and by the plain old liberalness of the university in general and the institutionalized liberal dogma here." He also added that no conservative student groups on campus received any school funding, largely because they are opposed to government handouts. Matt Strickler, a member of the Queer Student Cultural Center board, believes that the lawsuit is merely "part of a larger movement by the radical right to remove views that they disagree with from public universities." The groups targeted in the lawsuit are receiving legal counsel from the Lambda Legal Defense and Education Fund which filed a motion in April to intervene in the case on the side of the university, but this motion was denied in February 1999. Meanwhile, the case against the UM is on hold until Lorence's case against the University of Wisconsin is heard by the U.S. Supreme Court. The University of Wisconsin has lost in the lower federal courts. Lorence does not expect the Supreme Court to hear the Wisconsin case until February or March of 2000.

MISSISSIPPI

Columbus: Student poem

A Columbus high school's literary magazine was criticized by a school board member for giving one of its annual awards to a poem that suggested a homosexual theme. "Forbidden Love," by a 17-year-old girl, tells of a disappointing relationship with a lover who could never make her happy. She ends the poem by telling the lover to go, and concludes, "David was never happy with Jane. But he will be with Steve." Another award-winning poem was also objected to, presumably because the speaker in the poem is intoxicated. Charging that the poems sent the wrong message to students, Glenn Lautzenhimer, the school board's vice-president, requested that the teachers responsible for selecting the poems for an award come before the board to explain why taxpayers should pay for the publication of such poems in The Merlin, the school's literary magazine. However, The Merlin's sponsor, Jackie Brewer, said that the students on the magazine's staff had selected the poems, and were proud of their decisions.

Statewide: Same-sex marriage

After the Missouri Supreme Court declared the law that included the state's ban on same-sex marriage unconstitutional, state lawmakers immediately pledged to re-introduce the ban. The ban had initially been passed in 1996 as a last-minute amendment to a bill that dealt with a slew of different issues. A health care organization challenged the law because it objected to another of the law's provisions, which included term limit changes for officers of non-profit corporations and a repeal of limits on suing non-profit corporations, in addition to the same-sex marriage ban. The state Supreme Court upheld the ruling by a circuit court judge that the title of the bill was too broad. Although the law was struck down, the practical effect on gay men and lesbians was non-existent. Before the bill was passed, state law defined marriage as being only between a man and a woman. The 1996 law had expanded the ban by stating that Missouri would not recognize same-sex marriages performed in other states; however, no other state recognizes same-sex marriages. Sen. Peter Kinder, sponsor of the 1996 bill, pledged to launch another effort in 1999.

Statewide: University anti-discrimination policy

In October, student activists began pushing the University of Missouri administration to add protections for gay, lesbian, bisexual and transgendered students to the university system's anti-discrimination policy. Two of the school's campuses had actually added the language to their policies in the late '80s. When the university system passed a system-wide anti-discrimination policy in 1995, two other campuses opposed extending protections to gay and lesbian students, and "sexual orientation" was not included in the system-wide policy and was deleted from existing policies, although protections for other groups remained intact. In November, the Student Government Association (SGA) at the St. Louis campus passed a resolution denouncing discrimination on the basis of "age, disability, sex, color, national origin, veteran status, religion, race, sexual orientation, or gender orientation." It also pledged to lobby the UM Board of Curators to include sexual and gender orientation in the university's policy. Three weeks later, the Executive Committee of the Board of Curators held an open meeting to discuss the proposed policy change, and the feedback was favorable for extending the anti-discrimination protections to gay men and lesbians. Instead of voting on the issue, however, the Board of Curators met for six minutes and forwarded the question to UM President Manuel Pacheco for further review. In January 1999, Pacheco recommended adopting a general statement pledging to treat all people fairly, which he said would "provide and maintain a positive work and learning environment." The Board of Curators agreed, and voted 6-2 to draw up and adopt such a statement. Two dozen student protesters heckled the board after the vote was taken, leading to an unscheduled recess. One campus student association called the resolution "a disheartening loss for tolerance."

Jefferson City: Child custody

The Missouri Supreme Court denied a lesbian mother custody of her three children in a September ruling. No gay or lesbian parent has ever won a custody appeal in the state. This ruling overturned an appellate decision that had favored the mother, which had in turn reversed a circuit court decision that had denied her custody.

Janice DeLong, a Jefferson City substitute schoolteacher, had divorced her millionaire husband of eleven years and the father of her children, F. Joseph DeLong III, in 1995. Their marriage had been going downhill for some time, and both admitted to having affairs. The fact that Ms. DeLong's affairs were with other women proved to be a deciding factor in the custody battle. Macon County Circuit Court Judge Ronald M. Belt ruled in April 1996 that all three children, aged 5, 7, and 9, should be awarded to the father, because without therapy, he believed Ms. DeLong was "always going to be indiscriminately searching for stimulation and affection." He based his ruling on the fact that she testified to having four affairs during her marriage. Belt further ordered her to tell her two eldest children that she was gay, acting on the recommendation of Ken Lewis, a professional custody evaluator who believed it was necessary so the children could understand why their father was so angry with their mother. DeLong was also ordered by the court to keep "the homosexual lifestyle" away from her children, restricting her from seeing the children in the presence of any lesbians or female housemates, save one longtime family friend.

Citing Belt's apparent anti-gay bias, DeLong appealed his decision. A Kansas City appellate court ruled in favor of DeLong, approaching the case with the legal principle now used in 28 states that unless a parent's sexual orientation can be shown to be detrimental to a child, it should not be considered in a custody case. The children's father appealed the case to the state's Supreme Court. It handed down a decision overturning the appellate court, saying that sexual orientation was not the sole basis of Belt's decision awarding custody to the children's father. The court did, however, order Belt to come up with a less restrictive visitation plan. While the children were not permitted to testify in court, in a letter to one of the judges, Ms. DeLong's eldest child wrote, "It's like the judge is punishing us because he does not like our mom. Our mom is the greatest person....I think this prejudice in the world needs to stop. God loves everyone the same."

Liberty: Clubs banned

Pre-empting a formal request from students for a gay and lesbian student group, William Jewell College's president instituted a ban on all such groups at the school, citing its Southern Baptist roots as the reason. Christian Sizemore, president of the college, decreed over the summer that the school would not "provide recognition, endorsement or funds" for any gay or lesbian student clubs because it would be "contrary to our mission and purposes, which are deeply rooted in Baptist traditions." The issue had been raised by students during the spring semester when they notified the dean of student affairs that they were interested in organizing such a group and had secured a faculty sponsor. However, they did not make a formal proposal. One of the students who supported the creation of a gay/lesbian organization reacted to the ban: "It didn't surprise me, but it does disappoint me. They preach Christian values and unconditional love and acceptance. Basically, I think they are being hypocritical." College spokesman Raymond Jones explained that the college did not want to appear to condone something that the Missouri Baptist Convention, which donates $1 million annually to the school, had decreed was sinful. The convention's resolution on homosexuality reads in part: "Opposing the homosexual agenda is not gay-bashing but rather an affirmation of the Christian lifestyle," and directs Baptist institutions to "prevent granting special protected 'minority status' and privileges to homosexuals."

> "It's like the judge is punishing us because he does not like our mom. Our mom is the greatest person.... I think this prejudice in the world needs to stop."
>
> The eldest child of Janice DeLong, in a letter to the Missouri Supreme Court after DeLong was denied partial custody of her children because she is a lesbian.

St. Louis: Anheuser-Busch

In September, the anti-gay group Americans for Truth About Homosexuality lambasted Anheuser-Busch for sponsoring San Francisco's Folsom Street Fair, the culmination of Leather Week. Americans for Truth president Peter LaBarbera said, "Anheuser-Busch's sponsorship of a 'street fair' celebrating sadistic sex perversion shows just how low some in corporate America are willing to go to make a buck." Most of the proceeds from the street fair go to gay charities. After the event, which LaBarbera attended, Americans for Truth issued another press release, saying that the company should apologize to the American people for sponsoring the event alongside clubs that encourage anonymous sex acts. An Anheuser-Busch company statement says, "We diversify our marketing plans to reach a variety of adults who enjoy drinking beer...including the Gay and Lesbian community."

Stockton: School cancels Disney trip

In Stockton, a trip to Disney World by the high school band was canceled due to objections to Disney's "pro-gay" philosophy. Seven years of planning had gone into the trip, which would have been paid for by the band. The school board was required to approve the idea because district equipment would be used and the students would be covered by district insurance. In November 1997, members of the high school band and others were surprised and disappointed when Tom Landers, a member of the school board, would not agree to the trip because he objected on moral grounds to Disney's pro-gay policies, such as providing domestic partner benefits to its gay and lesbian employees. The school board did not vote at that time, but instead gave the students and parents time to come up with alternative destinations and/or "merits" of a trip to Disney World.

At a band meeting held in February, many parents argued that few of the town's children had ever traveled, and that this would be their opportunity to experience life outside of rural Missouri. Others touted the musical experience of performing and working with professional musicians in Florida. Others in the community backed Landers and said that to visit Disney World would be immoral. Outside the meeting where the school board was to decide the fate of the trip, members of Rev. Fred Phelps' Westboro Baptist Church from Topeka, Kansas, infamous for traveling throughout the nation to picket anything they consider to be gay-friendly, protested with signs portraying Mickey Mouse with the words "Rat Fag" written on them. At the hearing, the band revoked the request for the trip altogether. He cited community divisiveness over the issue, and suggested the band go to San Antonio instead.

MONTANA

Statewide: University funding threatened

In January, state Sen. Daryl Toews (R) threatened the University of Montana that state higher education funding could be cut if it offered the class "Queer Stories: Literature of Sexual Differences." The course was described as an examination of "literature by and about gay males, lesbians, bisexuals and transgender individuals." Toews, who chaired the Senate Education Committee, claimed that legislative support for school funding could erode unless the course was dropped. UM President George Dennison defended the course, saying that the subject matter was appropriate for college study and that the school should offer a broad curriculum. He also said that the course was intended to educate, not convert students. The course was ultimately dropped due to low enrollment; a UM dean said that it would be offered in the future should interest in the course increase.

NEBRASKA

Statewide: Republican gubernatorial campaign

From March to May, two of the Republicans competing to be the party's gubernatorial nominee seemed to be at war over who was the most homophobic. John Breslow fired the first shot when he ran a television ad in which he stated, "Let me tell you something I won't do. I won't let liberals allow men to marry men and women to marry women." Breslow went on to attack Rev. Jimmy Creech of Omaha, whose trial in church court for marrying two women had raised the profile of the same-sex marriage issue in Nebraska the previous year. He said Creech had "begun to make a mockery of our values, embarrassed us and our state." Breslow was quickly attacked by Andy Abboud, campaign manager for candidate Rep. Jon Christensen, who pointed to Breslow's 1982 support for adding "sexual orientation" to an anti-discrimination ordinance in Lincoln. Abboud claimed that this was clearly "the first step towards same-sex marriages" and that Breslow "wants to extend legal protection to people based on who they have sex with."

Abboud's cause was soon taken up by the Religious Right organization Traditional Values Coalition (TVC), which held a press conference to denounce Breslow's 1982 vote for equal opportunity for gay men and lesbians. Lou Sheldon, TVC's founder, charged, "It's all part of the same homosexual agenda," and that employers should have the right to fire people for "dysfunctional behavior" such as homosexuality. Breslow's campaign countered that fair hiring practices were not synonymous with gay marriages, and that his record was being distorted. Next, Christensen himself stated that he would personally use the office of governor to discriminate against gay men and lesbians. When asked at a televised forum whether he would hire a homosexual to a government position, commission or judgeship, he replied, "I would not — if I knew someone was a homosexual — I would not be appointing someone to a position of leadership. Because I believe it is important that that person model who I am as a person. They model my ideology, my belief system, my conservative values, my belief as a family man." Both Christensen and Breslow were defeated in the Republican primary by "moderate" Republican Mike Johanns, mayor of Lincoln, who also has said that he opposes homosexuality. Johanns went on to win the general election, defeating Democrat Bill Hoppner.

> "If I knew someone was a homosexual — I would not be appointing [that person] to a position of leadership."
>
> — Then-Rep. Jon Christensen, campaigning for governor of Nebraska, when asked in a debate if he would appoint gays to government positions.

Albion and Loretto: Churches reject pastor

Rev. Doyle Burbank-Williams, pastor of Dietz Memorial United Methodist Church, was rejected by Nehawka and Weeping Water United Methodist congregations because he supports covenant ceremonies for same-sex couples. The issue of same-sex commitment ceremonies has been especially inflammatory in Nebraska since 1997, when Rev. Jimmy Creech was charged with performing the same-sex commitment ceremonies in defiance of church doctrine. Creech was later acquitted by a church court, but was fired nonetheless by Nebraska Bishop Joel Martinez. Burbank-Williams, one of about 200 pastors nationally who have signed a pledge to defy the United Methodist Church's ban on performing same-sex commitment ceremonies, had said he would not perform such ceremonies in churches that objected to the practice. Farley Amick, a leader at the Weeping Water church, said Burbank-Williams would still not be welcome. "We don't want a pastor who believes this. It's a bad influence for the youth." When the former pastor of the two congregations, a popular evangelical minister, had been reassigned by Martinez, the churches had requested a conservative replacement. Omaha District Superintendent Ronald Croom had told the pastor-parish relations committee that Burbank-Williams was neither liberal nor conservative. Eventually, Martinez capitulated to the two congregations, withdrew Burbank-Williams' assignment, and appointed an interim minister until a permanent conservative replacement could be found.

Lincoln: Student group

Some students at Nebraska Wesleyan University were so opposed to having an officially recognized gay/lesbian/bisexual student group on campus that they made death threats to the student who wrote the bill asking for official recognition. Jonathan Judge, a heterosexual student with a passion for human rights issues, was asked by members of Plains Pride, a gay student group, to draft a bill asking for official status as a campus organization. Judge soon received two death threats on his answering machine, which he reported to police. "They personalized it quite a bit. Obviously they know what's going on and who I am," he said. This was the second incident of intimidation directed toward supporters of the group; about a month earlier, another student said he had been knocked to the ground and spit on by three individuals, presumed to be other students, who then called him a "fag lover." Plains Pride posters had also been torn down around the university. Despite the anti-gay tactics, the Student Senate voted 26-8 to recognize the group, and students and faculty staged a rally in support of Judge that was attended by several hundred people.

> "Sometimes we confuse the creeds and rules [of the church] with the real essence of loving God and each other."
>
> — Rev. Jimmy Creech, who lost his position at an Omaha church after performing a union ceremony for two lesbians.

Lincoln: Diversity proclamation

Lincoln Mayor Mike Johanns refused to sign a proclamation celebrating the city's diversity because it was drafted and presented to him by a gay group. The proclamation, which did not mention gay men, lesbians, or the Lincoln Pride Network (LPN), the organization that submitted the document, was the fourth such proclamation that the mayor had refused to sign in the past year. The LPN had hoped to use the proclamation at Lincoln PrideFest, an annual event put on by the organization. It read, in part, "no community can survive without the open, active and proud participation of all its members." The proclamation also declared June 20, the date PrideFest would be held, as "a day of pride in, and celebration of, the many parts that make our city whole." The mayor defended his refusal to sign the proclamation by saying, "They are asking me to proclaim something that somehow lends the credibility of my name to their cause. As mayor, I cannot condone what they ask me to condone. This is a lifestyle that, from a personal standpoint, I cannot condone." In November, Johanns was elected governor of Nebraska.

Omaha: Gay art ruled obscene

Three pieces of art with homoerotic themes were ruled to be "obscene" by a District Court judge and were ordered to be destroyed or removed from the state. In 1995, The Run, an Omaha bar, was being remodeled. During a safety inspection, the fire inspector saw the three artworks in question in a basement room, and, believing them to be obscene, called the police to report them. The police seized the paintings and charged that they were in violation of the city's obscenity laws. Police also seized 19 other paintings and sketches that had been on display at The Run. Terry Tippit, who owns both the bar and the art, argued that the pictures had artistic value and therefore should not be censored. The two sides agreed to allow a judge to render the final decision on the fate of the works, and, in the interim, Tippit removed the three most controversial works from the bar's walls. The city's lead witness decried the artistic value of Tippit's collection, saying, "you don't see great art in bars." Tippit brought a copy of Madonna's book "Sex" from the public library to illustrate the fact that images like the ones in his bar were indeed present in Omaha. While the judge did determine 19 of the works to be in line with community decency standards, he ruled three of the images obscene. All three depicted homosexual sex. The judge wrote in his ruling that he was "hard-pressed to find how these exhibits would be tolerated in Omaha, Douglas County, Nebraska."

Omaha: Same-sex commitment ceremonies

In May, Rev. Jimmy Creech of Omaha was notified by Bishop Joel Martinez that he would not be reappointed as pastor of First United Methodist Church (First Church) for reasons stemming from Creech's performing a same-sex commitment ceremony for two lesbians in 1997. Creech, who had been barred from the pulpit by Martinez since November 1997, had been tried and acquitted for performing the ceremony by a church court in March. Creech had argued that he was not guilty of disobeying church regulations, because although the Book of Discipline, which contains the Social Principles, is binding on pastors, the Social Principles, which address the issue of "homosexual union" ceremonies, are not binding. He also claimed that he had not presided over a "homosexual union" because although it was two women he joined, he was never told of their sexual orientation. He was found guilty of performing the ceremony, but was acquitted of violating UMC rules.

Almost immediately after Creech was acquitted, his opponents held a Laity Rally, which included members of First Church who had been worshipping in "exile" since Creech had performed the ceremony and others who opposed same-sex commitment ceremonies.

Signatures were gathered there for petitions to be sent to Martinez asking that Creech and his two assistant pastors be fired immediately or that they not be reappointed for the following year, and letters were later sent out asking for a review of Creech's trial. Less than two months after he had been cleared by the church court, Creech was informed that he had nonetheless lost his position as pastor at First Church. Martinez reportedly told Creech that the division within First Church, the division within the Nebraska UMC Conference over same-sex commitment ceremonies, and Creech's defiance of Martinez's order not to perform the ceremony were the basis for his decision. Martinez then gave Creech the option of asking for another Nebraska appointment, finding another appointment in another conference, or taking a leave of absence. Creech, who says he was surprised and devastated by the news, decided to take a leave of absence and move back to his home state of North Carolina with his wife.

After Martinez's decision, Creech said, "Sometimes we confuse the creeds and rules with the real essence of loving God and each other. What really matters is not our creed and rules. In the end, what really matters is how we treat one another." Creech stepped down from the pulpit June 7. On June 5, delegates to the Nebraska Conference passed a resolution directing congregations to "explore ministries that assist homosexuals who desire to leave the homosexual lifestyle, as well as minister to homosexuals who are comfortable with themselves and their sexual orientation." A second resolution affirmed "change" ministries that have been soundly denounced by both professional therapists and homosexuals who have lived through them. In August, UMC's highest court, the Judicial Council, responded to a request from Martinez and other bishops to hand down a definitive ruling on same-sex commitment ceremonies. The court ruled that pastors who perform such ceremonies can be charged with disobedience, and that the rule was binding on all UMC ministers.

On April 24, 1999, in Chapel Hill, N.C., Creech performed another commitment ceremony for two men. Because Creech was still a part of the Nebraska conference, complaints were filed with Martinez soon after. In July, official judicial proceedings were begun to investigate the complaints.

NEVADA

Clark County: Student harassment policy

The Clark County school district was persuaded by conservative Christian groups, including the Nevada Concerned Citizens (NCC), to delete any mention of specific types of harassment from a student harassment policy that was passed in April. The issue had been debated since December 1997, with civil rights organizations declaring that without guidelines as to what type of actions constitute harassment and which groups are protected under the policy, schools in the district would be unable, or unwilling, to enforce the policy. NCC President Kris Jensen argued that a blanket policy stating that the schools would not tolerate harassment would be sufficient. In February, a draft was proposed stating that harassment based on sexual orientation, race, color, creed, age, religion, national origin, handicap, marital or familial status would not be tolerated. The school board president had specifically said she supported listing "sexual orientation" because many administrators do not see it as a form of harassment. However, the language was deleted by the trustees, who were to forward their proposal to the board, after one trustee offered a blanket statement opposing harassment. "I feel the gay rights issue got blown out of proportion, frankly," she said, adding that the school district would oppose all forms of harassment. When the shortened statement came before the board, the two minority members both expressed concern over the lack of specific language. One commented, "We have teachers and administrators who need some sensitivity training. Let's be real here. I don't play games when it comes to kids." The board voted twice on the broad statement, passing it both times 4-2.

NEW HAMPSHIRE

Statewide: Gay-baiting in state Senate race

One week before election day, The Union Leader, New Hampshire's conservative newspaper, published a story tying Democratic state Senate candidate Rick Trombly to Minotaurs B.C. Inc., a club for gay men, and editorialized against his candidacy, saying he did not represent "family values." The club's statement of purpose reads, in part, that it is "a fellowship of members, primarily leather/Levis oriented whose purpose is to develop character and leadership in the spirit of friendship.... Charitable functions are as an important part to the membership as are the social functions." Attempting to capitalize on the potential for anti-gay backlash, the newspaper titled the breaking story "Trombly: Just Lawyer for Gay Club Linked to Fetishes." The title referred to links from Minotaurs' web site to another site on rubber fetishes. Trombley's home phone number was listed on the Minotaurs' web site as a resource to call for more information. When questioned, Trombly stated that while he did do pro-bono legal work for the organization, including helping it incorporate, he was not a member, and that his number had been printed in error. He refused to respond to questions about his sexual orientation, saying, "I don't think it's relevant to the campaign." The Union Leader emphasized the fact that Minotaurs B.C. held monthly "leather nights" at a Manchester members-only club and called its web site links "quaint homosexual fetishes and the assorted amusements of the gay lifestyle." Both Democratic and Republican state party leaders and Trombly's opponent spoke out against the sensational story, saying that they considered it to be irrelevant to the race. The Union Leader, however, used the information as the basis of their editorial against Trombly's candidacy, writing, "Voters in District 7 should ask themselves this question as they go to the polls next Tuesday: Does Rick Trombly represent the sound moral and family values that more than ever are needed in our elected officials?" On Election Day, Trombly defeated his opponent, incumbent state Sen. Amy Patenaude.

Manchester: New Hampshire Pride parade

The Christian Coalition was so outraged that Manchester was permitting the New Hampshire Pride parade to march down its streets that it organized a Traditional Family Values Rally in protest. For the past 10 years, the New Hampshire Pride parade had been held in Concord, but the chairman of New Hampshire Pride Inc. said that the parade moved to Manchester for more publicity and to challenge what they thought might be a less supportive community. "We felt that Manchester was somewhat more homophobic. I don't think Manchester has been as exposed to things as Concord." When the Board of Aldermen approved the Pride parade's permit, Shelly Uscinski, state chairwoman of the Christian Coalition, was present. She says the action moved her to stage an alternate event the same day to celebrate heterosexual marriage and families. "We are Christian and we think that homosexuality is wrong. We look upon what they do as unnatural and unhealthy," she explained. On June 20, the day of the Pride parade, the procession moved as planned, with events afterward in Veterans Park and McIntyre Ski Area. The Christian Coalition rally was in another park, but protesters showed up near Veterans Park with signs telling marchers to repent, and Christian Coalition members handed out biblical texts titled "Doom City" to people leaving the park.

NEW JERSEY

Statewide: Child custody rulings

Two similar custody cases in New Jersey had two different outcomes, initially resulting in one woman being denied rights with respect to three-year-old twins she had raised since birth. The woman, identified in court only as V.C., had entered into a relationship with another woman, M.J.B., who had been trying for eight months to become pregnant through artificial insemination. The two bought a house together and were married in a commitment ceremony, and when M.J.B. gave birth to the twins in 1994, V.C. was present in the delivery room. The two shared parenting duties, prepared wills and gave each other powers of attorney. When the two women ended their relationship in 1996, they worked out an informal visitation agreement that allowed V.C. to see the children every other weekend in return for child support payments. When M.J.B. tried to end V.C.'s visitation rights, V.C. sued for partial custody. In September, Essex County Superior Court Judge Phillip B. Cummis ruled that V.C. had no claim on the children because she was not related to the children through blood or marriage, and thus was legally a "third party." "New Jersey courts have typically held a third party seeking custody against the natural parent must prove unfitness or abandonment by the parent in order to terminate parental rights," Cummis wrote in his ruling. He also cited the fact that M.J.B. had intended to have a child before entering the relationship and that the couple's current animosity toward each other could be harmful to the children.

In early 1999, an appellate court heard the case and the three judges each came to dramatically different conclusions. Judge Edwin H. Stern wrote in the controlling opinion of the court that V.C. stood "in the shoes of a parent" in relation to the children, but did not think that granting her custody rights would be in the best interest of the children. Judge Stern ruled that he would award V.C. visitation rights, calling her a "psychological parent." In a dissenting opinion written by Judge Dennis J. Braithwaite wrote that "A psychological parent is someone other than a natural or adoptive parent who, when removed from a child, will cause that child severe psychological harm." He wrote that he did not believe that to be the circumstance in V.C.'s case, and that no visitation or custody rights should be awarded to her. Judge Barbara Wecker thought that V.C. had a right to seek joint custody in court and that, at the very minimum, she deserved visitation rights. Because she concurred with Judge Stern on the issue of visitation, those rights were awarded to V.C.

In Newark, however, another custody battle between two lesbians ended with Superior Court Judge Vincent Grasso granting R.E.M., the plaintiff, partial custody of the child. In this case, the couple had chosen a sperm donor together and sent out birth announcements together. After the birth of their son, S.L.V. went back to work while R.E.M. stayed home to care for the child. Grasso wrote, "The court is satisfied that R.E.M. has been able to show that she stands in the shoes of a parent to the child and should be accorded the status of parent in parity with S.L.V." Experts who follow custodial battles said that this decision went further than any other to date in granting broad custodial rights to a woman that is not the child's birth mother.

Statewide: Activists named to AIDS panel

Two representatives from powerful anti-gay Religious Right organizations were appointed by Gov. Christine Todd Whitman to the Governor's Advisory Council on AIDS. Sarah L. Rein, New Jersey director of Concerned Women for America (CWA) and Len Deo of the New Jersey Family Policy Council, a Focus on the Family affiliate, advocate chastity as the best form of AIDS prevention. Prior to the appointments, CWA had released a statement critical of the FDA's plan to begin testing a new vaccine and a new urine test for HIV, saying "The overwhelming cause of HIV/AIDS is risky behavior, such as homosexual sex and drug abuse." The report went on to say, "Recent studies have documented that advances in AIDS treatment have led to a rise in risky sexual activity among homosexuals," although no specific documentation of the studies was given. Rein claimed not to have heard of CWA's position on advancements in AIDS treatment, but said that they must have "a very good reason for it" and that as a state charter "our positions are always consistent" with the national organization. The two appointments came in the wake of a recommendation by the advisory council supporting clean-needle exchanges, which the governor does not support. Gov. Whitman had urged the council to investigate the rise of AIDS in women of child-bearing age instead. Both new appointees object to needle exchanges.

Warren: Substitute teacher denied reappointment

George DeCarlo, a former substitute teacher, sued Watchung Hills Regional High School District saying that the district had refused to allow him to continue teaching due to his sexual orientation, in violation of the New Jersey anti-discrimination law that covers discrimination based on "affectional or sexual orientation." DeCarlo began working as a substitute teacher for the district in 1992, and had received only positive reviews from his supervisors. While he never disclosed his sexual orientation, many students reportedly assumed he was gay, and directed homophobic comments toward him in the halls. Because the school did not cover gay men and lesbians in its anti-discrimination policy, he says, he did not report the incidents. However, in 1994, he finally complained to school administrators after becoming increasingly frustrated by the insults. One student was reprimanded, but within weeks, DeCarlo says, other students made anti-gay comments to his face. One of the students was suspended for one day. In June 1994, DeCarlo received a letter approving him to be a substitute in the district for the following school year. However, in September, he never received a request to teach. DeCarlo says that when he made inquiries to school administrators, they told him he had problems with classroom management. In January 1995, he was informed that he never should have been approved to teach in the 1994-95 school year, and that his services were no longer needed by the district.

DeCarlo filed a complaint against the school district with the state Division on Civil Rights. After an investigation, the agency found: "It is reasonable to conclude that complainant was denied reappointment as a substitute because of his sexual orientation and as an act of reprisal." DeCarlo then filed the sexual-orientation discrimination lawsuit against the district, ending the state agency's involvement in the case. In February, State Superior Court Judge Helen Hoens ruled that DeCarlo could not seek punitive damages from the school district, but that he could seek lost and future wages and compensation for emotional distress. The case is expected to come to trial in September 1999.

Statewide: Anti-discrimination bill

The New York State Senate once again prevented enactment of the Sexual Orientation Non-Discrimination Act (SONDA). SONDA would prohibit discrimination based on a person's sexual orientation in housing, employment, credit and public accommodations. SONDA was first introduced in the state legislature in 1970, and it has been passed by the Assembly each year since 1992. All other Northeastern states except Maine have such legislation. In May, the Assembly passed the bill again, this time by a 87-53 vote. Republican Senate Majority Leader Joe Bruno then refused to consider SONDA, despite the fact that the Senate Government Operations Committee's 11-1 vote to move it to the Senate floor.

Four New York newspapers wrote editorials in favor of SONDA, including the New York Daily News, which wrote about Republican opponents of the bill, "That they refuse to pass a law specifically because it would protect gays and lesbians is obscene." The group Pride Agenda urged then-U.S. Sen. Alfonse D'Amato to lobby the state Senate to pass the bill, and although he reportedly did talk to Bruno, his support was not enough. Senate Republicans refused even to discuss SONDA in their conference, and Bruno never called a vote on the bill, allowing it to die. The bill passed the Assembly again in 1999, by an even greater margin of 105 to 43, with even greater Republican support than the previous year. As of publication, it still languished in the Senate.

Nassau County: Employment discrimination

Jeffrey Mandel, a Queens resident, filed a lawsuit in December contending that he was fired in 1992 from his job in Nassau County as a salesman in the Cheyenne Software division of Computer Associates International Inc. due to his sexual orientation. In the lawsuit, Mandel also claims that his supervisor, Judy Vieco, created a hostile, anti-gay working environment through a series of homophobic comments she made to him. He claims in his suit that shortly after he was hired, he was asked to remove from view a photograph of himself and a male friend. The suit also claims that Vieco told Mandel that his commitment ceremony with his partner was inappropriate and that it would be inappropriate for him to invite co-workers to the ceremony. She reportedly also requested that Mandel's partner not drop him off at work within 100 yards of the Cheyenne Software premises and reportedly accused Mandel, without proof, of partaking in phone sex in his office during the workday.

> "If you call anybody a fag or a faggot, that's just a term guys use. It doesn't mean anything."
>
> — Rev. William Kalaidjian, then the New York Police Department's senior chaplain, after he caused a stir by using a slur in a speech at an awards ceremony.

Although a Computer Associates spokesman said, "The sole basis for his termination was performance-related," in late summer of 1997, Mandel received an outstanding performance evaluation. When he was fired a couple of months later Mandel says he was told unofficially that his firing was due to his sexual orientation. Mandel says he decided to approach Vieco to see if she would confirm the rumor. The Cheyenne Software division was moving to the Computer Associates headquarters location, and he says she told him, "In plain English, we don't want any homosexuals at the new company." Cheyenne Software was located in Nassau County, which has no non-discrimination laws to protect gay men and lesbians from being fired on the basis of sexual orientation. However, Computer Associates does have a non-discrimination policy that covers gays. Mandel's only recourse, therefore, was to cite the company's alleged violation of its own policy in his suit. However, attorneys from the Lambda Legal Defense and Education Fund, a group that works to protect civil rights for gay men, lesbians, and people with HIV, say that a fired gay employee has a much better chance of prevailing in a discrimination case when there is an anti-discrimination law on the books in the governing jurisdiction. Mandel's attorney, Lawrence Gershberg, said that Computer Associates had asked the court to dismiss the case because Nassau County's lack of an anti-discrimination statute nullifies any discrimination claim by Mandel against the company, regardless of the company's own policies. Gershberg argued that the company cannot have it both ways and must be held accountable to its policies. As of publication, the judge had not ruled.

New York City: Barnard College brochure

Lesbian and bisexual students at Barnard College saw an item on "Alumnae Achievement" in the student recruitment brochure as a slap in the face for its boast that graduates of single-sex women's colleges are more likely to marry and have children than female graduates of co-ed higher education institutions. Barnard senior Sandra Chefitz commented, "It suggested that Barnard is not any more proud of its gay students than the University of Alabama." Shannon Herbert, president of Lesbians and Bisexuals in Action at Barnard, explained that she objected to Barnard's reinforcing a bigotry already present in the American culture: "Marriage in our culture is seen as the pinnacle. There is a stigma attached to women's colleges, a stereotype that they produce unshaven, unmanageable, unruly women, or women who become lesbians." Herbert gathered 300 signatures for a petition to revise the brochure, which she presented to school administrators. School officials promised to revise the brochure and praised Herbert's resolve and forthrightness for challenging the college. Barnard's decision to revise the brochure was criticized by conservatives. A New York Post editorial called the move a "cowardly cave-in" and Barnard's administrators "truly silly." Radio personality Laura Schlessinger gave an anti-gay diatribe condemning Barnard's "lesbian activists" for being overly zealous and politically correct. She said, "I just wanted to make it clear that I am sick and tired and fed up with the tyrannical power of the gay and lesbian activists." In the same statement, she also called homosexuality a "biological error."

New York City: Police chaplain uses slur

The Rev. William Kalaidjian, the New York police department's most senior chaplain, referred to Thomas Hickey, a gay assistant district attorney, with an anti-gay slur during an awards ceremony. The ceremony was for Sgt. Thomas Kennedy, a police officer Hickey had prosecuted on charges that Kennedy had assaulted a car-theft suspect. In his speech for Kennedy at a banquet celebrating "Law Day," investigators say Kalaidjian called Hickey a "bum prosecutor who went after Sgt. Kennedy" and then said something to the effect of, "Oops, I almost called him what he is, that fag." Kalaidjian seemed to be oblivious to the insensitivity of his comments afterward, saying, "If you call anybody a fag or a faggot, that's just a term guys use. It doesn't mean anything." Sgt. Edgar Rodriguez, the president of a police officer support group called the Gay Officers Action League, learned of the chaplain's comments and reported them to his superiors, who then referred the matter to the Internal Affairs Bureau for investigation. Police Commissioner Howard Safir said, "I have a problem with anybody who uses any racial, ethnic, or sexual-preference derogatory comments. That's about all I have to say about that." Christine Quinn, executive director of the New York City Gay and Lesbian Anti-Violence Project, said of Kalaidjian's slur, "This sends a chilling message to gay members of the police force and to gay New Yorkers that the NYPD in full force isn't really standing there for us." After the Gay Officers Action League pressured the NYPD to remove Kalaidjian from his position with the department, he decided in May to retire from the police force.

New York City: 'Corpus Christi'

Terrence McNally's play "Corpus Christi," a production at the off-Broadway Manhattan Theatre Club (MTC), was the focus of a campaign organized by anti-gay activists and conservative Christian organizations that sparked bomb threats to the theater and death threats to McNally, the cast, and crew. The controversy focused on the play's protagonist, a gay Christ-like character, who is crucified as the "king of the queers." The conservative Catholic League for Religious and Civil Rights, whose president called the play "sick beyond words" and offensive to Catholics, sponsored a letter-writing campaign to protest the play. TWA, a corporate sponsor of the theater, withheld funds for the play. National Christian-right groups, such as the Mississippi-based American Family Association, also complained that the theater had received $80,000 in government funding from the National Endowment for the Arts. In May, several months before its planned premiere, the production was canceled due to what the theater called "security problems," which included threats to MTC and McNally. A

"Because of you we will exterminate every member of the theater and burn the place to the ground."

— From a message left on the Manhattan Theatre Club's answering machine during rehearsals for Terrence McNally's play "Corpus Christi."

threatening phone message said, in part, "Again, message is for Jew guilty homosexual Terrence McNally. Because of you we will exterminate every member of the theater and burn the place to the ground."

Several prominent members of the New York theater community defended the play and encouraged MTC to reinstate it; playwright Athol Fugard even considered bowing out of a planned production of one of his plays at the MTC. Eventually, MTC reversed its decision to cancel the play after the NYPD began an investigation into the threats. An op-ed in U.S. News and World Report by John Leo called the play "in-your-face Christian baiting." Patrick Buchanan wrote in the Washington Times, "Mr. McNally's play is nothing less than a hate crime of modernity directed against Christians, the moral equivalent of Nazis marching in Skokie." During an early preview performance of McNally's play, a group of about 100 protesters prayed and picketed outside the theater. They held signs that read, "You call this art?" "Don't support blasphemy," and "This is bigotry." Then Religious Right organizers from groups such as the Christian Action Network and the American Society for the Defense of Tradition, Family, and Property led a protest of some 3,000 on the play's opening night. Several civil liberties groups, including People For the American Way Foundation, engaged in a silent counter-protest supporting the First Amendment and free expression.

New York City: Domestic partner benefits

To the chagrin of anti-gay forces including Pat Robertson's American Center for Law and Justice (ACLJ), New York City Mayor Rudolph Giuliani signed an expansive domestic partners benefits ordinance in July. In May, Giuliani had made a campaign promise to gay and lesbian groups to pass citywide gay rights legislation. The mayor sponsored the domestic partnership bill along with Democratic City Council Speaker Peter Vallone. The legislation was mostly symbolic because many of its provisions already existed as executive orders by former mayors Ed Koch and David Dinkins, but it was nonetheless praised by most lesbian and gay groups for its breadth and for including all registered New York City heterosexual and homosexual domestic partners, whether they work for the city or seek access to city services.

> "The notion that two homosexuals shacked up in a Greenwich Village loft are the ... equivalent of a man and woman bonded in holy matrimony is palpably absurd."
>
> — From a New York Post editorial against a city ordinance providing benefits for domestic partners.

The legislation included a city registry recognizing domestic partner relationships, rights to succession by domestic partners in city-owned housing, partner visitation rights in city-run jails and hospitals, the inclusion of domestic partners as beneficiaries to all benefits won in collective bargaining labor negotiations, the right of domestic partner city employees to be buried together in the city-owned Canarsie Cemetery in Brooklyn, the right to death benefits of city police officers and other uniformed city employees for their domestic partners, and the right to inherit some city licenses from deceased partners.

Opposition came most visibly from the New York clergy. Roman Catholic John Cardinal O'Connor used his Sunday homily at St. Patrick's Cathedral to denounce the measure. He said, "Marriage matters supremely to every person and every institution in our society. It is imperative, in my judgment, that no law be passed contrary to natural moral law and

Western tradition by virtually legislating that marriage does not matter." On the day in June when the bill was passed by the City Council on a 39 to 7 vote, a group of two dozen Hasidic rabbis protested outside city hall and cast a biblical curse on the council members who voted for the bill. One rabbi read the biblical story of Sodom and Gomorrah, and Rabbi William Handler of Jews for Morality demanded "God to direct His wrath against the guilty parties."

Conservative columnist William F. Buckley wrote a column for the New York Post suggesting that the bill was anti-marriage, asking sarcastically, "Maybe we should eliminate marriage. Why not?" Another more pointedly anti-gay Post editorial stated, "The notion that two homosexuals shacked up in a Greenwich Village loft are the political, legal, societal and moral equivalent of a man and woman bonded in holy matrimony is palpably absurd." The ACLJ filed a lawsuit against the city claiming that the ordinance supersedes New York state law that has jurisdiction over marriage and domestic relations. And the New York Family Research Foundation issued a press release that said of gays and lesbians, "God judges their relationship by His divine laws and will recompense them justly."

New York City: On-the-job harassment

Two New York police officers filed a lawsuit against New York City, the New York Police Department, and several other officers for sexual harassment and violations of their civil rights. Thirteen-year veteran Joseph Baratto had joined East Harlem's 23rd Precinct in 1989 and was allegedly the target of relentless harassment because he is gay. Baratto asserts that he was the victim of verbal anti-gay harassment and that he was forced into his own locker, which was then locked on him by other officers on four different occasions. In addition, he asserts that on two occasions he was handcuffed and hung from a coat rack in the precinct lunchroom where he was subject to the ridicule of his co-workers and other officers once tried to physically force him to simulate an oral sex act with another officer. Steven Camacho, who is not gay, asserts that he was nonetheless the victim of sexual harassment by other officers simply because he was willing to work with Baratto. According to Camacho, other officers called him "Camacho the homo," drew pictures depicting Camacho engaged in sex acts with Baratto on precinct walls, and wrote graffiti on police station walls that read, "Camacho is a butt pirate." In the lawsuit, filed in October in Manhattan State Supreme Court, Baratto and Camacho seek unspecified damages. After an article critical of the department appeared in an official police publication, Camacho's superiors forced him to relinquish his gun and badge. He was later reassigned to the 10th Precinct in Chelsea after he filed a complaint with the Equal Employment Opportunity Commission. Baratto suffered a nervous breakdown, which he asserts was a result of the harassment, and was placed on restricted duty.

New York City: 'The Most Fabulous Story Ever Told'

After protesting against Terrence McNally's play "Corpus Christi," anti-gay Christian conservative groups next targeted Paul Rudnick's comedic play "The Most Fabulous Story Every Told," which was performed in the fall at the New York Theater Workshop. The play satirizes biblical motifs and substitutes two men, Adam and Steve, for the biblical Adam and Eve. Family Defense Council Chairman Howard Hurwitz said of Rudnick's play, "This abuse of the Bible is to be expected from people who are pro-gay. This is an outrage for religious people." The American Society for the Defense of Tradition, Family, and Property asked its supporters to flood the Minetta Lane Theatre, where the play was being performed, with postcards protesting the play. The recommended postcards read, in part, "If you continue with this presentation, be sure millions of Catholics will oppose it in one of the largest and loudest peaceful and legal protests ever seen." The Catholic League for Religious and Civil Rights criticized the New York Times for praising the play's "blasphemous elements."

New York City: Polish parade

A group of gay and lesbian Polish Americans was denied participation in New York City's Pulaski Day Parade in October. Members of Razem, a Polish gay and lesbian social organization, had marched in the 1996 Pulaski Day Parade carrying a banner that read, "Polish Gays and Lesbians together." In 1997, Polish priests complained about Razem's participation and threatened to boycott the event. Parade organizers compromised by allowing the group to march, but prohibited it from using the words "lesbian" and "gay" on their banner. The group decided the compromise was not fair and boycotted the parade altogether. This year, the group was banned from participating in the parade at all. Martin Sopocy, a member of Razem, said, "We sent our membership check to the parade board, and the check was returned. The letter attached said that because we insisted on advertising our sexual preference, we were not keeping with the ideals of the organization, and we were out."

New York City: Police break up Shepard vigil

New York City police officers broke up a midtown Manhattan vigil for murdered gay University of Wyoming student Matthew Shepard, assaulting numerous marchers and arresting more than 100. The organizers of the vigil, which was advertised through fliers, e-mails, and word of mouth as a political "funeral" for Shepard, had not obtained a permit to hold a march, as they had not anticipated the large turnout, which was estimated at more than 4,000. The police were similarly unprepared for the number of participants. When vigil participants began marching down Fifth Avenue, spilling into the streets from the sidewalks, the police began arresting marchers and also called for additional officers. An hour after the vigil began, some 1,600 officers were involved. Officers in riot gear struck out at marchers with their batons and protesters were later injured by police horses. More than 100 people were arrested. About 30 of those arrested were released from custody that day, and the rest spent the night in jail. Among those who spent the night in jail were John Irizarry, who says he was unable to take medication for AIDS complications that included kidney and heart disease. He and another man with AIDS say that they were denied food and water for hours while in jail, and that they were the subjects of anti-gay verbal abuse. Treated for dehydration after he was released, Irizarry said, "I'm really terrified right now. Whatever you do, you can't miss a dose of your medicine, it could definitely be life-threatening.... I had no idea whatsoever this would happen. I just went to a peaceful candlelight vigil." Mayor Rudolph Giuliani said he was sympathetic toward the cause that brought people to the vigil, but he was unapologetic about the police reaction and blamed the organizers of the vigil for failing to control the marchers. Said Giuliani, "I hope they just don't do the knee-jerk, advocate reaction and try to blame the police, but rather take some responsibility for their own actions. It's really a shame what advocates do. They distort the truth to fit their position."

New York City: St. Patrick's Day parade

For the eighth consecutive year, the Ancient Order of Hibernians (AOH), the sponsor of the yearly New York City St. Patrick's Day Parade, refused to allow gay and lesbian Irish groups to participate in the parade. The Irish Lesbian and Gay Organization (ILGO) submitted an application to march in the parade and carry a banner with the group's name, and the application was denied. ILGO also submitted a request for a New York City permit for a countermarch to be held simultaneously with AOH's annual parade, but the city refused to grant the permit. The U.S. Supreme Court ruled in 1995 that Boston's St. Patrick's Day parade was a private event whose organizers had a constitutionally protected right to exclude whomever they wanted. Unable to participate in the New York City St. Patrick's Day parade or to organize their own parade, ILGO members demonstrated along the parade route. First the group met on the steps of a library to denounce the parade organizers' discrimination against gay and lesbian Irish Americans, and to announce, "The AOH has repeatedly pursued an agenda of bigotry couched in the language of religious freedom and moral superiority." Approximately 100 ILGO members then moved to the start of the parade route on Fifth Avenue. Protesters held signs that read, "What is St. Patrick's Day without Fairies? A Sham," and they shouted, "Homophobia!" at Mayor Rudolph Giuliani for marching in the parade. About two dozen protesters were arrested during the parade. A parade official knocked down one protester and kicked two others while tearing up their signs and calling them a "disgrace" and "trash." He was not arrested.

New York City: Housing discrimination at Yeshiva

Two lesbian medical students at Yeshiva University's Albert Einstein College of Medicine filed a lawsuit against the school after they were denied campus housing with their respective partners. The suit was filed by the American Civil Liberties Union in New York

State Supreme Court on behalf of the students, Sara Levin and Maggie Jones, and the Einstein Association of Gays, Lesbians, and Bisexuals (EAGLB) at Yeshiva. The lawsuit, filed in June, charges discrimination based on sexual orientation and marital status, which is illegal under city and state law. The suit also seeks a change in Yeshiva's policy that denies campus housing to non-student unmarried same-sex partners of students, but does provide campus housing to non-student spouses of heterosexual students. In addition to unspecified damages, the lawsuit seeks compensation for housing and transportation expenses incurred by the plaintiffs, both of whom live with their partners in Brooklyn — a three-hour commute to and from the school — because non-campus housing near the medical school costs about twice as much as student housing.

Sara Levin spoke about the same-sex partner housing ban at Yeshiva: "Heterosexual, married couples get to take advantage of cheap rent and nice apartments close to school, while gay partners are not even acknowledged. My partner and I don't even have the option of marrying." Though Yeshiva was originally a sectarian Jewish school, its medical school is now secular. However, after Einstein's faculty/student senate passed a resolution in 1989 to secure housing rights and other benefits for same-sex couples, Yeshiva President Norman Lamm said, "Under no circumstances can Judaism permit homosexuality to become respectable." Matthew Coles of the ACLU's Lesbian and Gay Rights Project noted the irony of the Einstein Medical School's denying rights to its students. "It is sadly ironic that a college named for Albert Einstein, who was himself the victim of discrimination, is today engaging in its own brand of discrimination against its students," he said. The case was dismissed in 1999 on the grounds that the complainants failed to state a cause of action. The ACLU planned to appeal the case.

Rochester: Child custody court ruling

In June, a New York state appeals court in Rochester ruled that a lesbian had no custody or visitation rights with respect to her ex-partner's biological child. The court based its decision on the fact that the birth mother had neither surrendered, abandoned nor neglected her daughter, the conditions under which her parental rights could be denied. The couple had planned for the child together; the child's biological mother was artificially inseminated, and she gave birth to the baby in 1993. Before the partners separated, the non-birth mother had filed an adoption petition under which the biological mother would surrender her rights as the child's natural parent so that both partners could then adopt her and thus both be declared the child's parents. However, the two ended the relationship in 1997 before that motion could be filed. The non-birth mother then filed a lawsuit in Onondaga County Family Court seeking custody and visitation rights, and cited the failed adoption petition and her decision to have a partial hysterectomy in reliance on her partner's promise to have a child for both of them. The Family Court ruled in the plaintiff's favor and gave her temporary visitation rights with respect to the child. The child's biological mother then appealed the decision, and the appellate court ruled to overturn the previous ruling, saying the ex-partner had no legal right to the child. The lawyer for the child's birth mother said, "They said as a non-parent she basically has absolutely no rights under New York law."

Rochester: Priest excommunicated

A popular Roman Catholic priest, Father Jim Callan, was transferred from his position at Corpus Christi Church in Rochester in September, and later excommunicated from the Catholic Church, in part because he has performed gay commitment ceremonies. Having served at Corpus Christi since 1976, Father Callan revived a parish in decline by permitting a greater role in church activities for women, gay men and lesbians, and non-Catholics and by attracting younger Catholics through the parish's ministry to the poor. Under Callan, the parish of several hundred Catholics in 1976 grew to more than 3,000 by 1998. But Callan came under fire from Catholic Church officials for three violations of church dogma and traditional rules: he allowed his associate pastor, Mary Ramerman, to conduct religious rites usually reserved for ordained male priests; he gave Holy Communion to non-Catholics who attended Mass at Corpus Christi; and he blessed same-sex unions in commitment ceremonies off church grounds. When a gay couple from his parish came to him seeking a blessing of their relationship, "It wasn't in me to say no," said Callan. Over the years, members of a local traditionalist Catholic group, Citizens for a Decent Community, barraged the Vatican in Rome with accounts of Callan and his congregation acting in violation of church teaching. Vatican pressure on the Rochester diocese came to a head in September, when Callan was transferred from his ministry at Corpus Christi by Rochester's Bishop Matthew Clark. In December, Callan was suspended from his ministry indefinitely. Callan's supporters at Corpus Christi led numerous rallies and vigils asking for Callan's return, to no avail. After his departure from Corpus Christi, six church staff members were fired. Ramerman and other former Corpus Christi congregants began to hold their own religious services at a nearby Protestant church, calling themselves the New Faith Community. After Callan joined the new church, he, Ramerman, and their congregants were promptly excommunicated from the Roman Catholic Church.

> "I'm really terrified right now. Whatever you do, you can't miss a dose of your medicine."
>
> — John Irizarry, one of 70 people who attended a New York City vigil for Matthew Shepard and ended up spending the night in jail, where he was unable to take medication for his AIDS complications.

Saratoga Springs: Police officer alleges bias

A Saratoga Springs police officer, who alleges he was derided and harassed because he was perceived to be gay, sued the city and several fellow officers for $20.6 million for slander and sexual harassment. Robert C. Dennis, an eight-year veteran of the Saratoga

Springs force, asserts that he became the target of anti-gay harassment by his colleagues after he was honored for his involvement in a robbery investigation in 1992. According to Dennis, harassment consisted of references to Dennis as "queenie," and to his friends as his "boyfriends." Other officers allegedly ridiculed him by blowing kisses to him derisively over the police radio, stalking him, and telling members of the community that he was gay. Dennis claims that the harassment irreparably tarnished his reputation in the community and caused him "enormous emotional distress." He also asserts that a city employee told a youth organization with which Dennis was involved that he was "light in the loafers" and therefore "should not be considered as a chaperone for a camping trip the organization was having." His lawsuit claimed, "Mr. Dennis has suffered from sexual harassment from his co-workers, to the extent which is so objectively offensive so as to alter the conditions of his employment, and created a work environment which is, based on the evidence, actual discrimination based on sex." His attorney, Richard DiMaggio, said whether or not Dennis is gay has no real bearing on the case and that "it shouldn't matter. If someone is straight and they are called gay repeatedly, are they slandered?" Dennis' trial date is set for Dec. 1, 1999.

NORTH CAROLINA

Asheville: Events held to counter pride rally

The recently formed Community Council for Biblical Values held a series of events in Asheville in June to spread what it called the "good word" on traditional families and denounce the sins of homosexuality. Staged in direct response to the state's Gay Pride Rally, Families United for Biblical Values Weekend featured speakers such as ex-gay Michael Johnston and the Family Research Council's self-styled authority on homosexuality, Bob Knight.

Friday, Johnston spoke at a youth rally to kick off the events. Johnston, who contracted the HIV virus and asserts that he knowingly spread it to others for years, said that he finally gave up that "lifestyle" once he became convinced that his Christian faith required doing so. He is now an activist opposing homosexuality, warning his audience that "Hell is a real place" for those who make the wrong decisions. "God does not love everybody," Johnston said. "That's not what the Bible says."

Saturday's events included a seminar on homosexuality held at the West Asheville Baptist Church. Sunday brought another rally, which included speeches from U.S. Rep. Charles Taylor (R-N.C.), Knight, Johnston, and several ministers. During his address, Knight said, "Here in Asheville you're doing more than just attending a rally. You're striking a blow for freedom and for righteousness because, as you know, we are involved in a huge culture war in this country." He continued, "The gay advocates have said very clearly they want to take this town and remold it in their image."

Hendersonville: Child custody ruling

On July 30, the North Carolina Supreme Court handed down a 6-1 decision that revoked Frederick Smith's custody rights with respect to his two sons. Smith, a gay man who lives with his partner in Hendersonville, had held custody of his children since 1990, when his then-wife, Carol Pulliam, the mother of his children, left him to pursue a relationship with another man. Although the court found no ill effects resulting from the long-standing custody arrangement in general, or from Smith's relationship with his partner, it ruled that it was in the best interests of the children to live with their mother, who had remarried.

Pulliam brought suit for custody in 1995, upon discovering that Smith was living with another man with whom he acknowledged having a sexual relationship. A District Court judge sided with the mother and transferred custody, but that ruling was overturned in 1996 by the state Court of Appeals, which found no evidence of harm to the children. The state Supreme Court reversed the appellate court's decision on the ground that the children's exposure to affection and sexual situations between unmarried people, regardless of orientation, constituted "improper influences." One of the reasons given by the court was Smith's admission that he had engaged in oral sex with his partner (albeit behind the closed bedroom door) while the children were inside the house and that Smith refused to "counsel the children against such conduct." Oral sex is a crime in North Carolina. A lawyer with the Christian-right Focus on the Family affiliate, NC Family Policy Council, which filed an *amicus* brief on behalf of Pulliam, said, "If you are a regular bank robber and you keep your guns in the house and tell your kids it's a good way of life, that's not good. Raising a child means more than feeding and clothing. It should not include regular commission of criminal acts and telling children it's fine to do." Under oath, Pulliam also admitted to violating North Carolina's sodomy laws both before and after she was married.

> "We're backtracking ... to days when custody was taken away from a woman because she had a boyfriend and she was sleeping with him."
>
> — One of the lawyers for Frederick Smith, whose custody of his children was revoked by the North Carolina Supreme Court. Smith's ex-wife sued because he had a male partner.

The Supreme Court's decision broke with North Carolina's judicial practice of siding with stability — such as the five-year paternal custody arrangement — in favor of revisiting custody rights whenever new situations come to light, such as the mother's recent marriage or the father's new partner. In overturning the Court of Appeals decision, the state Supreme Court specifically overruled 18 prior decisions dating back to the 1960s. Many observers fear that the ruling, which was worded to avoid overt condemnation of homosexuality, will unduly affect other custody cases involving heterosexual parents as well as those who are gay or lesbian. "If anything, we're backtracking not so much in the area of gay parenting but to days when custody was taken away from a woman because she had a boyfriend and she was sleeping with him," said one of Smith's lawyers. "This is pre-'60s mentality."

The sole dissenter on the Supreme Court argued that custody should only be changed if the children were hurt by Smith's behavior. The court majority recited behavior by Smith which it "considers to be distasteful, immoral or even illegal and says this evidence supports finding of fact which allow a change in custody," he wrote in his dissent. "There is virtually no showing that these acts by the defendant have adversely affected the two children. The test should be how the action affects the children and not whether we approve of it."

Mecklenburg County: Judge comes out

Ray Warren, a Superior Court Judge and a Republican, held news conferences Dec. 9 to announce that he is gay. He said he believed the story would come out eventually, and he wanted it to emerge on his terms. Warren's coming out made him the first openly gay judge and first openly gay elected Republican official in North Carolina. Since then, many party members have voiced disapproval of Warren. The Mecklenburg County Commissioner said of the news, "This has been brewing for some time in Republican circles...I hope that Mr. Warren will turn from the destructive behavior that he obviously has been engaging in." The former county commissioner expressed shock, noting that Warren had claimed to be a Christian and pointed out what he claimed was a conflict between being a judge in North Carolina and openly breaking the sodomy laws of the state. The executive director of the state Republican Party issued a press release calling Warren a liar because of his claims to be a Christian. "Ray got up and made these comments about being a born-again Christian, and how he'd been a conservative all his life and really hit hard on family values," said the director, expressing sorrow for Warren's family and calling his behavior "deviant and destructive." Warren's announcement also provoked a formal response from the GOP leadership in the state, which released a statement accusing him of "using the Republican Party as a platform to spread his agenda."

Warren's term is up in 2002, and he is expected to face conservative opposition from his own party if he chooses to run again. The Christian Coalition, once Warren's ally, has been campaigning against him.

Winston-Salem: Phelps protests at Wake Forest

On Nov. 28, Rev. Fred Phelps of the Topeka, Kansas-based Westboro Baptist Church, along with about 13 supporters, protested at Wake Forest University over a statement in the school's 1998-99 Bulletin that reads, "Wake Forest rejects hatred and bigotry in any form and adheres to the principle that no person affiliated with Wake Forest should be judged or harassed on the basis of perceived or actual sexual orientation." The Westboro Baptists also protested the university's policy of allowing gay and lesbian student organizations, and Wake Forest Baptist Church's vote to allow same-sex unions. Holding anti-gay signs with messages like "God Hates Fags with God's Perfect Hate," Phelps and his followers failed to garner much support. Only a few families stopped to watch, most of whom, according to a university representative, did so only to teach their children a lesson about hate.

Before coming to North Carolina, Rev. Phelps and his church members had been protesting against Bob Jones University in South Carolina, which barred gay alumni from visiting the campus. Phelps protested the fact that the university even had gay alumni. After the Wake Forest protest, Phelps continued on to Lynchburg, Va., where his church protested against Jerry Falwell at his Thomas Road Baptist Church. Falwell, Phelps believes, has become too accepting of the gay community.

Winston-Salem: Same-sex union

Wake Forest Baptist Church (WFBC), open to gays for years, passed a resolution in 1998 acknowledging God's blessing upon all unions within its congregation, including those between same-sex couples. The vote was taken after a lesbian couple asked the church to bless their union. Southern Baptist Churches that openly affirm gay men and lesbians may not contribute money to the Baptist State Convention of North Carolina, and their "messengers" are not eligible to be seated at annual meetings.

The Baptist State Convention's president, Rev. Mac Brunson, had said the convention would end its relationship with Wake Forest Baptist Church if it voted to affirm same-sex marriages. WFBC's 90 to 33 vote taken Nov. 15 approved language that stopped short of affirming same-sex marriage, instead resolving that only God can bless relationships between two people. After the vote, Brunson said, "Regardless of how they phrase it, they're sanctioning same-sex marriage…. We can't condone sin."

Cincinnati: PFLAG speaker

In Cincinnati, group of parents and alumni were joined by national anti-gay organizations to protest a presentation on discrimination by a local member of Parents, Families and Friends of Lesbians and Gays (PFLAG) at St. Xavier High School. The PFLAG member had talked to the eleventh-grade "Social Justice — Morality" class at the Catholic school for many years, and both the school's principal and president defended her lesson in a letter. "The class seeks to help juniors form the conviction that discrimination is never justified. Our teachers have decided to frame this lesson in terms of discrimination against homosexual men and women because it is the form of discrimination that seems most common among our students."

The protesters organized a prayer vigil and held a news conference with two national anti-gay groups, Americans for Truth about Homosexuality (ATH) and Kerusso Ministries. One parent said that while the school was one of the best in the city, she was upset at the PFLAG presentation because "Catholic teaching says that sex outside of marriage is a sin, and that includes the homosexual lifestyle." Some seniors defended the class to the protesters. Said one student, "I think it's [the school's] obligation to present [PFLAG's] message of love and acceptance. That's what Catholicism calls us to."

The leaders of the anti-gay groups went on local talk radio to denounce the PFLAG presentation. Peter LaBarbera, president of ATH and Family Research Council's self-proclaimed "expert" on homosexuality, belittled the focus on discrimination and called for the students to be exposed to the "ex-homosexual" movement. "By hiding behind the simplistic theme of 'discrimination,' [the principal] is promoting a 'gay pride' agenda that naturally leads to immoral behavior. It is tragic that [the PFLAG member's] one-sided talks have probably confirmed more than a few boys in a homosexual identity that will cut their life short."

> "My heartfelt sympathy goes out to those employees who came to us and asked us to treat them like the majority of other citizens."
>
> — Columbus Mayor Greg Lashutka, after the City Council voted to repeal domestic partner benefits for city employees rather than see the issue decided by a ballot referendum.

Clermont County: Teacher reinstated

A U.S. District Court ordered that the Williamsburg School District to reinstate a sixth-grade teacher whose contract had not been renewed because he is gay. The school district denied that sexual orientation was the reason for its decision, but the U.S. District Court judge disagreed. In the ruling, the judge held that the board was motivated by bigotry, and that anti-gay hostility "can never be a legitimate government purpose." The teacher's lawyer said the decision and its award of more than $70,000 in back pay and damages was unprecedented. The school district is appealing the ruling.

Columbus: Domestic partner benefits

Just two months after passing them, the Columbus City Council repealed domestic partners benefits for city employees after opponents forced a citywide referendum on the issue. The City Council had voted unanimously in December to extend health benefits to the partners of gay, lesbian and heterosexual city employees. The ordinance's leading City Council proponent called the move "the right thing to do for the employees of the city."

However, a local Republican state senator and a conservative Democratic lawyer immediately teamed up to collect signatures to force a referendum. A local Religious Right organization, Mission: America, also jumped into the fray. "This legitimizes homosexuality and bisexuality by force of law and gives it legitimacy it should not have," said the group's president. Although most attendees of the next city council meeting supported the domestic partner policy, opponents collected more than enough signatures to force a vote. The opponents were aided by heavy media coverage of the signature collection efforts at local Christian bookstores. A local gay rights activist accused the petitioners of using scare tactics. "People told signers they need to sign the petition because 'Those homosexuals want to take our benefits away,' " he said.

Afraid of a divisive vote that would earn the city bad publicity, the city council voted unanimously in February 1999 to repeal the ordinance. A loss at the polls would also have meant that the council could not take the matter up again without another ballot initiative. After the vote, Mayor Greg Lashutka, who supported the ordinance, said the referendum would have "been significantly divisive to our community...My heartfelt sympathy goes out to those employees who came to us and asked us to treat them like the majority of other citizens."

Columbus: Student harassment policy

Despite the opposition of a local Religious Right group, the Columbus Board of Education passed an anti-harassment policy that included sexual orientation. A board member who had successfully opposed adding sexual orientation to the district's non-discrimination policy objected to this policy as well. The board developed the harassment policy in response to a lawsuit from an employee who claimed to have been harassed because of a disability. The new policy will be distributed to district employees and students.

Mission America, a local Religious Right newsletter, attacked the policy for "promot[ing] homosexual practices in schools." The editor lambasted the gradual acceptance of gay and lesbian issues through such policies. "Have we lost our minds? How can we support this behavior for our children? How can we continue to communicate that it is an inevitable and harmless 'orientation'? In fact, homosexual desire can be overcome, but if it is not, and our kids go down this road, it is one that is extremely high risk for disease, dysfunction and early death. Educators and parents deserve to know, and then be able to communicate, these facts to every child."

Kent: Preacher at KSU

A physical confrontation between Kent State University students and an anti-gay preacher led to criminal charges and a campus-wide debate about hate speech. The conflict occurred in the student plaza as students were setting up for a rally organized by two groups, the campus Lesbian, Gay, Bisexual Union (LGBU) and Kent Anti-Racist Action.

According to a press account, the preacher, Charles Spingola, set up camp shortly before the rally space reserved for the rally and refused to move. As students moved his chairs and signs, the preacher reportedly threatened to beat them up. He allegedly grabbed one student by the back of his shirt and then punched him when the student put his arm up in defense, breaking the student's nose and knocking a tooth loose. Police led Spingola away in handcuffs, but charges against him were dropped the next day. However, police charged two people involved in the rally with assaulting the preacher.

The campus LGBU held a rally to protest a verdict finding one of the students guilty of disorderly and disruptive conduct. A LGBU officer expressed dismay at the decision, saying that Spingola "insults, degrades and hits us....[the student] was just standing up to him for everyone else." Following the controversy, the university president reconvened the campus Civility Committee — first formed in 1994 following hate speech targeting African Americans, Jews, women and gay men and lesbians. University President Carol Cartwright said that she would not ban speakers from the student plaza, but asked the committee to consider recommendations to educate the community about hate speech and free-speech rights and to consider having a designated "free speech" space.

Summit County: Plea for dual parental status

The Ohio Supreme Court has agreed to hear the appeal of two lesbians who are seeking to both be legally recognized as parents of their child. The women have been together for more than 17 years, and have raised their 9-year-old daughter her birth. A common pleas court denied the non-biological mother's petition to adopt the girl, claiming that Ohio law required one mother to give up her legal status as a parent before another could adopt.

The women appealed the case with the help of the Lambda Legal Defense and Education Fund, arguing that their adoption petition should be treated like the adoptions regularly granted to step-parents. "This child shouldn't be penalized because her parents can't be married," said the Lambda attorney. "The child will benefit from the added security that legal recognition of a parental relationship provides, including both mothers having full authority to make medical decisions and giving their daughter many other legal, financial and health protections."

The appeals court ruled against the women, essentially saying that the law would need to be changed before a step-parent relationship between the two women could be legally recognized. The state Supreme Court has agreed to hear the case. Similar adoptions in cases of same-sex parents have been granted by courts in other states like Michigan, Minnesota, Indiana, Iowa and Illinois.

OKLAHOMA

Statewide: Bill to ban gays from school jobs

In April, the Oklahoma House of Representatives passed SB 1394, a bill to bar "known homosexuals" from working in schools. The bill had originated in the Senate as a measure prohibiting sex offenders from working in the public school system, and was amended in the House by Rep. Bill Graves (R-Oklahoma City) to include gay men and lesbians as well. Graves claimed that homosexuals were sexual criminals guilty of "consensual sodomy," which is prohibited by state law. He also said that many homosexuals are pedophiles who use schools as a "breeding ground" to "recruit young people" to become gay or lesbian. In addition to barring gay men and lesbians from working as school "support personnel," such as janitors or secretaries, the bill also prohibited schools from contracting with companies that employed gays. Furthermore, the bill would also prevent the state from contracting with any vendor that offered its employees domestic partner benefits. Graves' amendment was accepted without debate, and after the entire bill was passed unanimously it was sent back to the Senate. Graves told a local newspaper that his goal was to "drive [gays] back in the closet like the way they were." The Senate would not accept the amended bill, so it was sent to conference committee for revision. Graves' amendment was eventually stripped from the bill, which was then signed by Gov. Frank Keating in June. Gay men and lesbians convicted of sodomy are considered sex offenders and are still barred from employment in public schools under this law. A similar bill was passed and became law in the late 1970s, prohibiting teachers from performing "homosexual acts" in public and from "advocating, encouraging or promoting public or private homosexual activity." This law was struck down as an unconstitutional restriction on free speech in 1985.

> [The bill's goal is to] "drive them back in the closet like the way they were."
>
> — Oklahoma state Rep. Bill Graves, who inserted language into a bill prohibiting "known homosexuals" from working in schools. The bill passed the state House 100-0.

Tulsa: Phelps protest

Declaring that "Sodomites have seized control of Tulsa," Rev. Fred Phelps and his band of anti-gay picketers protested Tulsa's celebration of Gay and Lesbian Pride Week in June. Summoned to the city by a local white supremacist, Rev. Johnny Lee Clary. Phelps is based in Westboro Baptist Church in Topeka, Kansas, but frequently travels for demonstrations. Phelps was supposed to be joined in his protest by White Aryan Resistance leader Dennis Mahon, ex-Imperial Dragon of the White Knights of the Ku Klux Klan, who is usually escorted by a group of violent skinhead followers, which caused parade organizers to beef up security. Although Mahon never showed, the additional security was helpful in keeping Phelps and his followers at a safe distance from the marchers.

Statewide: Domestic partner benefits

Angry over a landmark court decision banning discrimination against gay men and lesbians in the workplace, the executive director of the Oregon Christian Coalition (OCC) and three conservative legislators are threatening to overturn through a voter referendum. OCC executive director Lou Beres decided to push for a ballot initiative because "We think there are a number of groups that will say the court stepped over the line on this one and trampled First Amendment rights."

The lawsuit involved three lesbian plaintiffs who were denied health coverage for their partners by their employer, Oregon Health Sciences University. The Oregon Court of Appeals ruled that the state constitution gives gay and lesbian state employees the right to health benefits for their domestic partners, making it the first court in the country to do so. The ruling is based in part on the Oregon Constitution's equal protection clause, which states that no law shall grant "any citizen or class of citizens privileges or immunities, which, upon the same terms, shall not equally belong to all citizens." The court held that gay men and lesbians are a class of citizens that "have been and continue to be the subject of adverse social and political stereotyping and prejudice."

Prior to the ruling, both the university and the state had voluntarily extended coverage to both same-sex and heterosexual domestic partners of employees. However, the state's implementation of the policy was contingent upon the Appeals Court decision. Oregon Citizens Alliance chair Lon Mabon denounced the Benefit Board's decision because "The government shouldn't be in the business of sanctioning immoral sexual behavior." Earlier in the year, Mabon and the Oregon Christian Coalition had unsuccessfully attempted to place an anti-same-sex marriage initiative on the Nov. 3 ballot.

Statewide: Oregon Citizens Alliance

Having failed to gather enough signatures to put its anti-gay "Family Act" on the November ballot, the Oregon Citizens Alliance (OCA) has filed a new anti-gay initiative for the 2000 general election. "We're never, never, never going to give up," vowed OCA head Lon Mabon. The OCA's upcoming initiative seeks to prohibit public schools from discussing homosexuality and bisexuality "in a manner which encourages, promotes, or sanctions such behaviors."

Mabon described the failed 1998 "Family Act" as a "comprehensive piece of legislation." He went on to say, "Our motivation isn't that we hate people or think ill of them. It is simply to put into law something that says the government can't promote something we think is wrong." The initiative would have amended the state constitution to define family as "one man and one woman in a marriage covenant and their children." It also called for the establishment of a public policy stating "the concept of the male/female relationship of sexual affection is that which is natural to mankind and male/female gender is determined at the moment of conception." The initiative would have prohibited same-sex marriages, prohibited domestic partner benefits for public employees, outlawed adoption by gay couples, prohibited sex-change operations, and virtually prevented lesbians and unmarried heterosexual women from becoming pregnant through sperm-donor programs by making sperm donors legally responsible for children born as a result of the procedure unless the responsibility was terminated by a court.

Mabon and the OCA have a long history of anti-gay activity, having placed or attempted to place five anti-gay measures on the ballot since 1988, when passage of OCA's Measure 8 repealed the governor's executive order prohibiting discrimination against gay men and lesbians in state government. However, many predicted that OCA's latest failure would finish the group. An alliance with the Oregon Christian Coalition may aid OCA's comeback. Though many conservatives, including former Christian Coalition head Ralph Reed, consider Mabon a political liability, Oregon Christian Coalition Executive Director Lou Beres disagrees. The Oregon Christian Coalition created a political

> "When the U.S. military is willing to hire gay and lesbian students, they are welcome to return to our schools."
>
> — Marc Abrams, vice chairman of the Portland School Board, which was pressured to lift its ban on military recruiting at high schools.

action committee to help Mabon collect signatures for his initiatives, and at the national Christian Coalition's 1998 conference, Beres attempted to get funding to support an anti-abortion initiative Mabon was working on at the time. Mabon was the Oregon Christian Coalition's first executive director when the chapter began in 1992.

Lane County: Domestic partner benefits

Lane County commissioners backed off a proposal to extend health benefits to the unmarried domestic partners of county employees following community opposition. All but one commissioner initially favored the proposal, but support dwindled after commissioners received numerous calls and letters in opposition to the proposal. While some commissioners cited questions about cost, Commissioner Cindy Weeldreyer said she opposed the proposition on moral grounds, saying "Not only do I have an obligation to the taxpayers, but I have a higher authority I'm obligated to [and] I think we've been here before in past societies. We've made some grave mistakes, and it has to stop somewhere."

The proposal, which would have included same-sex partners, was brought before the commission by the county's Human Rights and Affirmative Action Advisory Committee.

Commissioner Steve Cornacchia, one of the plan's strongest early advocates, admitted that numerous negative messages from constituents has caused him to back away from his earlier efforts to pass the measure. Believing that "this is big enough that the entire community has to weigh in," he proposed a public hearing in 1999. Cornacchia will leave the board in December, having lost his bid for re-election.

Portland: Job discrimination

In June, police captain Mike Garvey filed a federal lawsuit against the city of Portland, claiming that the mayor and police chief discriminated against him because he is gay. Garvey's lawsuit claims that Police Chief Charles Moose demoted him from commander in 1997, ostensibly for illegal personal use of city phones, but in reality motivated by "Moose's discriminatory animus towards gay males." In addition, the suit accuses Mayor Vera Katz of knowing of Moose's alleged homophobia and acting with "deliberate indifference" by not putting someone other than Moose in charge of decisions directly affecting Garvey. In response to the allegations, Katz cited the city-wide prohibition of employment discrimination on the basis of sexual orientation as proof that the city is a staunch supporter of civil rights. Prior to his demotion, Garvey, a 21-year decorated veteran of the Portland force had put on leave and investigated on charges that he had solicited male prostitutes. In August 1996, a Multnomah County grand jury refused to indict Garvey on the charges. He was then permitted to return to work, but he was demoted in early 1997. According to Garvey, Moose allegedly forbade him to call Moose at home because he was gay, and told Garvey he was not his "special friend." The suit also charges that during an internal affairs investigation Garvey was interrogated, "in a manner calculated to greatly embarrass and humiliate" him, about his sex life, including his sexual positions and the names of his partners. Garvey also charges that his safety was jeopardized when he was issued a squad car lacking a police radio, emergency lights and a siren, and that he was publicly humiliated by Moose, who later removed him from a ceremonial unit activated for the funerals of slain officers.

Portland: Schools defy military recruiters

Military officials and school administrators put pressure on the Portland Superintendent Ben Canada to lift two high schools' ban against on-campus military recruitment. Their actions re-ignited debate on the three-year old policy. The Portland School Board enacted the policy on the grounds that permitting military recruitment on campus supports discrimination against gay and lesbian students because the military won't allow known gays or lesbians to serve. Said one representative of Portland's U.S. Navy Recruiting Command, "We're not able to go into the Portland Public Schools and we think that's unfair...Portland is the only public school in the entire United States to have this ban. What makes them so special?"

Portland School Board Vice Chairman Marc Abrams, who vigorously supports the ban, noted that "When the U.S. military is willing to hire gay and lesbian students, they are welcome to return to our schools." He added, "The issue for us was employment discrimination. If I'm openly gay, can I sign up for the U.S. military? No! They are forced to lead a hidden life or be forced out."

While some school administrators and military recruiters argue that the policy unfairly deprives low-income and minority students of scholarship and career training information, in fact, recruiters are allowed on campus to bring recruiting materials to guidance counselor offices. The school board ultimately upheld its policy. In 1997, the state legislature approved a bill to lift the ban, but Gov. John Kitzhaber vetoed it, allowing the decision to remain with the local school board.

PENNSYLVANIA

Statewide: Anti-gay Senate candidate

Larry Murphy, the Republican Senate challenger to U.S. Sen. Arlen Specter (R-PA), campaigned against equal rights for gay and lesbian Pennsylvanians. Murphy accused advocates of domestic partner benefits of pursuing an unfair and unjustified "gay agenda." At a dinner sponsored by the North Huntingdon Republican Committee, he declared, "They took [their agenda] out of the bedroom and into the locker room, into sports, into the military and now, into the Boy Scouts....Thank God for the Supreme Court of California," for deciding that the Boy Scouts had the right to bar gays as Scout leaders and as Scouts. Murphy lost to Specter in the primary, 18 percent to 67 percent.

Allentown: Anti-discrimination ordinance

A bill to protect people in Allentown from discrimination in employment, housing, and public accommodations on the basis of sexual orientation has been indefinitely stalled. Despite accusations that protecting gay men and lesbians from discrimination would "encourage pedophilia...and contribute to society's moral decline," on Feb. 26, the Allentown Human Relations Commission unanimously urged the City Council to add sexual orientation to the city's human relations ordinance. Two previous attempts to pass such legislation failed outright since only one councilman would sponsor the latest bill, no further action has been taken.

Punxsutawney: Anti-gay harassment

A high school student in Punxsutawney filed a lawsuit accusing his gym teacher of anti-gay harassment and saying that the school failed to respond properly to his complaints of abuse. The student, who has kept his identity private, alleges that for two years his gym teacher, Gail Shields, harassed him — calling him "gay" and "queer." He also claims that these taunts prompted other students to follow the teacher's lead in him. The student eventually dropped out of school and was hospitalized for depression he says was caused by the harassment by both the teacher and other students. The student contends that school officials ignored his repeated complaints and pleas for help, and also failed to refer him to counseling when he was suicidally depressed. The student permanently withdrew from the school, and is now being educated at home.

After the suit was filed, lawyers for the opposition filed motions to force the student to use his real name in the suit and to open his parents to liability in the suit. The court denied the first motion, and as of publication, the second motion is still pending.

University Park: Penn State partner benefits

In University Park, Penn State President Graham Spanier rejected a recommendation by the State Faculty Senate for the first time since he took office in 1995, turning down their proposal to extend benefits to same-sex partners of university employees. In December, Penn State's Faculty Senate approved by a wide margin same-sex partner benefits for faculty members. Spanier, who had the final say in the matter, had said prior to the Senate Faculty vote that he would not approve the recommendation. He defended his position by saying: "Penn State is a state-related university that exists in no small measure because of the support we enjoy from the citizens of the commonwealth through their elected officials...I must report that there is insufficient support at this time in the Pennsylvania legislature" to extend same-sex domestic partner benefits.

RHODE ISLAND

Statewide: Sodomy law

Rhode Island was one of three states to repeal sodomy bans this year. Rep. Edith Ajello introduced a bill revising the state's "Crimes Against Nature" statute, which had previously outlawed sodomy and bestiality. The bill eliminated the phrase "either with mankind or" from the law. The state attorney general, Jeffrey Pine, wanted to keep the phrase in the statute in order to prosecute rape cases where lack of consent was difficult to prove. However, gay men in consensual relationships had been arrested under the statute, although they were reportedly not prosecuted. Ajello, noting that Delaware had continued to prosecute rapists without the phrase in its statute, managed to get the bill passed in the House by a 49-40 vote. It later passed the Senate 26-17 and was signed into law by Gov. Lincoln Almond on June 5.

Statewide: Tax-exempt status denied

Kathys' Group, a support group for lesbians with cancer, was denied tax-exempt status by the IRS in February unless the organization's mission was changed to better serve the "public good." Kathy's Group had sought 501(c)(3) non-profit status in order to expand the group, which now holds meetings twice a month for about 14 people, and provides the services of a therapist. Tax-exempt status is beneficial because it encourages donations from individuals who can deduct them on their tax forms and from charitable foundations that give grants exclusively to non-profits. After the initial request was denied, Kathy's Group enlisted the help of Lambda Legal Defense and Education Fund, which sent a letter to the IRS pointing out that many non-profit groups serve only segments of the population, such as the NAACP and AARP. Patricia Cain, a dean and professor of law at the University of Iowa, explained that as long as no racial discrimination is occurring, "The only other test is sufficient public benefit. If I set up a support group for the 10 lesbians in my neighborhood who are my friends, that wouldn't be a public enough purpose to get charitable donations. But if I set it up for all the lesbians in the state who have cancer, that's certainly a public enough purpose." In May, without explanation, the IRS sent a letter reversing its earlier decision and granting 501(c)(3) status to the group.

> "If the implication is that North Providence High does not have any homosexual students, I would be very shocked."
>
> — Marc Paige, addressing a committee that barred him from giving a speech at a high school. Paige, who is HIV-positive, gives lectures on how to avoid contracting the AIDS virus.

Cranston: Anti-gay campaign literature

In October, a father followed in his son's footsteps by disseminating anti-gay campaign literature targeting openly gay state Rep. Mike Pisaturo (D). Henry Archetto, the 1998 Republican candidate, is the father of Paul Archetto, the incumbent when Pisaturo defeated him to win his seat in 1996. The younger Archetto had made Pisaturo's sexual orientation the primary focus of his campaign, and apparently his father had the same goal this year. Henry Archetto sent a letter to all the registered voters in Pisaturo's district claiming that Pisaturo had introduced a bill to allow teaching about homosexuality in the public schools, proposed that condoms be distributed to high school students, sponsored a bill to allow gay and lesbian couples to marry and adopt children, and had co-sponsored the law repealing Rhode Island's ban on sodomy. Pisaturo did indeed co-sponsor the sodomy repeal law, and he did introduce legislation to allow same-sex marriages. However, it was already legal for gays to adopt, and he never advocated condom distribution, he only suggested that condoms be made available through a school nurse. He also did not suggest teaching students about homosexuality; he recommended that sensitivity training be offered to school staff on issues like anti-gay harassment and homophobia. Pisaturo, Rhode Island's only openly gay legislator, was re-elected in November.

Providence: Presentation barred from school

In September, Marc Paige of Cranston was barred, by a 7-0 vote from the School Committee, from speaking to North Providence high school students about the dangers of AIDS. Paige discovered he was HIV-positive in 1993, and since then he has spoken at dozens of colleges and high schools about avoiding the dangerous behaviors that can lead to contracting HIV, and what it means to live with the virus. He had been denied permission to speak at North Providence high school since 1995. "With 25 percent of new HIV infections occurring among teenagers," he said, "I believe you have a responsibility" to address the subject. After Cranston said this, the committee was silent. One man in the audience said, "I wouldn't want anyone to come in with an agenda and try to convince children that their personal lifestyle is acceptable or not acceptable." Paige reassured the man that he does not promote any sort of lifestyle, but when the committee asked Superintendent Marie Hanley for her opinion, she said, "The content of his presentation does relate in part to his personal life and personal lifestyle. ...That is in no way a criticism," she added. "Yes, I am a gay man," Paige responded. "I see an obsession with homosexuality here. If the implication is that North Providence High does not have any homosexual students, I would be very shocked." The committee voted immediately afterward not to allow Paige to address the school.

SOUTH CAROLINA

Statewide: Campaign for agriculture commissioner

Jim Gordon, a Republican candidate for state agriculture commissioner, campaigned against what he considered to be various threats to family farming, including same-sex marriage. "We can't have farming based on Bob and Bob being married and a new definition of marriage," he declared in May. He later said that the liberal media and Democrats were taking his comments out of context, but that he would continue to battle the "homosexual agenda." The correct context, he said, was "A homosexual couple is not a marriage." He then challenged Tom Turnipseed, the Democratic attorney general, to a debate. Turnipseed, who had been promoting hate crimes legislation that would include crimes against women and gays, declined to debate Gordon, saying, "If he can tell the difference between broccoli or turnips or green beans grown by a homosexual, then I'd like to know about it." Gordon also attacked gays for wanting "special rights," noting a court case in which a heterosexual man sued because he was not covered on his live-in girlfriend's health care policy because the company's domestic partners benefits were only available to gay and lesbian couples. Gordon claimed this was the gay agenda at work: "If they're successful in accomplishing their agenda, if we're going to give special rights to special groups, it's going to affect everybody." Gordon lost in the Republican primary to the incumbent, Les Tindal, who was unopposed in the general election.

Statewide: SCETV censors documentary

SCETV, a South Carolina public television network, decided not to show "Licensed to Kill," a documentary, saying that the film's violence was too graphic. In the documentary, film-maker Arthur Dong went into prisons to examine the minds and souls of men whose hatred of homosexuality motivated them to kill. The film won two top awards at the Sundance Film Festival in 1997, and was aired on many public broadcasting stations nationally. The film aired as a part of a Point of View (POV) series of films about "the plague of violence that is sweeping the nation." Although other films in the POV series were being shown on SCETV, the managers of the station said they felt that "Licensed to Kill" "would be unacceptable to the majority of our viewers."

> "If he can tell the difference between broccoli or turnips or green beans grown by a homosexual, then I'd like to know about it."
>
> — S.C. Attorney General Tom Turnipseed, in response to a campaign rival who said same-sex marriage undermined family farming.

The decision sparked outraged letters to the station. The station's vice president of communications, Kathy Gardner-Jones, said, "[W]e strongly agree that any hate crime, any incident of violence to any person — whether motivated by race, gender religion, or sexual orientation — is deplorable. This film, however, not only discusses the crimes, it shows brutal, gruesome police crime footage of the victim. In our view, it crosses a journalistic standard concerning the portrayal of violence." Dong says he added the footage of corpses to the film after early audiences left feeling sympathy for the killers. "It was because they didn't connect these men and their stories with their crimes. I had to balance that," he explained.

A personal essay by Arthur Dong appears on p. 18 of this book.

Columbia: Indigo Girls concert canceled

Irmo High School in Columbia canceled a free concert by the Grammy Award-winning group Indigo Girls last spring. The folk-rock duo had scheduled several free concerts at high schools across the South to share their knowledge about songwriting and the music industry. In addition to the half-hour concerts, the duo agreed to be interviewed by writers for the various schools' student papers. The tour had been going smoothly until Irmo parents complained to the high school principal that the concert was inappropriate because the two performers are lesbians. The principal then abruptly canceled the May 7 performance. Students were vocal on both sides of the debate. In a letter to the school newspaper, one student wrote, "I along with several other students and parents believe that it is wrong to have them at our school, simply because they are lesbians." The editor of the school newspaper criticized the decision: "I think it's a form of censorship. I'm conservative, I'm proud to call myself a Republican, but I don't think it's right to judge people. I think he [the principal] let the minority speak for the majority." She went on to point out that the school was not practicing what it preached: "Teachers preach to their students that they should be open-minded in this society, and then this close-minded, ignorant decision comes along and negates everything that they have stood for."

Some students in Irmo also suspected politics drove the decision. They expressed the view that pressure may have been put on the principal by the school board chair who was seeking the Republican nomination for South Carolina Superintendent of Education. The school board chair said it appeared that the Indigo Girls were promoting an agenda; he cited an article in an Atlanta gay newspaper in which they discussed their sexual orientation. Principal Gerald Witt defended his decision, saying, "I am not judging them.... I don't see us as a platform for community kinds of issues. We are an institution of learning." The Indigo Girls' manager remarked, "I'm just disappointed the authorities at the school buckled under pressure. I would like to think that they could stand up to it so the student body could see the value of that."

After the concert was canceled, students began organizing a walkout scheduled for the morning the Indigo Girls were supposed to have performed. Despite the principal's warning, the walkout began with 50 students, grew to 200, and, after someone pulled the fire alarm, the entire school emptied out. Eight students were suspended for eight days each, with two other students receiving lesser suspensions and dozens given detention.

Greenville: Bob Jones University

In October, Bob Jones University (BJU) in Greenville barred all gay alumni from setting foot on campus. The controversy arose when alumnus Wayne Mouritzen told a close friend and fellow BJU alumnus that he was gay. His friend, in turn, contacted the university. Mouritzen, who had been married for 36 years and who was a retired minister, was 60 at the time, and had reportedly only come to terms with his homosexuality in recent months. Soon after, BJU sent him a letter which read: "With grief we must tell you that as long as you are living as a homosexual, you, of course, would not be welcome on the campus and would be arrested for trespassing if you did visit." Mouritzen was shocked and angered. He remarked, "The Bob Jones letter also said, 'I need to get back to the Lord.' Well, I didn't know I had to get back because he hasn't left me. If anything, I feel even closer to him now. "A BJU spokesperson said that the letters were standard practice at BJU. He said, "We can't tell our alumni what they can and can't believe. But we can say, 'You've made your decisions-please do not return.'" Later, the school did say it would allow gay alumni to visit the school's art gallery, because to do otherwise could endanger the gallery's tax-exempt status. The university had lost its own tax-exempt status in 1970, when it refused to repeal its ban on interracial dating, and as a private university, it is exempt from many constitutional protections. The school claims that its ban on gays does not extend to non-alumni visiting the campus.

Although the incident resulted in an easily anticipated wave of protest from the liberal community, anti-gay crusader and BJU alumnus Rev. Fred Phelps also became furious with the university. Phelps brought his congregation from Westboro Baptist Church in Topeka, Kansas, to protest the "backslidden university of hypocrites" because he said the school was being too lenient towards gays, and that the fact that there were gay BJU alumni meant that the school was clearly not doing its job. Phelps claimed that when he attended, homosexuals would have been too intimidated to go near the school.

SOUTH DAKOTA

Spearfish: Student play censored

In Spearfish, students saw their chance of winning a statewide play competition disappear after censorship of the play due to its theme of tolerance for gays led the publishers to rescind permission for its performance. The play, "Removing the Glove," was an award-winner for the author, Clarence Coo, when Coo was in high school. The play never mentions homosexuality directly, but instead delivers its message of tolerance by means of an allegory, as one of the characters, in Coo's words, has to "finally admit that he is indeed left-handed."

Objections to the play came from a variety of sources, including religious leaders and students, who asserted that promoting tolerance for gay men and lesbians was pornographic and immoral. A local parent also claimed that his daughter did not bother trying out for the play because she had been told by other students that it was "probably not one she would want to be a part of based on its contents." He added, "The play that the school put on was promoting acceptance and normalcy of homosexuality. That, I don't believe, is the right of anyone but the parents to teach to their children." Others asserted that putting on the play was discriminatory toward students who could not participate based on their beliefs.

In an effort to win approval for the play to be performed as scheduled, the students deleted more than 20 lines of dialogue from the 26-page script. The publisher had agreed that if the $40 royalty and performance fees were paid, the students did not need to submit the revised script for the publisher's approval. The edited version was approved by the district's "Controversial Issues Committee" and by the school board in a 4-1 vote. Local opponents, who did not want the play performed at all, then inundated the publisher with phone calls, requesting that the company take a closer look at the editing. The publisher ultimately decided that the "adaptation or editing without permission did not agree with the author's original intent." Two days before they were scheduled to go to the competition, the students learned the trip would have to be canceled because the publisher had withdrawn its permission to perform the edited play.

The executive director of Free Americans Creating Equal Status of South Dakota, a statewide gay rights group, remarked, "This is a story of being left-handed in a right-handed society. The author was born in the Philippines, and may have experienced all kinds of intolerance. The message of tolerance can be applied in many ways...skin color, speaking a different language, just being different. The issue of homosexuality is not the real issue here except the fact that it's been made the issue by people who want to attack gays and lesbians on all levels."

TENNESSEE

Knoxville/Memphis: Indigo Girls concerts canceled

Two Tennessee high schools canceled free concerts by the openly gay Indigo Girls in May. The duo had scheduled several free concert dates at high schools across the South to share their musical experience, and also agreed to be interviewed by writers for various schools' student papers. In May, a high school principal in Columbia, South Carolina, had abruptly canceled a concert after parents complained that the concert was inappropriate because the two women are lesbians.

Within the week, two more free concerts by the Grammy-winning group were canceled in Tennessee. Officials at both schools cited profanity as the reason for the cancellations. One of the Tennessee principals claimed he had received a call warning him that the group had used profanity in a school appearance in April. He said, "The principal told me they sung the song that had the f-word in it and emphasized it. The concert went downhill from there." He said that upon calling the school to verify the story, he had discovered the singers' sexual orientation.

The band's manager asked if the principal would reconsider if the band promised not to use that word, but the principal refused to change his mind. A second school followed suit. That decision led to an after-school demonstration by about 50 students who claimed that the cancellation was not due to profanity at all, but was due to the duo's sexual orientation. "It's understood by everyone that the show was canceled because the Indigo Girls are gay," said the co-editor of the student newspaper. Another asserted, "Our point is that we have a right to listen to the music that we want to listen to, and sexual preferences shouldn't have [anything] to do with this." The editor of the Knoxville News-Sentinel agreed, writing that, "...the message to the children is: When you are trying to uphold Christian values, it's OK to lie about it." In both venues, the Indigo Girls performed alternate free concerts after school hours and off school property.

Nashville: Billboard defaced

In Nashville, a billboard put up by the local chapter of Parents, Families and Friends of Lesbians and Gays (PFLAG) was defaced with black paint weeks before the Pride Parade in September. The billboard, which read "Someone You Know and Love Is Gay!" was put up to counter a series of anti-gay "Truth in Love" newspaper ads that were sponsored by the Religious Right, and to commemorate Gay Pride Month and National Coming Out Day. Initially the incident was attributed to vandalism, but later the company that owns the billboard stated that the incident was due to the sign painter's desire to improve his original work. However, the painter resigned before he could repaint it, and the sign was left mostly blacked-out and illegible until the company could hire another painter to repair the damage. The local PFLAG spokesperson found the entire episode "suspicious."

Savannah: United Methodist Church

Claiming that the United Methodist Church does not condemn homosexuality strongly enough, the East End United Methodist Church in Savannah is withholding an estimated $15,000 from the denomination. The denomination teaches that homosexuality is incompatible with Christian teachings but that homosexuals are nevertheless people of sacred worth. Savannah church leaders believe the teaching should be amended to say that homosexuality is a sin requiring repentance. One lay leader explained the action, stating that "homosexuality is one of the things in the Bible we have to stand firm on. The Bible says it's an abomination."

Statewide: Adoption/foster care bills

Two bills in the state legislature sought to bar gay men and lesbians from serving as foster parents. Both bills were introduced in December after a state employee filed a legal challenge contesting her reassignment for inappropriately removing an infant from the foster home of a lesbian couple. One sponsor vowed to "leave no legislative stone unturned to make sure this bill happens." Amid the public controversy over the issue, Gov. George W. Bush (R) announced his opposition to gay adoptions.

A few months before the bills were introduced, the employee sued the state Child Protective Services agency seeking both her reinstatement and the agency's enforcement of the state's law against homosexual conduct (a Class C misdemeanor in Texas). She is receiving legal help from the Liberty Legal Institute, a Religious Right-affiliated law firm that "specializes in the defense of family autonomy, religious freedom, personal property rights and innocent life." Lumping gay men and lesbians with sexual "criminals," the employee said others at the agency agreed with her "that placing children in homes where there is sexual molestation, prostitution or other criminal sexual conduct is wrong."

One bill pending in the Texas legislature, sponsored by GOP Rep. Warren Chisum, would remove foster children from the homes of gay and lesbian foster parents, prohibit gay men and lesbians from adopting children in state custody, and mandate the scrutiny of prospective foster parents' sexual orientation. Rep. Robert Talton's (R) proposal goes even further, requiring authorities to investigate all current foster parents. Talton had earlier worked to keep gays excluded from the state's hate crimes law and Chisum had sponsored an anti-gay marriage bill the previous year. Both foster care/adoption bills have been referred to a House committee, though Chisum conceded in March 1999 that his bill had no chance of passing during the session.

Statewide: School board divests Disney stock

After a year of pressure from the Religious Right, the Texas Board of Education sold its stock in Walt Disney Co. The American Family Association (AFA) of Texas had sent board members excerpts of what it considered to be objectionable scenes from movies produced by a Disney subsidiary, including a film with lesbian themes, Chasing Amy. For quite some time the AFA has led the Religious Right in a national campaign that claims Disney is "one of the leading promoters of the homosexual lifestyle, as well as the homosexual political and social agenda in America today."

Some board members who voted to sell the stock claimed their decision was based on the overall sex and violence in the movies. However, one state representative who petitioned the board not to sell the stock noted that the AFA's main objection to Disney stemmed from its policy offering benefits to the partners of its gay and lesbian employees. "They've been out to get Disney for a long time," she said.

Statewide: Conservative Baptists split

Upset that the Baptist General Convention of Texas (BGCT) has not taken stronger stances against abortion and homosexuality, conservatives split with the more moderate body to form their own group, the Southern Baptists of Texas. The new convention immediately vowed to reject churches that condone homosexual acts or "have pastors or deacons that are practicing homosexuals." The schism culminated years of tension between moderate and conservative factions within the BGCT, which was one of the country's largest Baptist groups before the split. "I think we've got to get away from this thing of getting away from God's word," said the president of the new group.

Austin: Baptist church ousted

The Baptist General Convention of Texas ousted a small church in Austin, Texas, over its acceptance of gay and lesbian members. The Convention's executive board severed ties with the 90-year-old University Baptist Church after it ordained a deacon who is gay, criticizing the church's ministry to gay men and lesbians as an affirmation of homosexual practice. Though Pastor Larry Bethune denied that the church endorsed homosexual behavior, he acknowledged, "we do embrace homosexual persons as persons beloved of God."

This is not the first time that the University Baptist Church has broken barriers. Fifty years ago, this church became known as a leader of racial equality by integrating blacks and whites into the congregation. Many church members see their church's ouster as a chance to broaden the debate and for their ministry to grow. One 76-year-old churchgoer noted that "someone always has to be first," and vouched for her younger fellow parishioners, calling them "some of the nicest young men and women you'd want to know. Their lifestyle to us was they were devoted Christians and good friends."

College Station: A&M football player

At an annual bonfire celebration, a Texas A&M football player said he was glad to attend a school where "men like women and women like men." The player later expressed regret for his comment, calling it a "heat of the moment" remark that was not necessarily directed at anyone. The university president and the athletic director also apologized after the Gay, Lesbian, Bisexual and Transgendered Aggies lodged a complaint. The group's student leader suggested that sexual orientation be added to the school's non-discrimination policy.

The controversy also caught the attention of the virulently anti-gay Rev. Fred Phelps from Topeka, Kansas, who promised to protest Texas A&M's apologies outside the Big 12 championship game between A&M and Kansas State University. In a press release, Phelps said, "Kansas State should have no trouble beating a fag Aggie team, cowed by the Texas A&M fag student body into abject silence. When football players must give up free-speech rights to satisfy fags, they lose heart." Phelps also promised a trip to Texas A&M, saying that because "A&M has allowed fags to take it over, it is damned."

Carrollton: Article pulled from student paper

A high school principal in Carrollton stopped the student newspaper from running an article about student efforts to gain official recognition for a gay and lesbian support club. Dr. Lee Alvoid said she pulled the story because it was premature, since she was still researching whether the club could exist at the school. Describing the area as the "Bible Belt of America," the student editor of the newspaper saw a different reason, and threatened to sue the school. "They don't want awareness on the whole issue. They don't want the students and parents to know that the group is being formed so no one will show up to the school board meeting in the fall to support it."

Though she acknowledged that the article was factual and represented all sides of the issue, Alvoid also said she had to consider the story's potential impact. "Because of the nature of the topic and because of the conservative nature of the community, I didn't want a negative reaction before we even had a club. This is not just one of your normal teenage clubs," she said. The principal did say she intended to allow the story to run in the fall, after the club was approved or rejected by the school board. A year earlier the school board had delayed another high school's trip to Disney World because the theme park provides benefits to domestic partners of its gay employees.

The club was never formed, although the school does have a "support group" for gay, lesbian and bisexual students that is run out of the school's counseling office. In the fall, the returning newspaper staff decided not to run the story at all, saying that it was no longer newsworthy.

Dallas: Flip Benham at Cathedral of Hope

The head of Operation Rescue had to be escorted from the grounds of Cathedral of Hope Metropolitan Church in Dallas, one of the largest gay and lesbian churches in the nation, after church officials accused him of harassment. The Universal Fellowship of Metropolitan Community Churches is the only Christian denomination with a primary outreach to gay men and lesbians. Benham had previously denounced Cathedral of Hope in interviews, saying that its teachings are contrary to the Gospel. After he became belligerent during discussions with church members, Rev. Philip "Flip" Benham was given a warning ticket for criminal trespass. Benham and about a dozen followers had attended worship services without incident before the dispute. The senior pastor said that Benham was welcome to attend services any time but "if he disrupts things here again, we would have him banned." Benham called the visit the "beginning of a truth telling" mission and said that he and his followers will travel all over the country to other Metropolitan Community Churches.

Dallas: Gay prom

Protesters and police gathered outside a prom held especially for gay and lesbian youth in Dallas. About 50 teens came from around the region to a downtown Dallas hotel for the event, which was sponsored by the support group Parents, Families and Friends of Lesbians and Gays. Police closely watched a group of protesters from Heritage Baptist Church in Rusk County who were bearing signs saying that the teens were bound for hell. When two prom-goers staged an impromptu counterprotest by hugging in view of the protesters, they heard shouts of "Wicked!" and "See what they did in Sodom and Gomorrah!" One young attendee said that the protest "just makes us band together more." The organizers plan to make the prom a yearly event.

Dallas: Perot Systems

Two-time presidential candidate Ross Perot rescinded domestic partnership benefits at his company, Perot Systems, less than a year after he returned to the chief executive position. The company's previous head had instituted the policy at the end of 1996, citing the desire to attract, develop and recognize talented people. Perot reportedly complained about the decision at the time. According to Perot, the benefits policy was unfair because it didn't include people who share housing with roommates, but he added that expanding the policy to include them would be too expensive.

While the Human Rights Campaign decried the move as "totally unnecessary and mean-spirited," the Religious Right radio program "Family News in Focus" reported favorably on the first known company to rescind domestic partnership benefits. Peter LaBarbera, president of the anti-gay Americans for Truth about Homosexuality and editor of the Family Research Council's weekly publication "Culture Facts," commented on the program, "So many corporations are buying the homosexual line that they should treat gay employees like people who are married. I think the bottom line is the almighty dollar. But we will take the victory however we can get it."

Fort Worth: Anti-discrimination ordinance

A proposed amendment to Fort Worth's anti-discrimination ordinance that would have added protections for gay men and lesbians to existing safeguards against gender and race-based discrimination died in January 1999 for lack of support from city council. A similar effort suffered the same fate in 1992. The city's Human Relations Commission formally recommended the amendment. In a letter to the council, the chairman of the Human Relations Commission wrote that, "[g]ay and lesbian citizens of Fort Worth (as well as those perceived to be) are being discriminated against on a regular basis due to irrational fear of and prejudice against their sexual orientation." Had the measure passed, Fort Worth would have had one of the strongest municipal anti-discrimination laws in the state, banning sexual orientation discrimination in housing, employment and public accommodations. Opposition led by a former employee of the Texas Christian Coalition (TCC), however, helped convince the city council not even to consider the proposal.

> "There are a few reasons why we should discriminate against homosexuals. The number one reason is God."
>
> — A speaker from Choose Life Ministries, urging the San Antonio City Council not to expand the city's non-discrimination policy.

Meetings of the city council and the Human Relations Commission were packed with people expressing strong opinions on the matter and both sides quoted Biblical Scripture in support of their positions. Opponents largely argued against the measure out of the belief that homosexuality is morally wrong. The area chapter of the American Family Association presented the commission with petitions opposing the proposed ordinance and Operation Rescue head Flip Benham spoke against it on behalf of the Fort Worth Pro-Life Ministry. Said Benham, "We've done it with abortion. We're doing it with homosexuality. God says no."

In an alert sent to its activists, the Texas Christian Coalition trumpeted its role in defeating anti-discrimination measures in both Fort Worth and San Antonio. "Personally, I think the council showed reasoned restraint in the face of fierce pressure to force Fort Worth citizens to conform to current notions of political correctness," said the TCC's Fort Worth organizer.

Fort Worth: LCR barred from GOP conference

For the second time in a row, an organization of gay Republicans was denied exhibit space at the Texas Republican Convention in Fort Worth. A party spokesman called the Log Cabin Republicans "extremists," saying that "the Republican Party is not going to allow individuals like the Log Cabins or the KKK or any other hate group that are in direct conflict with our philosophy a forum to spread their hateful message. We don't allow pedophiles, transvestites or cross-dressers, either," he added. The Texas LCR director said that "being a gay Republican in Texas is a little like being a black Democrat in Mississippi in the 1950s. You're involved in a party that doesn't really want you, where you're excluded, discriminated against, segregated."

The Log Cabin Republicans, who had elected more than 50 delegates and alternates to the state convention, protested the party's decision with a "Rally for Liberty" next to the convention hall. They were met by demonstrators bearing signs with sayings like "Fags, Queers & Sodomites: Go Home to San Francisco" and "The Gay life = AIDS, then death." Log Cabin opponents also tried to drown out speakers as they read statements from supportive GOP officials including U.S. Reps. Chris Shays, Connie Morella, Jim Kolbe and Wayne Gilchrest. One speaker, a GOP activist whose son was a gay delegate, heard someone shout over her speech, "Your grandson is a sodomite and you're both going to burn in hell!" LCR made a videotape of the rally, On the Front Lines, which it is distributing to Republican officials around the country.

> "Being a gay Republican in Texas is a little like being a black Democrat in Mississippi in the 1950s. You're involved in a party that doesn't really want you."
>
> — The director of the Texas Log Cabin Republicans, which was denied exhibit space at the state GOP Convention in Fort Worth.

The situation mirrored the events of the 1996 convention, where the LCR was turned away but not treated quite so poorly, according to the group's president. The group sued the Texas Republicans after the 1996 convention but the state Supreme Court ruled against it, saying that the party is a private organization. The dispute added to a national debate over whether the GOP should embrace a "big tent" philosophy, including differing viewpoints on social issues. The Traditional Values Coalition's Lou Sheldon commented, "There's no problem with the big tent. But you don't want a bunch of mush in the tent so that the pegs in your tent can't stay up."

If the convention did not make the Texas GOP's attitude toward gay men and lesbians clear enough, the official state party platform left no doubt. It states: "The Party believes that the practice of sodomy, which is illegal in Texas, tears at the fabric of society, contributes to the breakdown of the family unit, and leads to the spread of dangerous, communicable disease. Homosexual behavior is contrary to the fundamental, unchanging truths that have been ordained by God, recognized by our country's founders, and shared by the majority of Texans. Accordingly, homosexuality should not be presented as an acceptable 'alternative' lifestyle in our public education and policy."

Houston: Sodomy charges

Two Houston men were arrested for violating a Texas law that prohibits same-sex sodomy, beginning a legal challenge that many hope will end the discriminatory law. The case began when an estranged friend of the two men called in a false police report of a crazed man with a gun. When police entered the apartment through an unlocked door, they found the two men having sex in the bedroom and arrested them under the 119-year-old law. The two men initially pleaded no contest, but then appealed it to the next court with a motion to quash the charges. The judge dismissed the motions and fined them each $200. With the help of the Lambda Legal Defense and Education Fund, the two men have filed new appeals, challenging the law on the grounds that it violates their rights to privacy and equal protection under the Texas and U.S. Constitutions. The case is on appeal to the Texas Court of Appeals. A bill to repeal the law was introduced in the state legislature in November, but it was referred to the Criminal Jurisprudence committee and no further action had been taken on it by the end of the legislative session.

The Texas case began shortly after the Georgia Supreme Court struck down that state's sodomy law as violative of the Georgia Constitution. These developments have heartened gay activists but galvanized Religious Right support for the laws. Both the Texas Eagle Forum (EF) and Family Research Council (FRC) put out opinion pieces on national wire services defending the laws for "protecting" society. FRC's Steve Schwalm and EF's Cathie Adams claimed that the end of state sodomy laws would contribute to the spread of AIDS. Wrote Adams, "Denial of natural law and common sense by our modern society has permitted this horrible disease (AIDS) to wreak havoc on every segment of society." In addition, both Schwalm and Adams said the laws should remain on the books in order to keep schools from presenting information about homosexuality and to prevent same-sex marriages and adoptions. Schwalm claimed that the laws "have never created 'sex police' in private bedrooms," but have been used to "keep homosexual curricula out of schools" and "to prevent homosexuals from acquiring children."

Houston: Anti-discrimination executive order

Houston Mayor Lee Brown was sued by a Houston City Council member and a conservative businessman after he signed an executive order prohibiting discrimination against lesbians and gay men in city government. Council member Rob Todd and conservative activist Richard Hotze claimed that Brown lacked the power to add sexual orientation to the city's existing law. Their lawyer also called the executive order a "slap in the face of democracy," claiming that it illegally reversed a 1985 referendum that overturned a similar measure passed by the city council in 1984.

Both Todd and Hotze claimed that the content of the executive order was not their reason for suing. However, Hotze and his family were heavily involved in the 1985 campaign to overturn the original 1984 measure, organizing a "straight slate" of candidates to oppose the city council's passage of the anti-discrimination ordinance. Hotze is a force in city politics, largely through his group Conservative Republicans of Harris County, and he believes that government should be limited to "God-ordained duties." Todd joined the suit at Hotze's request and had already come out against adding sexual orientation to the anti-discrimination ordinance. The head of the Houston Gay and Lesbian Political Caucus noted that "in all the years [Hotze] has been involved in politics in Houston, he has never questioned the mayor's right to issue executive orders until it comes down to employment equality for gay city employees."

A state district court judge ruled that the mayor did not have the power to issue the executive order, but also ruled that only Todd had standing to file the suit. A panel of appeals court judges heard the case in September; but no decision has been issued as of publication.

San Antonio: Anti-discrimination ordinance

In the face of intense lobbying by Religious Right activists, the San Antonio City Council stopped short of voting on a proposal to include sexual orientation in the city's nondiscrimination policy. A council member had proposed the measure after members of local and national gay rights groups asked him to do so, but he withdrew the measure shortly before a city council meeting when it became clear that he lacked the votes to pass it.

Although the item was pulled from the agenda, the council allowed protesters to speak on the issue. One speaker from Choose Life Ministries said, "There are a few reasons why we should discriminate against homosexuals. The number one reason is God. He says it's wrong." The Religious Right activists and their supporters on the council made an unsuccessful attempt to bring the measure up for a vote after it had been pulled, a possible violation of Texas' Open Meetings Act that a local newspaper columnist called "a clear case of trying to rub the faces of the defeated into the dirt." A spokesman for the protesters called the evening "a victory for God."

The protesters were spurred on by the broadcasts of a local Christian radio host, television and radio ads run by fundamentalist churches, and by e-mail and other alerts from the local Christian Coalition, the Texas Christian Alert Network and the Christian Family Network. The radio station went so far as to pitch a tent outside city hall. Adam McManus, the talk show host who made the proposal a daily topic of his show, said, "Are we next going to protect pedophiles and bestiality?"

San Antonio: Arts funding

The Esperanza Peace and Justice Center, sponsor of a local gay and lesbian film festival, is suing the city of San Antonio for violating the First Amendment when it cut off the center's funding in 1997 following a campaign against the center by Religious Right organizations including the Bexar County Christian Coalition and the Christian Pro-Life Foundation. The lead attorney for Esperanza stated, "The city allowed prejudice and favoritism to influence their arts funding decision and that violates the United States Constitution." The suit alleges that the City Council gave in to pressure from the right-wing groups who called the center's work "anti-family values," "pro-homosexual" and "pro-abortion."

> "Homosexual behavior is criminal in Texas.... it's bad for the individual and bad for society, like drug use."
>
> — Allan Parker, president of the Texas Justice Foundation, criticizing a San Antonio high school for allowing same-sex couples at its prom.

While the mayor and City Council members claimed that the overall reduction of arts funding was necessary to provide other city services, Esperanza was the sole arts organization to have all of its funding cut; other organizations received cuts of up to 15 percent. Although the local Department of Arts and Cultural Affairs had rated Esperanza as the most qualified of the arts funding candidates, the mayor criticized Esperanza as being a political, not artistic, organization. He said, "They seem to go way beyond what people want their money spent on. That group flaunts what it does, it is an in-your-face organization. They are doing this to themselves." More than 25 organizations dedicated to the arts and civil liberties signed a statement in support of Esperanza. It read, in part, "Cultural funding must not be used to endorse a single culture or to penalize disfavored political viewpoints." The suit is scheduled to be heard in federal court in October 1999.

San Antonio: Homophobic article

After attending a sensitivity training class about homophobia, a local police officer published an article in the magazine of the San Antonio Police Officer's Association condemning homosexuality, causing concern in the city's gay and lesbian community. The officer wrote, "presumably someone at City Hall, the police department or the federal government is pushing the homosexual agenda on us." Citing numerous verses from the Bible, the officer said, "It seems as though the homosexual community's agenda is to throw out as much filth as possible and eventually we will get to the point where it will just be accepted as common practice. Well it is wrong. It's still wrong in the Bible. Jesus still hates it."

> "The city allowed prejudice and favoritism to influence their arts funding decision."
>
> — The attorney for Esperanza Peace and Justice Center, which sued San Antonio for cutting off its funding. Esperanza sponsors a gay and lesbian film festival.

Lesbian and gay rights leaders expressed disappointment and police officials quickly pointed out that the opinion piece did not reflect any official position. The police association's president said, "We don't want the city's gay and lesbian community to think we condone the article. In fact, we've had several officers who called and complained about it being published." The article's message of intolerance was magnified by the fact that it came on the heels of the stabbing of a gay man that was considered a hate crime by police. A month later, police officers met with concerned members of the gay community in hopes of further easing tension between the two groups.

San Antonio: School prom

A San Antonio high school's policy of allowing only opposite-sex couples to attend the senior prom was successfully challenged by two female students this year, drawing fire from a Religious Right organization. Marshall High School's principal explained that the policy was instituted because of previous problems with groups of boys who came alone and flirted with the dates of other boys. "We never had an intention to discriminate against anybody," he said. After meeting with class leaders, the policy was changed to allow a senior to buy two tickets and take the person of his or her choice.

Allan Parker, the president of the right-wing Texas Justice Foundation, lambasted this solution, saying "[t]eachers and counselors at the school should be steering children toward a healthy choice." He further explained, "Homosexual behavior is criminal in Texas. It's criminal because it's bad for the individual and bad for society, like drug use. Homosexuals have a much shorter life span, because it is an unhealthy lifestyle."

Wichita Falls: Book controversy

Two children's books that were held hostage by a local minister and began a city-wide controversy are once again accessible in the children's section of the Wichita Falls public library. The library had purchased the books, "Heather Has Two Mommies" and "Daddy's Roommate," in response to patron requests for reading materials that discuss gay and lesbian parents in a "tasteful, positive light." Rev. Robert Jeffress, pastor of the First Baptist Church, who began the fight to have the books removed, explained his objection: "We object to sodomy because it is against the law, and is responsible for the greatest epidemic in history. AIDS is a gay disease that has spilled over into our society." He decided that the only way to keep the books out of young hands would be to keep them himself. He later wrote a check for $54 to pay for the books and for the fines incurred, arguing that keeping the books was a form of civil disobedience to protest the spending of tax dollars on "filthy" books.

The Wichita Falls Times Record News editorialized against Rev. Jeffress' actions, prompting him to preach about the controversy in his Sunday sermons, which are also televised on a local station. He compared banning the books with censoring material on pedophilia and the censorship of cigarette advertising: "What's the difference between that ad censorship and a lifestyle that kills tens of thousands of people?" He also predicted the City Council would face defeat in the next election unless it removed the books from the library. Rev. Jeffress then asked members of his congregation who would pledge to write letters in support of the books' removal to raise their hands, reminding them, "You can't lie in church." Eventually, a vote was held among the deacons at his church to request that the City Council remove all books from the library that "promote and/or sanction homosexual behavior." The Wichita Falls City Council does not have the power to order the library adviser to remove materials from the library's collection, although it could institute a policy defining acceptable reading materials for the library.

Another pastor, who claimed that God pronounced the death penalty on gay men and lesbians, eventually lodged a formal protest against the books. This required the Library Review Board to review the books and make a formal recommendation to Library Administrator Linda Hughes as to what should be done. During the review process, Jeffress said he would revise his original request to have the books removed from the library outright, and would accept a "compromise" in which the books could be kept in an adult-restricted area or behind an employee's desk. However, Hughes made it clear that these were not options she would consider, as she felt that it would unreasonably compromise the privacy of those who wished to look at the books.

The board's decision was announced at a meeting attended by about 90 citizens. The meeting was reportedly marked by shouts and grumbles from the crowd; one woman even had to be escorted to her seat by a police officer after she took the floor out of turn. At the beginning of the meeting, there was a 15-minute period of public testimony on the books. The majority of the board voted to leave "Daddy's Roommate" in the children's section and recommended moving "Heather Has Two Mommies" to the juvenile section which is intended for older children, or to the adult bookshelf because it discusses artificial insemination. Two of the nine board members supported leaving "Heather..." on the children's bookshelf. After the vote, one board member defended her votes to keep the books, saying, "I am a mother. I am a grandmother and a great-grandmother. I feel I can help my children understand the lifestyles of other people. And, may I say, I am a Christian. Believe it or not, I am." Hughes' final decision was to move both books to the juvenile section. She explained that moving the books to the adult section would invite children to search among other adult titles. Ironically, the effort to remove the books had resulted in an increase in copies being made available to the public. The library was swamped with requests for the books, which meant that according to policy, more copies had to be purchased. In addition, citizens supportive of the two books donated 22 copies of each. Rev. Nancy Horvath, an openly gay citizen that vocally opposed Rev. Jeffress, said that the press coverage had opened people's eyes to the gay men and lesbians in the community. Horvath, who is minister of the Metropolitan Community Church, a church that ministers primarily to gays, said, "[The church has] been here 11 ´ years, and the community doesn't know it. I would say we have probably gained people [because of the controversy]."

In response to Hughes' decision, Jeffress asked his congregation to "vote out the infidels who would deny God and his word," challenging City Council members to step in and remove the books from the library. In February 1999, after months of debate and several proposals, the council voted 4-3 to adopt a policy whereby a children's book could be moved to the adult section if 300 library card holders signed a petition saying that they had read the book and objected to having it in the children's section. Petitions were filed, and the books were moved to the adult section. On July 20, however, the books were returned to the children's section, at least temporarily, after 19 residents represented by the American Civil Liberties Union sued the city, asserting that the policy and the petitions violated their First Amendment rights. As of publication, the hearing on the challenge to the policy had not occurred.

Statewide: Same-sex marriage

Gov. Mike Leavitt and Attorney General Jan Graham clashed over joining an *amicus curiae* brief urging the Vermont Supreme Court to uphold Vermont's refusal to recognize same-sex marriages. Both Leavitt and Graham oppose same-sex marriage, but Graham believes that the federal Defense of Marriage Act is sufficient to protect Utah's prohibition of same-sex marriage. Central to the controversy is Lynn Wardle, author of the *amicus* brief, co-author of Utah's 1995 law against same-sex marriage, and advocate for the Eagle Forum, the Religious Right group created by Phyllis Schlafly. Wardle called the governor's office over Graham's failure to join his brief, whereupon the governor attacked Graham's strategy as insufficient to defend Utah law against potential legal challenges from out-of-state same-sex couples. Graham wrote back to the governor that "It is only when the Eagle Forum is at your door that you have contacted me about any case. The Eagle Forum's interest makes the case 'important' to you." She also asked, "Why do you allow them to push you around?" The decision not to sign the *amicus* brief came as Utah's dominant church, the Church of Jesus Christ of Latter-day Saints, was urging church members "quietly to promote legislation that will ensure traditional marriage."

Statewide: State House election

During her campaign for state assembly, Democratic candidate Jackie Biskupski became the target of attacks by the Religious Right organization Eagle Forum and a group called Citizens for Strong Families (CSF) because she is openly lesbian. One week before the election, CSF, with the support of Utah Eagle Forum Leader Gayle Ruzicka, sent a letter "urging voters in our district not to elect a lesbian as our standard-bearer." The flier also claimed that homosexuals subvert fidelity in marriage, lure young people into becoming homosexual, and have no respect for traditional morality. Ruzicka, who helped "out" Biskupski during her 1997 bid for a seat on the Salt Lake City Council, commented, "Once we found out about it, we helped get the word out...Why wouldn't we? It is certainly our business when a candidate is committing sodomy and living a blatantly immoral lifestyle."

Earlier in the campaign, an anonymous flier threatening to expose Biskupski's 1997 campaign contributors was widely circulated. Despite the fliers and negative campaigning, Biskupski won her seat by a margin of 61 to 39 percent to become Utah's first openly gay state legislator. Reacting to Eagle Forum's actions, Biskupski's Republican opponent commented, "With people like Gayle Ruzicka involved, it almost makes me want to be a Democrat...I don't think I would have won. But she cost me about 10 points. Somehow the party has got to get a leash on her."

Provo: Middle school 'wish ceremony'

Just one week after the murder of gay University of Wyoming student Matthew Shepard, a Provo middle school student shocked his schoolmates and the community during the school's annual "wish ceremony" by wishing that "gay men be crucified on Main Street and lesbians be burned at the stake." The ceremony is part of Centennial Middle School's character education program; students are divided up into "packs" of 20, and members of each pack pick a wish they all agree on and a representative to read it. The principal suspended the student for three days and showed a school-produced video on tolerance and encouraged discussion of the statement. Gayle Ruzicka, head of the Utah chapter of

Phyllis Schlafly's Eagle Forum, said she did not think that speaking out against homosexuality creates hatred or intolerance. "It's our obligation to speak out on immorality...I don't think that causes hate. It's the in-your-face politics and attitudes of a handful of militant homosexuals that makes people mad." While some commended the principal for his swift action, the student who reported the incident suggested the school was more worried about "damage control" than promoting acceptance or condemning homophobia, noting that the principal misrepresented her mother and her to the media as being motivated by the desire for publicity.

Salt Lake City: Anti-discrimination ordinance

The Salt Lake City Council voted in January to repeal the city's one-month-old anti-discrimination ordinance, because it included the term "sexual orientation." The ordinance had passed in December 1997 despite lobbying by prominent Christian right leaders such as Utah Eagle Forum President Gayle Ruzicka, who told council members that she and her organization were concerned that their children could come into contact with gay city employees in schools, parks, and city swimming pools. One University of Utah professor testified that "Homosexuality is a perversion. It will always be an abomination before God."

Central to the repeal effort was Councilman Bryce Jolley, who argued that the law unfairly singled out gay men and lesbians for protections that should be extended to everyone. Further, he claimed there was no evidence that a discrimination problem against gay and lesbian city employees existed, calling the ordinance a political gesture to placate the gay and lesbian community.

Although Jolley said "a person's personal life is their business" and that no employee should be discriminated against, his critics pointed to a list of questions on the ordinance he sent to legal experts as proof of his bias. Among the questions are: "Should the city clarify that it believes it is in the best interest of society that sexual relations occur only between persons who are lawfully married?" and "Would it be helpful to establish a program for city youth to encourage them to resist and overcome homosexual orientation?"

In the months following the ordinance's repeal, the city council passed a scaled-down version of the ordinance that requires employment decisions to be based on "job-related criteria" and specifically defines "the status of having a lifestyle which is irrelevant to successful job performance" and "the status of being in or outside of an adult interpersonal relationship or a family relationship" as not being job-related criteria. "I have to call this the beat-around-the-bush ordinance," said Councilwoman Deeda Seed, who helped push through the original ordinance. "The goal for some [council members] is not to say 'sexual orientation,' and it doesn't say it." Also disappointed with the compromise was Councilwoman Joanne Milner, who said, "We're hedging. We are not addressing a lifestyle. We're talking about discrimination."

Salt Lake City: Student clubs

Protests over a presentation by the Gay/Straight Alliance at East High School's multicultural assembly marked the latest episode in a controversy that has received national attention since 1996, when the Salt Lake City School Board voted to ban all extra-curricular school-sponsored clubs rather than permit students to form a Gay/Straight Alliance.

Approved by the school's principal, the presentation prompted an investigation by the district and a proposal to limit future multicultural assemblies to ethnicity or geographically defined groups. Protesters claimed the presentation indoctrinated their children in the homosexual lifestyle without their consent. "This is propaganda," declared one parent from the right-wing America Forever Foundation, which has threatened to sue. "Most parents don't understand that this is the tip of the iceberg." East High Principal Kay Peterson defended his position, saying, "I see people stand up and dodge bullets and not take responsibility. You're not going to see a man here do that. If anyone's to blame, look right here...[I did] what I felt at the time was legal and right."

This latest controversy came in the midst of a lawsuit brought by the Utah and Northern California ACLU chapters, Lambda Legal Defense and Education Fund and the National Center for Lesbian Rights on behalf of Gay/Straight Alliance members and East High students Ivy Fox and Keysha Barnes and their parents. The lawsuit was filed after the school board eliminated all 46 extra-curricular clubs in 1996 rather than grant the Gay/Straight Alliance's 1995 application for club status. The board acted in response to pressure from the Utah chapter of Phyllis Schlafly's Eagle Forum, which called on schools to ban all clubs rather than allow gay and lesbian student organizations to exist. The school board decision also precipitated state legislation requiring school boards to prohibit student organizations that involve human sexuality.

> "It is only when the Eagle Forum is at your door that you have contacted me about any case.... Why do you allow them to push you around?"
>
> — Utah Attorney General Jan Graham, in a letter to Gov. Mike Leavitt. After being lobbied by Phyllis Schlafly's Eagle Forum, Leavitt had asked Graham to join an *amicus* brief urging the Vermont Supreme Court to uphold that state's ban on same-sex marriages.

Filed in March 1998, the federal lawsuit claims that the Salt Lake City School Board discriminated against certain clubs by permitting some extra-curricular clubs to meet, such as the Future Business Leaders of America and Future Homemakers of America, while excluding such groups as the Young Democrats and Young Republicans, Students Against Drunk Driving, an environmental club, Polynesian Pride, the Star Wars Club and the Gay/Straight Alliance.

In November 1998, U.S. District Senior Judge Bruce Jenkins declined plaintiffs' motion for a preliminary injunction that would have allowed the Alliance members to use the public address system, post meeting notices and conduct outreach while their case was pending. He also ruled that school board members' motivations in banning the clubs may not be considered at trial as that would represent an unnecessary judicial intrusion into legislative autonomy. Since the plaintiffs are barred from proving an intent to discriminate, the Gay/Straight Alliance now must prove discriminatory harm. An earlier attempt at mediation between the Alliance and the Salt Lake City School Board failed to resolve the issue. In March 1999, the plaintiffs filed a motion for partial summary judgment on the Equal Access Act and First Amendment claims. A hearing on the motions took place on April 16, 1999. As of publication, the court has not issued a decision.

Spanish Fork: Lesbian high school teacher

In Spanish Fork, a group called Citizens of the Nebo School District for Moral and Legal Values wants to take its battle against a lesbian teacher to the Utah Supreme Court. The plaintiffs claim that veteran psychology teacher and coach Wendy Weaver is morally unfit to teach because she is a lesbian. The battle began in 1997, when Weaver was forced by the school district to sign an order that prohibited her from discussing her sexual orientation with anyone in the school community and removed her as coach of the girls' volleyball team. Weaver successfully sued the district for violating her constitutional rights of free speech and equal protection. A U.S. District Court judge awarded her damages and ordered the school district to rehire her for the coaching position; citing family reasons, Weaver declined to return to Spanish Fork High School as a coach.

"It's in the Bible — homos should die."

— A sign outside the courthouse where a lawsuit against gay Utah teacher Wendy Weaver was being heard. The protest was held by the America Forever Foundation.

Citizens of the Nebo School District for Moral and Legal Values then sued Weaver, claiming she was morally unfit to teach and that she had violated state law and teacher certification requirements. The judge dismissed these claims. However, he let stand two students' claims: one student objected to Weaver's characterization of a Mormon tradition as social rather than religious and to Weaver's suggestion that her then-husband read books besides the Book of Mormon to their children. A second student claimed her personal and religious rights were violated because she would not have undressed in the locker room in Weaver's presence had she known that Weaver was a lesbian. Lawyers for both the citizens group and Weaver have asked the judge to dismiss both counts, in the plaintiffs' case because they want a "clean" appeal to the Utah Supreme Court. Matthew Hilton, the plaintiffs' lawyer, is most interested in arguing the seven dismissed counts. Hilton stated that the suit does not focus on Weaver's lesbianism, but rather her alleged unlawful use of psychology tests in her psychology class. However, three of the seven dismissed counts claim that Weaver's lesbianism violated Utah's teacher certification requirements because Weaver may be in violation of the state's sodomy law by living with her partner.

Conservative voices in the state have responded to the controversy in various ways. The Utah chapter of Phyllis Schlafly's Eagle Forum laid the groundwork in pushing the legislature to enact three laws — the 1993 Constitutional Freedom in the Schools Act, the 1994 Family Education and Privacy Rights Act, and the 1996 Responsibilities of School Employees and Limitations Regarding School Clubs Act — that are key in the lawsuit against Weaver. A newly formed group called the America Forever Foundation organized anti-gay demonstrations at the courthouse. One court protester expressed his opposition with a sign reading "It's in the Bible — homos should die." And on the legislative front, state Rep. Bill Wright (R) announced that he will introduce a bill to strike down or weaken compulsory education laws now that a federal judge has ruled in Weaver's favor.

A personal essay by Wendy Weaver appears on p. 44 of this book.

VERMONT

Statewide: Same-sex marriage

In 1997, three same-sex couples sued their respective town clerks for refusing to grant them marriage licenses, challenging a 1975 ruling by the state's attorney general advising town clerks that state law defined civil marriage as between a "husband" and "wife." Chittenden Superior Court Judge Linda Levitt ruled that there was no fundamental right to same-sex marriage and that gay men and lesbians were not being discriminated against. The six plaintiffs then appealed to the Vermont Supreme Court, which heard the case on Nov. 18. The plaintiffs assert that aside from the fundamental right to marry, they are also being denied the protections, obligations and benefits that go along with civil marriage. They rely principally on the state's "common benefits clause" which states, in part, "[G]overnment is, or ought to be, instituted for the common benefit, protection, and security of the people, nation, or community, and not for the particular emolument or advantage of any ... set of persons," arguing that the state has to show that "legitimate purposes" are served by limiting marriage to opposite-sex couples.

During oral arguments, the plaintiffs stated that the current ban on same-sex marriage is strikingly similar to the former ban on interracial marriage-while it may be socially accepted, it is not just. The state argued that prohibiting gay and lesbian couples from marrying is essential to "supporting marriage and protecting it from potentially destabilizing forces" as it could lead to cases where two brothers could marry. The state also asserted that marriage is "a unique social institution based on the sexual communion of a man and a woman" aimed at providing stable homes for children and that "[t]o say [otherwise] would be to say there's absolutely no connection between marriage and procreation." However, the attorney for the plaintiffs countered that "[i]f the state's concern is about protecting children, then that would be protected by allowing these couples to marry," noting that two of the three couples who brought the suit had adopted children. In addition, one of the judges on the panel suggested that with advances in medical technology, same-sex couples could eventually be able to procreate, and if so, then by the state's argument, it would advocate same-sex marriage. And the procreation argument also suggests that marriage be limited only to heterosexual couples who can, or plan to, procreate — so sterile people or octogenarians would be excluded.

The state also denied that any discrimination was taking place. Although the state's lawyers conceded that the right to marry was indeed a fundamental right, they claimed that it was only the right to marry someone of the opposite sex. "There's no benefit given to males that isn't given to females," argued the assistant attorney general. One of the five justices on the panel, however, inquired, "Why isn't that gender discrimination? A man can't marry a man because he is a man." As of publication, the court has not issued a ruling in the case.

Take it to the People (TiP), an organization that wants to "preserve traditional marriage," vowed even before the hearing to push the legislature to change Vermont law to guarantee that same-sex marriage could not be legalized, or to let voters decide the issue via a ballot initiative. The earliest possible date for such an initiative, however, would be in 2000. TiP President Mary Schroyer explained her reasons for opposing allowing gay and lesbian couples to marry: "Homosexuals want to change the definition of marriage. It's not a matter of being loving and committed. It's setting the best example for our children that we can."

Henrico County: Child custody battle

In Henrico County, known for a 1995 court decision that separated a mother and her son solely because the mother was a lesbian, a lesbian mother was awarded continued custody of her two children in July. Judge Sharon Breeden Will had pledged from the start to view the case like any other custody battle, despite a 1995 Virginia Supreme Court ruling affirming that judges can consider sexual orientation as a factor in custody cases. The children, aged 6 and 8, had been living with their mother since 1996 when her divorce from her husband became final. The two parents agreed to a friendly visitation policy, and all was well until the fall of 1997, when the ex-husband filed for full custody based on his claim that the mother's relationship with her female partner, with whom she lived, would hurt the children. After reviewing the evidence, Judge Will found that it would be in the best interests of the children to remain with their mother and her partner.

Lynchburg: Phelps protests Falwell

Rev. Fred Phelps of Topeka, Kansas, brought about 12 of his followers to Lynchburg in November to denounce Rev. Jerry Falwell for being too soft on gays. Phelps has picketed all across the country to share his message. "God hates fags," he said. "That's a profound theological statement. This nation needs to hear more of that, more than it needs oxygen and bread." Phelps had decided to target Falwell, the founder of the now-defunct Moral Majority, who is normally not considered a friend of gay men and lesbians, because Falwell had criticized Phelps' protesting at Matthew Shepard's funeral. Falwell had also said that God loves everyone, even homosexuals, which

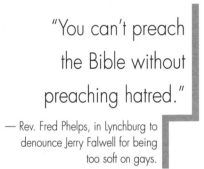

"You can't preach the Bible without preaching hatred."

— Rev. Fred Phelps, in Lynchburg to denounce Jerry Falwell for being too soft on gays.

Phelps said made him a heretic. He said, "We're just preaching the Bible — and not this kissy-pooh stuff Falwell is putting out. You can't preach the Bible without preaching hatred." Falwell ignored the protest as best he could, but commented, "Even the most unenlightened believe that God is love..."

Richmond: Newspaper rejects ad

The Richmond Times Dispatch refused to run an ad by the Richmond Organization for Sexual Minority Youth (ROSMY) promoting scholarships for gay, lesbian, bisexual and transgendered youth. The ad in question read: "College scholarships for gay, lesbian, bisexual, transgendered youth age 21 and under apply to Richmond Organization for Sexual Minority Youth (ROSMY) 804-355-1699." The Times Dispatch would not give a specific reason for refusing to run the ad, but said that it was entitled to refuse any advertisement that could be "objectionable, questionable, or controversial" to its readers. When a reporter from the GLBT publication Our Own asked for a copy of the newspaper's gay-related advertising policy, Times Dispatch President Albert August told him, "You're on your own there, bud."

Suffolk: Gay man barred from church

In April, Rodney Clements' membership at Nansemond River Baptist Church in Suffolk was revoked because he is gay. Clements had recently been featured in a Port Folio Weekly article about the female impersonation show that he co-owns with his partner, Carlton Greene. Timothy L. Piland, the Senior Pastor at Nansemond Baptist, read the article and immediately sent a letter to Clements informing him that the church had met and unanimously agreed to expel him. The letter said that because Christians are to "abstain from all appearance of evil," he could no longer be associated in any way with the church, although it was understood that he had not been involved in the church for years. The letter went on to say that Piland was acting out of love and that he urged Clements to repent and cease to be homosexual, which would allow the church to welcome him once again. Clements wrote a letter to a local newspaper to respond to Piland. He wrote, in part, "whether you are straight, gay, or bisexual, God created us all. And as long as we are living productive lives, monogamous relationships, giving back to our communities, supporting positive ventures, working hard, paying bills, striving for sound principles, treating people with respect, and sharing real love (not the fake stuff) — then God is pleased. God accepts us — all of us."

WASHINGTON

Statewide: American Baptist Church NW

The American Baptist Churches of the Northwest, part of the 1.5 million-member American Baptist Church (ABC), voted in May to adopt a resolution proclaiming that homosexuality is inconsistent with Christian teachings. However, separate resolutions that would have declared that the church only supports sexual relationships composed of "one man and one woman in a monogamous marriage relationship," and allowed the church to dismiss congregations that do not conform to this principle, were withdrawn. Two Seattle American Baptist churches were at the center of the debate. Seattle First Baptist and University Baptist are "welcoming and affirming" churches that welcome gay, lesbian and bisexual members and clergy and support the affirmation of gay and lesbian same-sex relationships as well as other gay rights issues. The two churches were targeted by an ABC-Northwest pastor who wanted to create a procedure that would allow the Northwest Baptists to expel the churches for not adhering to the Scripture in their teachings. The pastor withdrew his requests after the broad resolution was adopted. ABC is generally more open to different interpretations of the Bible and Christian faith than its more conservative counterpart, the Southern Baptist Convention. ABC also believes in local autonomy for individual churches. For these reasons, ABC did not take action to reprimand or dismiss Seattle First Baptist and University Baptist. University Baptist's gay co-pastor, the Rev. Tim Phillips, said, "People are afraid of either homosexuals themselves or what homosexuality means. But I can't help but believe if Jesus were here now, he would be most present to people like me who were most excluded from the church."

Statewide: Metcalf-Cammermeyer House race

In the race for 2nd District U.S. Representative, incumbent Rep. Jack Metcalf (R) made homophobic statements about his Democratic opponent, retired colonel and former Army National Guard nurse Grethe Cammermeyer, who is a lesbian. Cammermeyer was discharged from the military in 1992 after she revealed her sexual orientation. In 1994, after a bitter court fight, she won back her position. In a fundraising mailing, Metcalf charged that Cammermeyer was "the Lesbian Army National Guard colonel who was recruited by the Democratic Congressional Campaign Committee, especially ultraliberal Rep. Barney Frank, to move into our district and run against me." He also referred to her as a "spokesperson from the Lesbian lifestyle" and said that because she was his opponent, the race had become a "life and death struggle for the spiritual and cultural heritage and future of our country." In addition, Metcalf insinuated that a re-broadcasting of the film "Serving in Silence: The Margarethe Cammermeyer Story," was a political ploy to boost Cammermeyer's campaign. NBC executives asked Seattle affiliate KONG-TV not to air the movie, citing the fact that Cammermeyer was running for Congress. A Metcalf campaign spokesman noted, "It is poor judgment on their part and an attempt to manipulate the political process." He offered no evidence that Cammermeyer was behind the programming decision, but said that Glenn Close and Barbra Streisand, who produced the made-for-TV movie, had contributed money to Cammermeyer's campaign.

The Washington State Labor Coalition, the state's primary labor umbrella group, voted not to endorse Metcalf because of the anti-gay statements he had made against Cammermeyer. Metcalf did have the support of Christian Right organizations; he has always scored more than 80 percent on the Christian Coalition's candidate scorecards. After winning their respective primaries, Metcalf and Cammermeyer signed a "code of campaign conduct" in which they promised not to vilify each other. Cammermeyer lost the race to Metcalf in November, 45 percent to 55 percent.

Statewide: Same-sex marriage

In January, state legislative Republicans gave Democrats an ultimatum: either pass a ban on same-sex marriages in the legislature or the measure would become a ballot initiative. The Defense of Marriage Act (DOMA)'s sponsor, Republican Rep. Bill Thompson of Everett, explained his reason for supporting the bill: "Homosexuality is not a lifestyle; it is a death-style." Republicans claimed to have enough votes to pass the bill but feared a veto by Democratic Gov. Gary Locke. Many opponents of the bill feared that a ballot initiative could be divisive to the state and unduly expensive. Openly gay Rep. Ed Murray (D) commented, "My personal opinion is that a ballot measure will be a disaster for this community." The Legal Marriage Alliance, which also opposes DOMA, urged Locke to veto the bill, and its director John Wilkinson said, "We ask the governor to continue to support all families and to oppose and veto any legislation that hinders a group of individuals from the fundamental right of civil marriage." The bill passed in early February. Locke vetoed the bill as promised, but veto was overridden in both the House and Senate on votes of 65-28 and 34-11, respectively. Locke said, "No governor likes to have a veto overridden. But at least this issue does not go to the ballot. I did not want a divisive, bitter campaign. I did not want contributing members of our society vilified or used for false fears and scapegoating."

Statewide: University diversity program

Washington State University officials canceled a June conference on issues facing gay and lesbian youth because they said they could not "provide a safe and supportive environment" for the attendees. Another reason for canceling WSU's We Are Family II Camp Queer conference may have been pressure from the Washington State Legislature's Conservative Caucus, which has worked closely with the Religious Right group Christian Alert Network on other issues. The Conservative Caucus threatened to withhold funding for WSU if it did not cancel what the caucus labeled an effort at "homosexual recruitment." One e-mail announcement for the event that said organizers were hoping for a large turnout was used by conservative Republican state legislators, including Sen. Val Stevens, as evidence "that recruitment of children into the lifestyle was central to the homosexual agenda." Rep. Marc Boldt (R) asked, "What will the university's position be if an AIDS-free child goes there, only to return HIV infected?" Sen. Harold Hochstatter (R) said he considered it to be WSU's official promotion of a "lethal lifestyle," and Rep. Bob Sump (R) chided WSU for "inviting children to the university for a public celebration of immorality," saying he anticipated the "opportunity next legislative session to trim away" WSU's budget. Sump also said he planned to use his powers in the State House to defund WSU's Gay/Lesbian/Bisexual/Alliance (GLBA) because it helped organize the event and was a "recruitment center" for gay youth.

Despite conservatives' calls for budget cuts at WSU, Melynda Huskey, the director of the GLBA, noted that no state monies were used to fund the event, which was financed by a grant from the Pride Foundation, other private donors, and attendees' conference fees. The anti-gay Christian Alert Network sent out an alert urging its members to protect their children from "sodomite aggression" like this conference. The alert told parents: "GET YOUR CHILDREN OUT OF THE GOVERNMENT SCHOOLS!" Huskey said the decision to cancel the conference was made out of fear that attendees might have faced threat of or actual violence by attending. She said, "We were getting phone calls and letters from paramilitary groups, from Exodus International, Operation Rescue, and so forth." Her response to the notion that a purpose of the conference was "homosexual recruitment" was, "I don't know how to make someone gay and I don't know anyone else who does either."

Statewide: Student harassment

A "safe schools" bill to help foster a learning environment free from harassment was killed in committee. The bill would have required the Superintendent of Public Instruction to devise criteria for implementing policies that help create such an environment, which schools would then discuss with students and train school employees to enforce. HB 2271, sponsored by openly gay state Rep. Ed Murray, would have covered all students, including gay men and lesbians. The Safe Schools Coalition, which supported the bill, cited numerous cases of harassment and violence against gay and lesbian students, from name-calling to gang rape. The coalition said a law was needed because teachers and school administrators had been blind to these cases of anti-gay student harassment. Said Murray, "This bill is for the numerous high school students I hear from who are beat up and harassed because they're gay or lesbian. We've got to stop it. This bill builds on our anti-harassment law and says that we will not tolerate it in our schools either." House leaders told Murray that his bill would not even be considered and Republican House Education Committee Chair Rep. Peggy Johnson refused to hear the bill. Murray said he would reintroduce the bill in the next session.

Seattle: Discussion of homosexuality in schools

A well-known Seattle anti-gay advocate has taken on a new crusade in her fight to protect Seattle's children from what she calls a "homosexual menace": the Internet. Linda Jordan claims she is focusing her attention on homosexual pornography on the Internet because "I think there is a double standard. There is no heterosexual pornography on the Internet and yet they justify homosexual pornography." Jordan made her mark as a member of Parents and Teachers for Responsible Schools, a conservative group that opposed a private donation of funds last year to Seattle area public schools. The donation was intended for the purchase of children's books, such as "Heather Has Two Mommies" and "Daddy's Roommate," that depicted gay families in a positive way. The grants were eventually accepted, and the furor died down.

> "I challenge the diversity platform.... I don't believe in a 'live and let live' mentality."
>
> — Rob Taylor, director of the "ex-gay" Metanoia Ministries, at a Seattle event protesting gay city officials.

Jordan continues to pursue her goal of eliminating any discussion or depiction of homosexuality in public schools, and says: "I don't think homosexuality should be addressed at all in elementary school because I don't think it is age appropriate. If it is discussed, then I think both sides should be represented, which is that some people think homosexuality is immoral from a religious point of view and others think it is dangerous physically because a lot of people die at a young age from engaging in homosexuality. You cannot talk about gay issues without talking about sexual desire and sex and that's not appropriate." Jordan claims that the school district and public officials are exposing schoolchildren to child pornography and homosexual pornography on the Internet, and that city officials are either derelict in their duties or co-conspirators against these children. She has issued a number of press releases charging various city officials with usurping parental rights by "abusing the public school classroom in order to legitimize same-sex intercourse in the minds of other people's children."

Jordan also wrote to the newly inaugurated mayor of Seattle to alert him to pornography she had found on the Internet. She then went on to imply that city council member

Tina Podlodowski, whose partner works for PlanetOut, a gay youth website, was somehow linked to "hardcore pornography and pornographic stories depicting sadomasochism, incest, and some pedophilia." She also contacted Podlodowski directly to "inform [her] about King County and the City of Seattle's affiliation with, and tacit endorsement of, organizations and businesses that produce or affirm homosexual pornography ." Both the mayor and Podlodowski replied to the letters, reaffirming their own commitment to responsible use of the Internet. The council member also expressed her concern as a parent: "As a mother whose children will likely have more Internet interactions than even I can imagine, I share your concerns regarding seemingly benign links from what I as a parent might consider acceptable sites . I should emphasize that there are many painfully closeted gays and lesbians, both young and adult, who find empowering information through the Internet and through libraries. Yes, there are also sites and books you and I might find unsuitable for our children. I think that one of the best ways a parent can help a child is to teach a strong sense of self-worth and an ethic that says exploitation is wrong."

Seattle: Anti-gay coalition

A coalition of anti-gay organizations staged a "brown bag" luncheon rally at the Dome Room in Seattle's Arctic Building to protest the gay civil rights movement and gay city officials. Among the groups that attended were the Crusade for Traditional Family Values, Operation Rescue, Metanoia Ministries and Ex-Homosexuals. Only ten representatives of these groups attended the meeting, exhibiting tremendous hostility toward gay men and lesbians. Their particular target was lesbian Seattle City Councilwoman Tina Podlodowski, who has championed gay and lesbian civil rights. Podlodowski attended the event, as did about 40 gay and lesbian city employees. The anti-gay activists in attendance tried to promote the idea that homosexuality is simply a lifestyle choice, that most Americans oppose gay and lesbian civil rights, and that homosexuals must recruit new gays and lesbians to swell their ranks in society because they cannot have children.

Podlodowski, a mother of two, countered the anti-gay rhetoric and defended the need for civil rights protections. The literature the anti-gay groups distributed was especially vitriolic. One Operation Rescue flier read, "A dark cloud is gathering, casting a foreboding shadow over the Land of Liberty. The Gay community has openly declared war on American culture... The truth is that Biblical Christianity cannot coexist, tolerate, or condone homosexuality. To do so is to invite the wrath of God upon America . If the homosexual agenda prevails, this nation will be forced to outlaw and prosecute Christians." The main speaker at the meeting was Rob Taylor, the director of Metanoia Ministries, a group aimed at converting gay men and lesbians to heterosexuality. Taylor says he is an ex-homosexual. He attributes what he calls his former sexual orientation to being molested by an uncle and being too attached to his mother after his parents divorced. He told the small audience, "My reason for being here today is not about diversity. I challenge the diversity platform. I don't believe in a 'live and let live' mentality. I am here to defend the belief that a person does not have to be gay, it is a choice."

Seattle: PFLAG ads vandalized

Ads from a city-wide campaign of the Seattle chapter of Parents, Families and Friends of Lesbians and Gays (PFLAG) was "the most vandalized Metro transit ad in recent memory," according to the group. The ads appeared on 34 Metro Transit Buses that run in the Capitol Hill and University District neighborhoods starting in June as part of Gay Pride Month. According to a PFLAG press release, "the campaign aims to bring an uplifting and supportive message to troubled families and their children, while spreading the word about the role PFLAG can play in easing those troubles." One ad read, "We Love Our Kids Just the Way They Are It's OK To Be Gay," and pictured of a group of people representing the benefits of PFLAG involvement for families and their children. The other ad read, "When Your Mom Says It's OK, But She Doesn't Want to Talk About It It's OK To Be Gay," and showed a picture of a mother and son struggling to talk with one another. During the first 10 days of the ad campaign, six bus ads were defaced, costing PFLAG $400 to print replacement ads. Tawney Collins-Feay, the co-president of Seattle PFLAG, lamented, "Apparently there is some truth to recent polls which show that gays and lesbians are the most hated group in America. But those polls also showed that things are getting better every day, and that gives us hope."

Spokane: Bills on bias, domestic partners

The Spokane City Council considered two gay and lesbian civil rights proposals this year: an anti-discrimination ordinance and a domestic partners ordinance. Both proposals received considerable opposition from the Religious Right. The domestic partners ordinance would have allowed domestic partners to register with the city. The Rev. Ron Johnson, executive director of the conservative group Citizens for Common Sense and pastor of the Indian Trail Community Church, was a leading activist in opposing both measures, gathering 4,400 signatures for a petition opposing them. Johnson says he believes people choose to be gay, and that homosexuality destroys families through promiscuity and immorality. He contended that "[gays and lesbians] should not be given equal status with legitimate, protected people by making this behavior a civil right" and that the ordinance was "clearly harmful to the individual, to the family, and to society." The city council tabled the matter without debate, and supporters of the measure accepted that it would end up in "parliamentary purgatory."

The anti-discrimination ordinance would have banned discrimination in housing, employment, and public accommodations not only on the basis of sexual orientation but also on the basis of gender identity and source of income. The city council debated the legislation for months, and opponents weighed in from several angles. Some opponents thought the ordinance would be too costly and bureaucratic for the city to enforce, while others gave overtly homophobic reasons for opposing the measure. Some realtors and landlords feared the source-of-income clause would require them to rent to unsavory clientele. The vice president of one rental association did not want her members to be obligated to rent to gay men and lesbians and stated, "Civil rights should not be given to deviant behavior." Mayor John Talbott, who had allotted an anti-gay activist 20 minutes to speak at a meeting when all other speakers were given only three minutes, said, "We're being asked at the city level to create a new, protected class. An ordinance is not the right answer at this time." Opponents of the ordinance postponed a vote on it until January 1999, when it was finally passed. The ordinance took effect in February 1999, and its opponents have mounted a campaign to overturn it.

Tacoma: Gay-bashing

Tacoma police were accused of withholding evidence of an anti-gay hate crime in Tacoma in August. Teenager Dan Dover said he was severely beaten by a group of teens who called him "faggot." Tacoma police refused to classify the incident as a hate crime, and allegedly omitted the anti-gay slurs from the police report. Dover, a heterosexual 16-year-old student at Wilson High School, was walking home from a baseball game with a friend when, he says, a carload of youths drove up alongside them. According to Dover, one of the passengers got out of the car and, when he saw Dover and his friend, called out to the people still in the car, who allegedly began shouting "fag," "faggot," and other terms at Dover. Dover says the other occupants then got out of the car and began beating him; Dover's friend ran off and escaped with no injuries. Dover was beaten unconscious and received a scar beneath his eye. Dover and his family reported the crime to the police, and three men were charged with assault. Dover and his mother, Ave Maria Dover, requested that the Tacoma police label the incident a hate crime because of the homophobic comments. Dover told the police that the teenagers had uttered the word "faggot" three times, and in his personal written statement, he also stated that their comments included "faggot." Yet when the suspects were being arraigned, Dover and his mother discovered that the homophobic words that he had cited in his statement and in his conversation with police had been removed from all documents. The Tacoma police said they had lost Dover's statement. Ms. Dover accused police of purposely omitting the information. "They still haven't found my son's statement, and are stubbornly refusing to acknowledge that my son was called a faggot during the attack. The police are just plain

> "If Jesus were here now, he would be most present to people like me who were most excluded from the church."
>
> — Seattle Rev. Tim Phillips, when the American Baptist Churches of the Northwest adopted a resolution saying homosexuality is inconsistent with Christian teachings.

lying, and I'm surprised at their boldness. I guess I thought you couldn't do this kind of thing today, because I thought we had more scrutiny of the police. It's unbelievable," she said. Ms. Dover also said that the prosecutor's office advised her not to question the police because doing so would hurt her son's case, as police would be testifying in court. However, Ms. Dover refused to back down on the family's claims against the police, saying, "Danny has said he is absolutely determined to pursue this. He said that he personally experienced what it is like to be attacked because of homophobia, and he wants other people to know what happened."

Thurston County: Anti-discrimination ordinance

Gay and lesbian rights groups in Thurston County lobbied unsuccessfully for a second year for a countywide anti-discrimination ordinance. In 1997, the groups Lavender Action and Equality Washington (formerly Hands Off Washington) urged the county Board of Commissioners to enact an ordinance protecting Thurston County gay men and lesbians from discrimination in housing, employment, government services, and public accommodations. Washington state has a law protecting gay men and lesbians from hate crimes but not from discrimination. The groups had been prompted to act when a gay entrepreneur lost his lease for his restaurant and bar, Rendezvous. The businessman said he believes this occurred because Rendezvous had a gay clientele, although the landlord claimed that financial reasons for his decision. The Board of Commissioners opposed enacting the anti-discrimination ordinance, saying the county did not have enough money to enforce it. Commissioner Judy Wilson said, "There's absolutely no reason on God's green earth to have an ordinance you cannot enforce." Commissioner Diane Oberquell added that such an ordinance "would just be a feel-good thing."

Whatcom County: GOP expels transgendered person

In March, a transgendered member of the Whatcom County Republican Party was expelled for ardently supporting Initiative 677, Washington's gay and lesbian civil rights voter initiative. Sheila Richardson, a Canadian immigrant who became a U.S. citizen in 1995, explained her involvement in the Republican Party despite the fact that the party, and particularly its local chapter in Whatcom County, is unreceptive to the gay, lesbian, bisexual and transgender communities: "I joined the Republican Party because I am a conservative person. I agree with Republican Party politics except I am fully in support of civil rights. I don't consider support for civil rights to be a political issue. It's just basic human decency."

When Whatcom County GOP member Rev. Gary Small, a local preacher and leader of the Committee to Stop Pro-Homosexual Policies, found out that Richardson was an activist in Equality Washington, a group that lobbies against anti-gay civil rights legislation and initiatives, he sponsored a resolution to expel Richardson from the Whatcom County GOP by refusing to accept Richardson's $100 membership renewal. According to Richardson, "I've never tried to hide the fact that I'm transgendered. They guessed it. They knew I was supportive of Hands Off Washington. I gathered signatures for the campaign during the past year and wrote letters to the editor supporting Initiative 677. Then in the August meeting of the Republican Party, Rev. Gary Small stood up and wanted the party to go on record as opposing Hands Off Washington. I came up off my seat and defended [the] community. So they figured it out." Two-thirds of the Whatcom GOP committee members voted to oust Richardson and to return her donation. One committee officer said, "Returning money to someone whom we know actively supports a radical homosexual group is not only the right thing to do, but it would be unethical to do otherwise." Richardson was saddened and disgusted when the Whatcom County GOP then issued a press release referring to her as a man. The 1998 Whatcom County Republican Party platform contains the following anti-gay plank: "WE FURTHER BELIEVE that the promotion of equal justice is not served by granting special privilege or protection to any group based on their sexual orientation."

WEST VIRGINIA

Statewide: Same-sex marriage

Although the state already bans same-sex marriage, a bill was introduced in the state legislature in March to also bar any recognition of same-sex marriages performed outside of the state. The proposed legislation was added by the House Judiciary Committee to a bill dealing with marriage license applications. Citing the impending ruling from the Hawaii Supreme Court, Delegate Steve Harrison (R) said, "It's very important that this be passed this year." The measure died in conference committee about a week after it was proposed.

WISCONSIN

Statewide: Tammy Baldwin House race

The race for Wisconsin's 2nd Congressional District had national implications for both gay-rights and anti-gay groups. Then-state legislator Tammy Baldwin was the first woman to run as an openly gay candidate and win a seat in the U.S. Congress. Baldwin beat her Republican opponent for an open seat with 53 percent of the vote. Though the race eventually focused on a wide range of issues, the early focus was on Baldwin's sexual orientation and on the homophobia of one of her Republican opponents, Ron Greer. Greer narrowly lost the GOP primary to a moderate Republican, Jo Musser.

During the primary, Greer sent out an inflammatory fundraising letter warning of Baldwin's "radical anti-family agenda." The letter said: "1998 could be the first time in American history that a left-wing lesbian is elected to Congress!....she's got her sights set on Washington

D.C. And believe me, they don't come any more radical than her." According to Greer, Baldwin's "radical agenda" included, "legalized homosexual marriages, government-enforced racial quotas, skyrocketing tax increases, partial birth abortions and million-dollar welfare schemes." The attack drew fire from Greer's Republican opponents, including Musser, who said, "the God I know loves everybody." Greer responded, "What I'm criticizing is her homosexual political agenda....That's something I think is fair game."

Behind Greer's candidacy was a slew of Christian right organizations. Greer's anti-gay beliefs made him a darling of the Religious Right in 1997 after he was fired by the Madison Fire Department for insubordination. The contributor list for his legal defense fund formed the base for Greer's campaign. His bid for Congress was personally endorsed by Focus on the Family's James Dobson, he consulted with the Family Research Council's Gary Bauer and had the support of local anti-abortion groups. The Baldwin campaign faced other anti-gay attacks as well. Protesters attempted to picket her announcement speech with anti-gay and anti-abortion signs, and Wisconsin Christians United promised to work against her. WCU leader Ralph Ovadal sent Baldwin a letter before she even declared her candidacy. "We certainly have no intention of sitting as quiet bystanders while you assume an office which would put you in a position of direct authority over us and our loved ones," the letter said.

After losing the GOP nomination, Greer flirted with calling for a recount and running a write-in campaign. He sought the help of national and local right-wing supporters, but decided against the campaign when he could not raise enough money. Greer was the only Republican candidate not to endorse the Republican nominee, Jo Musser, in the general election. He complained of her support for abortion rights and "lack of clarity on the homosexual agenda." Eager to get a last word on Baldwin, he told reporters that she "represents all that is dangerous to the culture." However, Greer pledged further action for two other GOP candidates in the state and said he may work for the Christian Coalition in the future on grassroots campaigns in Wisconsin.

While running for Congress, Greer was also fighting in court to be reinstituted by the fire department on the grounds that the firing violated his free speech rights. Shortly after he lost the Republican primary in September, Greer lost his bid to get his job back. In ruling against Greer's request for an injunction, the judge said that the fire department would be likely to prove its case against him.

A personal essay by Rep. Tammy Baldwin appears on p. 16 of this book.

Statewide: Reggie White's speech

Football star Reggie White, who is also an ordained Baptist minister, took on another high-profile role in 1998: acting as the Religious Right's celebrity spokesperson against homosexuality. The Green Bay Packers defensive end gained national attention for his controversial remarks in a March 25 speech in front of the Wisconsin Assembly. White's comments condemning homosexuality and detailing his beliefs on racial differences stunned lawmakers who had just given him a standing ovation. "Homosexuality is a decision, it's not a race," said White. "People from all ethnic backgrounds live in this lifestyle. But people from all ethnic backgrounds are also liars and cheaters and malicious and back-stabbing." White also said that allowing homosexuality to "run rampant" is one of the ways that the country is getting away from God. On the subject of racial differences, White told the assembly that blacks are "gifted in worship and celebration" and like to dance, and whites "were blessed with the gift of structure and organization." According to White, Hispanics' talents lie in "family structure" as "they can put 20 or 30 people in one home," and Asians have creativity and invention, "they can turn a television into a watch."

> "People from all ethnic backgrounds live in [the gay] lifestyle. But people from all ethnic backgrounds are also liars and cheaters and malicious and back-stabbing."
>
> — NFL player Reggie White, in a speech to the Wisconsin Assembly.

After much public criticism, White publicly apologized for parts of his speech, saying that his intent was "not to demean anyone." "But I do not apologize for standing on God's word when it comes to sin in my life and others. My attitude is to hate the sin and love the sinner," he added. Soon after his comments, CBS television decided not to hire White as a commentator for football games. White's wife Sara told the ABC news magazine "20/20" that "[CBS was] too scared of the Sodomite community....Well you know what? Shame on them! I feel sorry for them because they can't stand the truth." The Whites also taped a commercial in Hawaii in July in support of the anti-gay marriage ballot initiative. In the ad, Reggie and Sara White urge voters to support the proposed constitutional amendment allowing the legislature to prohibit same-sex marriage.

Also in July, White was featured in one of a series of three full-page newspaper ads placed in the Washington Times and USA Today bought by a coalition of 15 Religious Right groups, including the Christian Coalition, Family Research Council, Concerned Women for America, American Family Association, and the Center for Reclaiming America. Janet Folger, director of the Center for Reclaiming America and coordinator of the ads, said, "[White's] been treated horribly.... He's standing firmly and courageously, speaking the truth on this issue." The ad, which features a large photo of Reggie White in his Packers jersey, defends his comments on homosexuality saying, "If you really love someone, you'll tell them the truth." When a gay rights group complained about the use of an official NFL jersey in the ad, White was reprimanded for "an improper use of his uniform." Nevertheless, a second ad ran with the same picture.

All of this earned White the enthusiastic support of Religious Right groups, which have interviewed and honored him repeatedly. When the Family Research Council awarded White its "Family, Faith and Freedom" award, White told the audience at the Washington, D.C. award ceremony that believers in God need to reclaim education and mass communications because they have been taken over by the wicked and the devil.

Statewide: Same-sex marriage

A bill that would bar the performance or recognition of same-sex marriages and deny health benefits to same-sex partners of local and state government employees was passed by the Assembly in May 1997. Opponents of the bill, sponsored by Rep. Lorraine Seratti (R), were quick to point out that same-sex marriages are already illegal in Wisconsin. The bill died in committee in the Senate on April 1, 1998, after heated hearings. Seratti used the issue in her successful re-election campaign later in the year. She taped a radio ad touting her sponsorship of the bill and criticizing her opponent for having an openly gay Assembly candidate campaign for him. The ad asked voters not to be "influenced by [her opponent] and his gay activists from Madison." Serrati was re-elected in November.

Barron: Book censorship

Four books with gay themes were removed from high school library shelves in Barron. A woman who no longer had any children in high school requested the removal of "Baby Be-Bop" by Francesca Lia Block, "When Someone You Know is Gay" by Susan and Daniel Cohen, "Two Teenagers in Twenty" by Ann Heron, and "The Drowning of Stephan Jones" by Betty Greene. Karen Williams' long campaign to have these and other books removed began when she asked the librarian specifically for books about gay lifestyles. She was not satisfied with the four removals, stating, "There are other trashy books that need to come out." She later requested that four other books, including John Steinbeck's "Of Mice and Men," be removed as well.

Though a reconsideration committee recommended retaining all four books, Superintendent Vita Sherry decided to remove "Baby Be-Bop" and "When Someone You Know is Gay" upon appeal. Sherry objected to the second book's "attempts to use biblical verses to defend homosexuality," which she said would lead students "to think that they are free to interpret the biblical references in any way they wish." Sherry concluded that this "viewpoint does a disservice to Barron's religious community." The school board then voted 7-2 to remove the two other books. During the board's deliberation on the matter, one school board member asked why the books were there in the first place and said, "we have a responsibility to dumb down the education of our children. We don't need the language of the Harlem streets in the Barron district." The president of the school board shared his opinion that homosexuality is "learned behavior" and said, "We're basically obligated by the taxpayers to remove these types of books to protect the children."

After the school board denied a request to return the four books, three high school students and their parents filed a lawsuit in federal court Feb. 16, 1999, seeking to have "Baby Be-Bop" and "The Drowning of Stephan Jones" returned to the library. Days before a district judge was to hold an injunction hearing on the constitutionality of book banning, the district agreed to return the two books to the shelves and refrain from removing any other materials the school board alleges to contain "irreligious, immoral or dangerous" ideas while the lawsuit is pending. The school board stipulated that it was doing so not as an admission of guilt, but rather to avoid unnecessary litigation.

Hamilton School District: Teacher harassment

In December, a gay teacher filed a federal lawsuit against the Hamilton School District for failing to respond to severe harassment he says he endured from students, parents, fellow teachers and administrative staff during his tenure at the school from 1992 to 1995. The middle school teacher said that he reported the harassment-including a death threat from a student-and sought to have the district's anti-discrimination policies enforced, but that no action was taken.

> "We have a responsibility to dumb down the education of our children."
>
> — A member of the Barron School Board, which voted to remove gay-themed books from its libraries.

Word began to spread that the teacher was gay the year after he was hired, during the 1993-94 school year. According to the lawsuit, constant verbal harassment with slurs like "faggot" and "queer" soon followed. The teacher says he began to seek professional help and repeatedly requested a transfer to another school, but "each request was either ignored or denied," according to court papers. The teacher further asserts that when he reported that a student threatened to kill him because he was gay, the associate principal told him that "we can't stop middle school students from talking." "Boys will be boys," she reportedly said. The teacher accepted a transfer to an elementary school in 1996 despite his concerns that younger siblings of the same students attend the school.

Madison: Anti-gay ads

A series of newspaper advertisements highlighted the ongoing public controversy over gay and lesbian rights in Madison. First, a number of pastors were targeted with anti-gay fliers after they signed "A Madison Affirmation," a gay-friendly document that was sponsored by about 75 area clergy. The document embraced "gay and lesbian persons as our neighbors" and children of God. A local group of conservative Christians, Wisconsin Christians United (WCU), responded by distributing fliers comparing the clergy to wolves in sheep's clothing. WCU's

Ralph Ovadal denied that the actions were motivated by hatred, but lambasted "homosexual activity," saying "it brings the judgment of God on a country that allows it to exist openly."

A local anti-choice group also joined the fray, adding anti-gay rhetoric to its roster. Dane County Right to Life took out ads in both of Madison's daily newspapers with the red headline: "Just the Facts: AIDS & the Homosexual Lifestyle." The ads featured outdated statistics on HIV transmission, claims of successful "conversions" of homosexuals through religion, and discredited statistics claiming that the average life expectancy of gay men and lesbians is no more than 45.

Madison: Billboards

A prominent local anti-gay group conducted an anti-gay billboard campaign, leading to a vigorous community debate and the eventual passage of a tolerance resolution by the Madison City Council. Wisconsin Christians United chose June, traditionally Gay Pride month, to post five billboards saying, "Homosexuality is not a family value, Homosexuality is a sin!" WCU director Ralph Ovadal said the purpose of the campaign was to "reverse the tide of evil that's infiltrated our country." Ovadal elaborated, "These are dark times we live in. Christians need to battle against evil, so that we can live in a world that's not taken over by these sexual perverts." Many also tied the billboards to a rise in hate crimes. The executive director of the gay advocacy group Outreach noted that there were no hate crimes in Madison before June 16, but that there were eight reported in the month that the billboards were on display.

The billboards stirred up opposition in Madison, including a protest by more than 200 people in front of the City-County building, editorials by both of the city's daily papers, and a swath of lawn signs in front of people's houses reading, "Madison Supports Its Gay & Lesbian Community." Hundreds of people gave the city council a standing ovation after it unanimously passed a resolution proclaiming Madison to be a city of tolerance in response to the billboards.

The campaign garnered Ovadal generous media coverage and the Religious Right organization Focus on the Family also covered the controversy on its radio show. Gay rights groups later appropriated Ovadal's tactic; local chapters of Parents, Families and Friends of Lesbians and Gays (PFLAG) in Milwaukee and Fox Valley put up billboards with their own positive message later in the summer.

Madison: Domestic partner benefits

The Madison School District extended health insurance benefits to teachers' unmarried partners, spurring both a lawsuit and a bill in the state legislature to stop the move. The lawsuit was filed by five residents, including the wife of a prominent conservative minister, claimed the district had no statutory authority to add the benefits. The minister's wife emphasized moral objections, saying that the plaintiffs "thought [domestic partner insurance] would be damaging to the traditional family structure." As of publication, the case had not been resolved.

GOP Rep. Steven Nass also tried to stop the school district with a bill to deny state funding to local governments providing domestic partner benefits and bar the state from offering them. Local governments could only offer the benefits if they relied on property taxes or other revenues, and they would still have to report annually to the Legislature on the benefits' cost and how many people applied for them. Nass said that he introduced the bill because the school district's decision "really undermines the parents and their promotion of marriage to their children." The bill died in committee.

Madison: Folklife Festival

Will Fellows, the author of a gay-themed book, was asked to alter his presentation at the Wisconsin Folklife Festival in Madison. The book, titled "Farm Boys," is a compilation of memoirs of gay men growing up on Midwestern farms and was named one of the best books of 1996 by Esquire magazine. The director of the Wisconsin Arts Board decided that the presentation would be altered to include other non-gay participants, saying, "We have no one else discussing their sexuality. It didn't fit what we've been doing for two years...." Fellows withdrew from the festival, explaining: "It would have undercut the integrity of my presentation. The disturbing irony is that a tremendous amount of gay energy has gone into the Folklife Festival."

Madison: Gay Pride rally

An airplane banner that read "Homosexuality is sin" was Wisconsin Christians United leader Ralph Ovadal's contribution to Madison's gay-pride rally. Ovadal had promised a "surprise" a week before the rally, just as he ended an anti-gay publicity campaign featuring billboards with a similar message. The crowd of 2,500 responded to the banner with boos and catcalls. One state assembly candidate who addressed the rally thanked Ovadal for his activities, saying, "Ralph, you've done more to organize lesbians, gays, bisexuals, transsexuals and their straight allies than anyone I know, and I thank you."

Madison: Landlord demands signs be removed

An apartment manager asked two women to remove two pro-gay signs from their apartment windows after receiving anonymous complaints that the signs were "offensive." He cited a vague apartment rule banning "any sign...in or about the premises." Reading "Madison Supports Its Lesbian and Gay Community," the signs had been produced in response to a citywide anti-gay billboard campaign sponsored by Ralph Ovadal, head of Wisconsin Christians United, and were a common sight in people's yards. The women refused to take them down, noting that plenty of Green Bay Packers signs and religious decorations were posted in other windows.

The manager said that he was "caught between a rock and a hard place," and that a lot of people "don't like gays and lesbians, period, and they can be meaner than hell." One of the women explained her position, "Every time I had to go down the highway, I had to look at those [anti-gay] signs. Those people have a right to free speech, but so do I." The director of the Tenant Resource Center called the rule "questionable" and said the landlord should be "concerned about a lawsuit for discrimination."

Madison: Student fees suit

A federal appeals court ruled against the University of Wisconsin at Madison's use of mandatory student fees to fund many student groups, including the Lesbian, Gay and Bisexual Campus Center. Three students filed the suit in April 1996 with the aid of a Religious Right organization. The students objected to 18 campus organizations, claiming that their activities ran contrary to their beliefs as conservative Christians. The decision mandated that the university find a way of collecting fees that would ensure that individual students' fees do not go to groups with which they disagree. The U.S. Supreme Court will hear the case during its October 1999 term.

The lawsuit was funded by the anti-gay Alliance Defense Fund, a group founded by Religious Right leaders James Dobson, Rev. D. James Kennedy, and Donald Wildmon among others. The students' lawyer, Jordan Lorence, is from the right-wing Northstar Legal Center. Lorence called the funding "ideological pork barrel spending for groups already in power at the universities," and said that the University of Wisconsin would be "the first big domino to fall." Lorence and the Alliance Defense Fund are also working on a similar suit against the University of Minnesota.

Mukwonago: Protest against pro-gay clergy

In July, a local Religious Right group demonstrated against Rev. Mark Stahlhut, a minister in Mukwonago who had signed a document, along with about 85 other ministers in Madison, calling for an end to discrimination against gay men and lesbians. Approximately 20 members of Wisconsin Christians United (WCU) protested at the village's busiest intersection with fliers and banners that read "Homosexuals Repent or Perish" and "Homosexuality is Sin." "It's a sin, and it can be very damaging," said WCU's leader Ralph Ovadal. In response to the fliers, many drivers yelled obscenities at the protesters while others shouted anti-gay epithets in support. WCU paid for an anti-gay billboard campaign weeks before the protest and had been traveling the state for months with the same message.

Stahlhut said that he had the overwhelming support of his church membership, but expressed tolerance for the beliefs of WCU and Ovadal: "He's just trying to do what he thinks is right. He just knows a different God than I do." The minister met the protesters, gave them cups of ice water and told them that he stands only for love. According to newspaper accounts, Ovadal poured his water into the grass and told the minister that he was preaching heresy and that "part of that love is warning the wicked."

Platteville: Anti-Disney parade protest

In Platteville, a local Religious Right group protested Disney's pro-gay policies at a Fourth of July parade organized by the corporation. Collegians Activated to Liberate Life, a national network of anti-abortion college students, planned to march in the parade and hand out pamphlets urging a boycott of the company. Disney selected Platteville in a nationwide search for their first "Hometown parade," and the protesters saw an opportunity to protest the company's donations to Planned Parenthood, domestic partnership benefits for employees, and involvement in television shows like "Ellen" and "Nothing Sacred." The protest organizer charged Disney with carrying out "a systematic assault on the moral foundations of western civilization," and said the company had "sunk deep into the mire of anti-family filth, rejecting the laws of God and attempting to render the violation of small-town values an art form."

The protesters drew help from the American Family Association (AFA), a leading force in the Religious Right's on-going national boycott of Disney. The AFA Law Center threatened the Platteville City Manager with litigation for allegedly denying the protesters parade access, though the city said it was simply a miscommunication and granted the protesters a slot.

APPENDIX   Incidents Indexed by Category

The 292 incidents described in this edition of *Hostile Climate* are grouped into the states where they took place. To give a sense for how the incidents occurred within certain types, we have indexed them according to the eight categories outlined below. Some incidents could be accurately classed within more than one category (for example, a student play that was censored could be classed both as Censorship or as Education/Academic). In those instances, the incident is marked with an asterisk in the index below. In each category, the incidents are listed alphabetically by state, as they appear in the report.

CATEGORIES:

Anti-Discrimination Ordinances: 32 incidents

These are incidents at the national, state, or local levels involving efforts to pass or revoke laws, ordinances or policies prohibiting various forms of discrimination based on sexual orientation. Includes any of the following areas: housing, employment, public accommodations.

Censorship: 20 incidents

These are incidents in which the freedom of expression for individuals or institutions is challenged due to anti-gay bias.

Culture War: 36 incidents

These are incidents of general intolerance that demonstrate the larger cultural and societal attack on the interests of gay men and lesbians.

Education/Academic: 76 incidents

These are incidents occurring in an academic or educational setting or incidents involving the services of academic professionals.

Employment: 36 incidents

These are incidents involving discrimination based on sexual orientation in the workplace. They include several disputes over proposals to offer domestic partner benefits.

Marriage and Family: 40 incidents

These are incidents in which the status of gay and lesbian relationships and family come under attack. They include incidents in which pro-gay legislation or judicial decisions were targeted.

Politics/Government: 44 incidents

These are incidents in which elected officials use anti-gay rhetoric to further their political power or to diminish their opponents, and incidents where officials create or uphold governmental policies that are hostile to the interests of gay men and lesbians.

Religion: 32 incidents

These are incidents in which religious leaders or institutions marginalize the status or interests of gay men and lesbians within their congregations and denominations.

INDEX:

CULTURE WAR

EDUCATION/ACADEMIC

EMPLOYMENT

MARRIAGE AND FAMILY

POLITICS AND GOVERNMENT

RELIGION

People For the American Way Foundation's
1999 Hostile Climate Team

Lead Researcher
Tia Sumler

Director of Research/Andrew Heiskell Library
Carol Keys

Editor/Essays Coordinator
Will Heyniger

Additional Research
JS (Jim) Adams
Sean Cain
Rachel Egen
Joshua Hilgart
Heather Kneiss
Erica Lasdon
Kareem Murphy
Leigh O'Sullivan

Additional Editing
Nancy Coleman
Peter Montgomery
Judith Schaeffer

Designer
Diahann Hill

Printer
Harris Lithographic

To order additional copies of this book, visit:
www.HostileClimate.org
Or contact:
People For the American Way Foundation
2000 M St. N.W., Suite 400 ∎ Washington, D.C. 20036
800/326-PFAW ∎ pfaw@pfaw.org ∎ www.pfaw.org